FERNANDO M. BASABE

Japanese Youth Confronts Religion

A SOCIOLOGICAL SURVEY

Japanese Youth Confronts Religion

A SOCIOLOGICAL SURVEY

BY FERNANDO M. BASABE, PH.D.
PROFESSOR OF SOCIAL PSYCHOLOGY
SOPHIA UNIVERSITY
AND
CO-DIRECTOR OF THE SOPHIA UNIVERSITY
SOCIO-ECONOMIC INSTITUTE

in collaboration with

ANZAI SHIN, PH.D.
PROFESSOR OF SOCIOLOGY OF RELIGION
SOPHIA UNIVERSITY

and

ALPHONSO M. NEBREDA, PH.D.
DIRECTOR, EAST ASIAN PASTORAL
INSTITUTE OF MANILA

PUBLISHED BY

Sophia University, Tokyo
IN CO-OPERATION WITH

Charles E. Tuttle Company
TOKYO, JAPAN & RUTLAND, VERMONT

REPRESENTATIVES
Continental Europe: BOXERBOOKS, INC., *Zurich*
British Isles: PRENTICE-HALL INTERNATIONAL, INC., *London*
Australasia: PAUL FLESCH & CO., PTY. LTD., *Melbourne*
Canada: M. G. Hurting, Ltd., *Edmonton*

Published by the Charles E. Tuttle Company, Inc.
of Rutland, Vermont & Tokyo, Japan
with editorial offices
at Suidō 1-chōme, 2-6, Bunkyō-ku, Tokyo
in cooperation with
Sophia University
7, Kioi-chō, Chiyoda-ku, Tokyo

Library of Congress Catalog Card No. 67-28418
First printing, 1967
Second printing, 1968

PRINTED IN JAPAN

THE VOYAGERS' PRESS, TOKYO

Acknowledgments

THE *present study is a joint research by Professors Anzai Shin, Alphonso Nebreda and myself; but I alone take full responsibility for the analysis and presentation of the results of our inquiry.*

The authors are deeply indebted to all those who in one way or another lent them every kind of cooperation, particularly to the present and past officials of SUSEI *(Sophia University Socio-Economic Institute), who from the start supported and encouraged this research with their understanding and interest.*

In the name of the authors I want to extend our gratitude to many colleagues of Sophia University, G. Barry, F. Lanzaco, E. Skrzypczak, M.E. Gallagher as well as to Rev. F. Keogh for their intelligent and devoted assistance in the translation of the Japanese excerpts from the students' reports.

We must also acknowledge the valuable help which we obtained from Professors Saitō Kin'ichirō and Antonio Sagristá for the statistic planning, analysis and evaluation.

Finally a tribute of thanks is due to Miss Sudō Hiroko who for a year and a half wholeheartedly took care of the main secretarial work for this research aud to Mrs. B. Glazer who made the last revision of the English text.

FERNANDO M. BASABE
SOPHIA UNIVERSITY
TOKYO, JULY, 1967

Contents

Chapter One
THE PROBLEM AND METHODOLOGY OF
THE PRESENT STUDY

THE aim of our research was to study exclusively one of the most important elements concerning the attitude of contemporary Japanese youth toward religion—that is, whether the attitude toward religion was "favorable" or "unfavorable." Our purpose, however, was not limited to reaching a flat conclusion, such as "The young Japanese student holds a favorable (or unfavorable) attitude toward religion." Our intention was to provide a detailed analysis of the different elements which make up the "favorable" or "unfavorable" attitude. Furthermore, we intended to investigate the roots of such an attitude. Our questionnaire was designed to achieve this goal; but at the same time it was constructed in such a way as to provide indirectly another significant element related to any religious mentality. This element is the degree of "subjectivity" or "objectivity" involved in the concept of religion. In other words, we hoped to find out whether the Japanese student envisages religion merely as a subjective matter or whether he recognizes in religion some elements which clearly appear as objectively independent of human thought and feelings.

During the course of preparation of the inquiry, we held several meetings with Japanese experts on religious problems. These contacts proved to be most valuable. As a result, we would like to clear up from the outset some difficulties discussed with these experts in regard to our study.

First, it seemed impossible to try to ascertain simply the "favorable" or "unfavorable" attitude of man toward religion. The word "religion" has a very wide range of meaning, and it includes all religions from the most ancient and traditional, such as Buddhism or Christianity, to the most recent with just a few years of existence. The same word "religion" is used to signify very primitive forms of religious behavior entangled with many superstitious elements, as well as to designate highly cultural religions endowed with great intellectual refinements. Hence, you can show a "favorable" or "unfavorable" attitude toward this or that particular form of religion, but it seemed impossible to obtain an indiscriminately general attitude toward whatever forms are included in the generic name of religion.

We frankly admit that this difficulty made us question many times, at the beginning stage of our research, the advisability of carrying out our study. Nonetheless, it was precisely during this preparatory period of our work that we found a satisfactory solution to the problem. At that time we analyzed

A

about 600 students' reports on religion which were made available to us prior to our inquiry. These reports were written by the students of Sophia University for the religion class, a compulsory subject during the first two years of general education. During the last three years, several professors of religion, at the beginning of the school year, had asked their students to write a report on their ideas about religion.

A careful analysis of these reports has shown us that in the mentality of contemporary Japanese youth some basic ideas clearly emerge about religion as such, without regard to a concrete form embodied in a particular religious denomination. It would be very hard, if not impossible, for a person with good religious background to answer our questionnaire indiscriminately. Such a person would immediately make the necessary distinctions, asking, in turn, what is the specific form of religion we have in mind, in order to be able to give an appropriate answer in regard to his personal approval or disapproval to the question formulated in the inquiry. This, however, is not the case with the Japanese youth of today.

Obviously, the young Japanese realizes that there are differences among the various forms of religion. But, some basic ideas on religion in general prevail in his mind which reveal a general attitude toward whatever falls under the religious phenomenon, especially in connection with the general content of the world "religion" regardless of any specific form such as Buddhism, Christianity, contemporary New Religions in Japan, or any other concrete religion. Hence, the difficulties which might naturally arise in the case of the individual versed in religious matters when asked to answer a set of given questions on religion, should not be projected to the case of other individuals who are not endowed with similar religious education or training. The same questions which sound ambiguous, with a variegated range of meaning, or even seem illogical to a given group of subjects, might not offer any particular difficulty to a different group of persons. We have been able to come to this conclusion after our pilot-tests, numerous interviews, and the use of other technical means which were employed to ensure the validity of our questions, as will be explained in detail further on in this monograph.

A second objection, based on the situation of the present Japanese student, was raised against our intended study. We were told that today it is practically impossible to try to investigate the attitude of Japanese youth toward religion, because to investigate an attitude presupposes that such an attitude exists. However, it was claimed that the postwar generations in Japan have no attitude in religious matters and only absolute ignorance prevails.

We agree to the fact that often times we meet unscientific questionnaires devised to detect attitudes which actually are not existent in the group of subjects under investigation. We do not think, however, that this is the problem in our case. We acknowledge the fact that contemporary Japanese youth has not received any religious education in the schools, nor, in the majority of cases, even at home. Nevertheless, in spite of this, it is a fact that either on account of the general atmosphere permeating Japanese society today, or because of private reading and informal converstations among friends, or because of the influence of some ideas commonly presented in textbooks, directly or indirectly on religion, freshmen students come to the university not only with certain vague and fluctuating attitudes toward religion in general, but they possess some convictions very clearly defined in their minds and deeply rooted in their hearts to such a degree that it is very hard to uproot or transform them.

Let us quote just one single instance out of the many cases that we could choose from materials collected on this matter. The following paragraph is a direct translation of a report written by a student who entered the university straight after high school, and joined the Economics Department. This report was written 15 days after entering the university, at the end of April, 1966:

> At present, I cannot believe in the existence of what Christians call God. And the reason is this. When man feels weak, oppressed by the fear of death, by the fear of Nature, and has to struggle through the hardships of life, he develops occasionally a capacity for thinking and constructing several objects on which he can lean, and he imagines something that can answer his outcry for help. It is this "something" which man calls god and makes an absolute. This product of human weakness is the legacy of ancient generations of men who felt relieved, saved by means of this belief. I cannot accept the existence of God. Nevertheless, because of the fact that I am also weak, there are times when I will also cling to some absolute, something like God; and in fact when I did it sometimes in my life, my heart could obtain peace. In such moments of life, I think that it does not make any difference about the nature of the object on which man leans, the object in which he believes. After all, if man feels saved it does not matter what means he uses. Therefore, I think that for contemporary men it is altogether irrelevant what the religion is they believe, be it either Christianity, or Buddhism, or Islam, or any other one.[1]

[1] 現在，私はキリスト教でいう神の存在が信じられません。それは，死を恐れ，大自然を恐れ，苦であがいている弱い人間，その人間にたまたまものを想像し，考える能力があったので，何かにすがろうとし，何かに助けを求めようとする，その対象に神という絶対者をつくり，それを信ずることによって，救われた気持になった大昔の人達の所産であると考えるからであります。私は神の存在を信ずることは出来ません。しかし，私も弱い人間の一人ですから，何か，神の様な絶対者にすがりたくなる事があり，そうして，すがった時に何か心に落着きの様なものが得られます。それで，私はその信ずる対象，すがる対象が何であってもよいと思います。それはただ人間の心が手段を問わず，救われればそれでよいからです。ですから，現在世界の人が信じている宗教がキリスト教であろうと，仏教であろうと，回教であろうと又，他のいかなる宗教であろうと，かまわないと思います。

Another difficulty that was suggested to us is the fact that the purpose of our inquiry involved a bias, that it suffered from a clearly Western and specifically Christian prejudice. This difficulty was proposed by a competent scholar in religious studies who has, himself, conducted several religious inquiries. We tried to find out exactly what he meant by this "Western, specifically Christian prejudice." His answer was that it is scientifically meaningless to ask about the objectivity of religion.

Although we respect this opinion, we cannot agree with it. Certainly, the aim of the positive sciences is not to attempt to prove or to disprove the objectivity of religion. Nonetheless, we fail to see that there necessarily exists any scientific difficulty in trying to find out whether the mentality of a given group of individuals involves an objective or purely subjective conception of religion. We would even dare to suggest that it is in such an opinion as that of our contestant that we can detect an underlying basic prejudice. Some Japanese scholars of religion easily tend to assume that religion is a purely subjective phenomenon. A more impartial position, it seems to us, would be just to offer the possibility to the individuals who are the subjects of the inquiry to freely express their opinions in either direction, without prejudging the matter in question as being subjective or objective.

Finally, we would like to point out that the purpose of our inquiry has not been a study of the religious attitudes of Japanese students. In this sense, the object of our analysis is not what, in a conscious or unconscious manner, may be found about religiosity in the Japanese soul. To state it differently, we did not study the so-called "religious attitude" in strict technical terms. Consequently, we did not analyze the "religious soul" of Japanese university students. Our only purpose, as we have already stated, was limited to the investigation of some fundamental aspects of the attitude held by the Japanese university students toward religion.

Our inquiry was distributed among first-year university students. Our intention was, as mentioned above, to study some religious factors existing today in university freshmen—that is, what is their attitude in regard to religion after they graduate from high school.

We have limited the field of our research to the student population of the Tokyo area, including also the prefectures of Kanagawa, Chiba and Saitama. Later on in this monograph we shall explain the chosen sampling and the methodology followed in determining this sampling. The target of our inquiry was constituted of some 8,000 students.

As an appendix to our study, we shall include the results obtained from other partial inquiries, which could be properly called preparatory materials for further studies on the subject. It goes without saying that such results are not representative of the whole student population. These partial inquiries were limited in scope. Our purpose was to investigate some of the students' ideas about God, an after life, and morality.

1 *Preliminary steps in the preparation of the inquiry*

T H E preliminary step in our inquiry was the attempt to collect and study previous similar inquiries that had been made in Japan in the last ten years. We limited our exploration to the religious inquiries made among youth, high school and especially university students.

In order to obtain the necessary information, we contacted the Department of Religion of the Ministry of Education, the Research Center on Youth Problems attached to the office of the Prime Minister, the Central National Committee of Youth Problems, the National Research Institute of Educational Problems, and other regional and local institutions dedicated to the study of youth problems.

Then we asked for information from the centers of religious research, the secretariats of different national associations for religious studies, psychological studies and educational studies.

Afterwards, we wrote to 104 universities all over Japan, to their different departments and research institutes, in order to find out whether any religious inquiries had been made in their universities and whether the results of such inquiries could be made available to us.

Finally, we tried to gather and screen available materials on religious inquiries among youth that have appeared in religious, educational and ethical journals, as well as in other general or cultural magazines, including newspapers.

We want to express here our sincere gratitude for the great spirit of cooperation that we met everywhere. Out of the 104 universities which were contacted, 76 sent back replies. In many instances, the replies included not only the particular materials available at that university, but also valuable information was added regarding other existing data that could be obtained from other universities or institutions. Thanks to such valuable cooperation, we have been able to collect a great number of these religious inquiries which were made in the last ten years.[2] We are well aware that the collected material is not exhaustive. We know, for example, that a number of different religious institutions, and many of the so-called "New Religions" in Japan, have recently conducted various religious surveys. Unfortunately, however, the results have not been published and they remain private information for the exclusive use of the respective religious denominations. Hence, these materials have not been made available to us.

After the postwar religious crisis which led to the prohibition of all religious teaching in schools and universities, there has been a kind of general inhibition, although it is gradually disappearing, in conducting surveys with

---

[2] The first appendix to this monograph is a list of the principal surveys on religion conducted among the youth, which we were able to obtain and which aided us in the preparation of this work.

a specific religious content and purpose. Actually, the surveys published about postwar youth problems are counted in the hundreds. Nevertheless, specific religious surveys are few as a whole, although we find in many inquiries of a general nature—on morality, youth ideals, personal problems of contemporary youth, etc.—two or three questions touching directly on religious problems. Usually, these questions ask whether the individual thinks religion is necessary for man, and whether he believes in a particular faith.

The second step in the preparation of our survey was the analysis of approximately 600 reports on religion, written by students of Sophia University in the last three to four years. All these reports were written on the general topic of religion by first-year students who freely expressed their opinions about the given subject. From these materials, we gathered the most significant passages and we tried to classify the students' opinions in groups and categories. Often times, these different categories do not reflect a clear distinction of ideas about religion, but rather they express almost the same ideas in very sharp characteristic statements but with different nuances.

Finally, we arrived at the formulation of the questions. Based almost exclusively on the above-mentioned student reports, and trying to keep their own expressions as much as possible, we could formulate 143 questions representing different opinions about religion in general. The approval or disapproval of the opinions stated in these questions would reveal a favorable or unfavorable attitude toward religion. The answers to many of these questions would also indicate clearly to what extent the religious conception of the student was merely a subjective one.

2 *Technique of our attitude scale construction*

WE have followed Likert's method, called the method of "summated ratings." It is a simple method for attitude scale construction and, although imperfect, we think it is sufficiently accurate for the purpose of our study.

Likert's method is concerned with investigation of an attitude toward a single problem. In other words, all the questions are purported to the same goal and they have the same object. In our case, all the questions are centered on the word "religion." Moreover, all the questions are aimed at finding a favorable or unfavorable attitude toward religion in the subjects of the inquiry. Precisely because it is a matter of numerous questions about the same topic and concerned with a single attitude toward this very topic, it is relatively easy to discover the different nuances in this attitude, and even possible to detect the motives or reasons underlying such an attitude.

In Likert's method, a great number of questions are formulated which can be divided into two main categories: questions whose positive answer presupposes a favorable attitude, and questions whose positive answer presupposes an unfavorable attitude. In order to determine more accurately the degree of favorability or unfavorability, the answers to the proposed questions are divided into five-grade marking units: *Strongly agree, Agree,*

Don't know, Disagree, Strongly disagree. The values 4, 3, 2, 1, 0 are assigned respectively to each of these answers in the case of positive questions, and inversely, the values 0, 1, 2, 3, 4, are assigned to the answers of the negative questions. The final grade obtained by each individual on the scale of attitudes is the corresponding sum of all his points for each given question.[3]

The proper selection of the questions posed a problem of the utmost importance. The decisive factor which has to be ensured in any inquiry is that the questions enjoy a high coefficient of validity and reliability. In other words, it is absolutely necessary that the questions really measure the attitude under study, and only this attitude, not a different one. And, second, it is required that the questions be such that the answers given to them always appear constant. If the subjects of the inquiry answer the same questions in a different manner each time the questionnaire is presented to them, it is evident that the proposed questions lack reliability.

In order to ensure the required validity for our questionnaires, we have taken recourse to several methods. First, we contacted 15 experts in religious and psychological studies, and presented our questionnaire for their qualified opinion and criticism. Then, we retained only those questions which met with the practically unanimous agreement of the experts concerning the ability of those questions to measure a favorable or unfavorable attitude toward religion. This method is called "Experts' judgments of content."

We have made use also of the "measurement of known groups" technique—namely, we distributed our questionnaire to two different groups of university students whose attitude toward religion was known to us beforehand: one group with a highly positive attitude; and the second one, very negative. The first group was constituted of 30 university students, all candidates for the Catholic priesthood. The second group also included 30 students, completely unrelated to each other, whose unmistakenly negative attitude toward religion had been clearly expressed in the course of

---

[3] The Likert method has the inconvenience of conferring the same points to responses to all questions. This means that whoever has replied "strongly agree" to a statement extraordinarily favorable to religion gets four points, which is exactly the same score given to another who responds in the same manner to a second statement also favorable to religion but not as favorable as the first. The same thing happens when the statements are of a negative tenor. Hence, the total score of every individual subject does not indicate clearly the subject's true attitude towards religion. Thus, the same score can be made by different subjects whose attitudes are quite different from one another. The total score of an individual subject will not show us which are the questions accepted and which are the ones rejected. Due to all the above, we have chosen to do away with these scores in the analyses of the results that we shall reveal in following chapters. Instead, we shall offer a detailed study of the obtained results in each and every one of the postulates formulated for the survey. In the shortcomings of the Likert method, see: D. Krech, R.S. Crutchfield & E.L. Ballachey, *Individual in Society*, New York, McGraw-Hill Book Company, Inc., 1962 pp. 153-156; Allen E. Edwards, *Techniques of Attitude Scale Construction*, Appleton-Century-Crofts, Inc., New York, 1957, pp. 156-157.

private interviews. The questions with answers reflecting an almost complete unanimity of opinion in each group, but with opposite significance, were retained; and other questions which elicited answers not too different in either group were rejected.

We used, finally, the method of "item analysis" which is commonly used in connection with the Likert method. We distributed our questionnaire to 100 first-year students at Sophia University, and we obtained the average grade which each student achieved in the total number of proposed questions, following the 0-4 grading system explained above. Then, we chose the quarter of students with the highest score and the quarter of students with the lowest, and we carefully analyzed the answers of these two groups to each question, according to the formula

$$t = \frac{\bar{X}_h - \bar{X}_1}{\sqrt{\dfrac{S_h^2}{n_h} + \dfrac{S_1^2}{n_1}}}$$

where $\bar{X}_h$ = the mean score on a given statement for the high group;

$\bar{X}_1$ = the mean score on the same statement for the low group;

S_h^2 = the variance of the distribution of responses of the high group to the statement;

S_1^2 = the variance of the distribution of responses of the low group to the statement;

n_h = the number of subjects in the high group;

n_1 = the number of subjects in the low group.

The value of "t" is a measure of the extent to which a given statement differentiates between the high and the low groups. As Edwards points out: "As a crude and approximate rule of thumb, we may regard any "t" value equal or greater than 1.75 as indicating that the average response of the high and low groups to a statement differs significantly, provided we have 25% or more subjects in the high group and also in the low group."[4] We have applied this formula to all the questions distributed to the students belonging to both groups, the high and the low group, and we kept those questions only in which the "t" value appeared to be the highest, between 2.90 and 9.10.[5]

We tested the reliability of the questionnaire with the "equivalent forms" method. In this method, we compared the results of two different questionnaires given at the same time to the same group of subjects. The questions of both questionnaires were practically identical in content, but formulated differently. The coefficient of correlation between the parallel questions of each questionnaire will show the reliability of each question. After applying this test to our survey, we retained only those questions with a coefficient of correlation higher than 0.89.

---

[4] Allen L. Edwards, *Techniques of Attitude Scale Construction*, Appleton-Century-Crofts, Inc., New York, 1957, pp. 152-156.

[5] This "t" value for each question of the inquiry is given in detail in the second appendix to this monograph.

As the concrete result of all these preliminary tests, 36 questions were selected out of the 143 questions originally formulated. Some of these 36 questions even underwent a slight change in their final expression.

3 Sampling

We conducted two surveys. The first was carried out during the month of April, 1966, among the freshmen of Sophia University (Jōchi Daigaku). The second was made the following month among the freshmen from universities in Tokyo and the prefectures of Kanagawa, Chiba and Saitama. The same questionnaire was used in both surveys.

No sampling problem was encountered in the Sophia University survey, since it was intended to cover the entire student population by making the survey during the regular Religion class hour. According to official records, Sophia had a freshman group of 1,808 as of April, 1966, of whom 1,298 were men and 510 were women.[6] The questionnaire was handed out to 1,137 boys and 497 girls, these being the number of students present at the time of the survey. Of these, 1,120 young men and 495 young ladies returned their completed forms. The distribution of the total respondents, by sex and by academic faculty, follows:

TABLE I

	Liberal Arts	Law	Economics	Languages	Sciences	Total
Boys:	236	182	183	246	273	1,120
Girls:	306	14	9	153	13	495
Total:	542	196	192	399	286	1,615

The sampling method employed in the second survey was the "replicated sampling method" advocated by W. E. Deming, the famous American statistician.[7] In Tokyo, there are 96 universities, while there are 23 others in the prefectures of Kanagawa, Chiba and Saitama. Excluding Sophia, therefore, we covered an area with 118 universities, offering a combined total of 250 faculties. The sampling was carried out in two phases: first, according to university and faculty; then by individual student.[8]

The 250 faculties were divided into two large groups, Liberal Arts and Sciences. Each group was then subdivided according to university type into

---

[6] Not included among these 1,808 students are the 35 aspirants to the Catholic priesthood who enrolled in the University's Department of Philosophy. We excluded this small group from our survey sample.

[7] W. Edwards Deming, *Sample Design in Business Research*, John Willey and Sons, Inc., New York, 1960.

[8] The concrete planning of the sampling for our survey was entrusted to the J. Walter Thompson Company under the direction of Professor Kinichiro Saito, Head of the Department of Economics, Sophia University.

State, Local and Private. The following step was to find out the theoretical total of students which, according to the Ministry of Education, should be enrolled in these faculties. This total was then divided into 10 equal parts or "zones."

From each of these "zones" a subject was chosen at random, and the faculty to which each of the 10 thus chosen happened to belong was made a part of the sample. From each of the faculties thus determined, the sampling of individual students was to be taken, the resulting group to become the first sub-sample. Following the same procedure, a second group was formed to constitute the second sub-sample. In this manner, 10 sub-samples were finally selected.

The above method offered the possibility of 100 faculties being chosen from among the total of 250; but actually a number of faculties were chosen two or more times so that the survey covered subjects from 83 faculties. In some faculties, however, the number of students were so few that we combined two or three into one unit for purposes of the survey. The final tabulation showed 67 faculties from 46 universities.

We next proceeded to the selection of the sample of individual students. For the basic unit, we employed systematic sampling to select 40 students from each faculty. But, from those faculties which had been chosen several times in the prior sampling, not only were 40 students to be chosen but this number was to be multiplied by the number of times such a faculty had been chosen previously.

All these computations were based on the theoretical number of students each faculty was supposed to have, according to the criterion of the Ministry of Education. The actual cases, however, showed the real number vastly different from the theoretical, particularly in the private universities. Thus, we had to introduce some changes in the manner of determining the basic group. When the actual students in any given faculty were more than the theoretical enrollment, we chose more than 40 from it; and when the enrollees were fewer than the theoretical number, we chose less than 40. The changes thus made were in proportion to the excess or deficit in number.

In order to establish a sound foundation for the sampling of individual students, we requested the different universities to kindly furnish us with the lists of students in the faculties in which we were interested. At this point, we would like to express our gratitude for the wonderful cooperation we received from the respondent institutions everywhere. Only two—the National University of Yokohama and the International College of Commerce—offered objections to our request; thus, we were forced to exclude the students from these two universities from our survey. In all, we succeeded in selecting samples from 44 universities, as presented below:

TABLE 2

University	Faculty	Sample Size
A *State Universities*		
1 University of Tokyo	Letters I	40
	Letters II-III	48
	Sciences I	81
	Sciences II-III	41
2 Tokyo U. of Foreign Languages	Foreign Languages	48
3 Tokyo Gakugei University	Teacher Training	43
4 Tokyo U. of Agriculture & Tech.	Agriculture & Tech.	82
5 Tokyo University of Arts	Fine Arts	42
6 Tokyo University of Fisheries	Fisheries	38
7 Tokyo U. of Merchant Marine	Merchant Marine	39
8 Ochanomizu Women's University	Letters and Education	52
9 Saitama University	Education & Economics	95
10 Yokohama Municipal University	Commerce	82
B *Private Universities*		
a *Religiously affiliated universities*		
11 Saint Paul University (Anglican)	Sociology	91
(Rikkyō)	Economics	151
12 Aoyama Gakuin University (Prot.)	Economics	70
13 Kantō Gakuin University (Prot.)	Engineering	47
	Economics	60
14 Meiji Gakuin University (Prot.)	Economics	105
15 U. of the Sacred Heart (Cath.)	Letters	43
16 Komazawa University (Buddhist)	Economics & Commerce	195
17 Kokugakuin University (Shinto)	Letters, Politics & Economics	193
b *Non-religiously affiliated universities*		
18 Nihon University	Law	74
	Science & Engineering	175
	Humanities & Sciences	256
	Agriculture & Veterinary Medicine	163
19 Nihon College of Phys. Ed.	Physical Education	200
20 Nihon Dental College	Dentistry	69
21 Hōsei University	Economics	84
	Letters	73

22	Tōkai University	Engineering	82
		Sciences & Oceanography	83
23	Tokyo College of Sciences	Engineering & Pharmacy	94
24	Tokyo College of Pharmacy	Pharmacy	93
25	Tokyo College of Economics	Economics & Bus. Adm.	92
26	Chūō University	Sciences	86
		Economics	158
		Law	243
		Commerce	70
27	Kitazato University	Hygienics & Pharmacy	78
28	Waseda University	Commerce	43
		Politics & Economics	375
29	Gakushūin University	Law	55
30	Meisei University	Engineering	89
31	Musashi Institute of Technology	Engineering	51
32	Kunitachi Music College	Music	110
33	Keiō University	Economics	59
		Commerce	193
		Engineering & Medicine	113
34	Kōgakuin University	Engineering	140
35	Tōhō Gakuen School of Music	Music	82
36	Meiji University	Law	64
		Politics & Economics	116
37	Seikei University	Engineering	49
		Letters, Politics & Economics	92
38	Senshū University	Economics & Bus. Adm.	94
		Law and Commerce	102
39	Kanagawa University	Law, Economics & Languages	112
		Engineering	229
40	Dokkyō University	Econ. & Foreign Lang.	84
41	Japan Women's College	Home Economics	103
42	Ōtsuma Women's College	Home Economics	81
43	Tokyo Electrical Eng. U.	Engineering	57
44	Kokushikan University	Law, Letters & Phys. Education	104

Total: 44 Universities and Colleges;   63 Faculties;   6,586 Students

It is estimated that an additional 213 subjects should have been chosen from the faculties of the two universities which did not allow us to examine their student registers. This would bring the total sample to 6,799 students. The actual total of university freshmen in universities and colleges within the areas of Tokyo, Chiba, Saitama and Kanagawa lies between 135,000 and 137,000. Multiplying our total sample by 20 gives us a product of 135,980. This shows that, within a sampling error of ±0.6%, our sample total relates to the total student population according to the ratio 1/20. Our sample of 6,799 is considered of optimum size and representative of the entire population of our survey. By looking into the results of our sub-samplings and the standard deviation of the total, we shall be able later to determine scientifically the degree of reliability of the survey.[9]

4 *Completion of the survey and percentage of responses*

As mentioned above, in the case of the subjects from Sophia University, we followed the simplest way of contacting them by handing them the questionnaire during the religion class. The number of responses has been given in preceding pages.

This procedure was not possible with the subjects from the other 44 universities. There was no alternative except mailing the questionnaire, and this step made us fear that the responses would greatly decline in number. Thus, starting on June 10, we began sending the questionnaire through the mails to the 6,586 students, with an explanatory covering letter. Of these, 277 were returned because of wrong addresses. Among the 6,309 who received the forms, 3,734 answered promptly. Such a high rate of response, 60% of the mailings, is an unusually high precentage of returns for surveys by mail. Of the responding 3,734 addresses, 48 had to be discarded because they did not belong to the faculties chosen in the sampling. This left 3,686 valid responses.

Next, another sampling was made among the students who did not respond. One-third of the 2,575 non-responding students were chosen at random; the 921 subjects thus selected were taken to be statistically representative of the 2,575. Thus, by multiplying by 3 the results to be obtained later, we would arrive at a legitimate total, representative of the part of the original sample which had failed to answer the first mailing.

To these 921 students was sent a letter by special delivery urging them to please fill in and mail back the questionnaire previously sent to them. Those failing to reply were sent follow-up telegrams. To complete the round-up, field men were sent to personally interview the subjects in their homes or at their universities. The following is the outcome of these efforts: 180 subjects were not at the addresses we had for them, and were not even known to the people at those addresses. Of the remaining 741, we received responses from 582, representing 80% of the 741. The rest could not be contacted in any manner. Of these, 74 were not in any of the three times that field men went to visit them; the other 73 lived too far away to be reached by our contact men. There is no basis whatsoever for the thought that these last

---

[9] Appendix III gives the analysis of the Standard Error of the Estimated Percentages., pp. 148–50.

mentioned students would differ much in their religious thinking from the other 582 who responded. And then there were 12 who refused to answer at all when contacted. From the 582 replies received, 15 were rejected because the respondents did not belong to the faculties chosen in the sampling.

We consider the above results, when multiplied by three, as validly representative of the 2,575 who did not answer the first letter. Thus the 3,734 who answered the first letter, plus 582 × 3 gives us 5,480. This total is more than 90% of all who had received the questionnaire. Since we have to reject from this 48 plus 15 × 3, or 93, for the reasons cited above, our total becomes 3,686 plus 567 × 3, which leaves us a total sample of 5,387 subjects.

Furthermore, if we are to assume that those whom we were unable to contact would not introduce any bias on the value of the survey, and, on the contrary, if we are to assume further the possibility of a bias among the potential subjects from the two universities which declined to cooperate with us in the survey, as well as among those who absolutely refused to fill in the questionnaire, then statistical calculations indicate that the number of respondents among the 567 should be multiplied by 4.4 to arrive at the real value of all the responses. From this, we would find that of the 6,799 who composed the total original sample, we know the replies of 3,686 plus 567 × 4.4, or of 6,180. This again gives us 90% of the total sample. Of these, 5,178 are men and 1,002 are women.

Chapter Two
GENERAL ANALYSIS OF THE RESULTS

W E shall begin by making a general analysis of the replies to the 36 questions which were the nucleus of the survey. In this analysis we shall consider separately the male subjects and the female subjects.

Since such a general analysis will be incomplete, we shall proceed afterward to more detailed analyses. We shall look into the responses of the university students according to various criteria, such as: the university at which they were enrolled; the faculty in which they were registered; the geographical area from which they come; the high school at which they completed their secondary education; their life ideals; the religion they now belong to, if any; and others. All of these investigations should reveal to us some of the factors which may exert some influence upon the religious thinking of these youths.

We would like it understood that in the course of the following explanations, whenever we mention the term "Total Results" we shall mean the general results of the survey conducted in the 44 universities of Tokyo and surrounding areas, but excluding the results obtained from Sophia University which will be given separately. These totals have been obtained using the statistical computations explained in the foregoing pages. We shall likewise continuously refer to Group A and Group B in the survey. By Group A, we shall mean those students who responded to the first letter by mailing their completed questionnaire forms soon after they received them; and by Group B, we shall mean the 567 subjects upon whom it was necessary to exert some moral pressure to obtain responses.

A. STUDENTS' NEGATIVE ATTITUDE TOWARD RELIGION

1 *Religion is unnecessary for those who have self-confidence*

AMONG the opinions of a negative character concerning religion, what seems to be the most representative of the typical Japanese student is the inclination to believe that religion is completely unnecessary to those who have confidence in themselves, to the strong-willed, to those who know how to meet their problems and solve their difficulties without having recourse to external support.

The text of the statement as presented to the young students read as follows: "Religion is unnecessary for those who have self-confidence." The replies obtained differ significantly according to whether the respondent was a young man or a young lady. Because of such deviation, we shall present the

TABLE 3A

Boys:	TR(5,178)	GA(3,066)	GB(480)	SU(1,120)
	%	%	%	%
SA:	36.7	38.2	34.4	31.2
A:	27.1	24.7	30.6	29.0
TA:	63.8	62.9	65.0	60.2
SD:	7.0	7.9	5.8	9.9
D:	17.2	18.5	15.2	19.9
TD:	24.2	26.4	21.0	29.8
DK:	12.0	10.6	14.0	10.0

results separately. We shall first look into the replies by the male students.[10]

We consider the percentages of the Total Results to be truly representative of the whole student population of our survey, as proven by the statistical method we have followed, and as corroborated by the results obtained from the partial groups of the survey, the groups A and B and the group at Sophia University. Furthermore, if we consider these students according to the region from which they have come, or divide them into the universities in which they are enrolled, or take them according to the faculty in which they are registered, we find the same percentages, as above, holding true. We shall look into this aspect later.[11]

Such facts very clearly show that, without fear of contradiction, we may make the affirmative statement that between 60% and 65% of the freshmen are in favor of the thesis indicated above. Such being the mentality of the majority of the young people, we believe that we can also presume that the group of students who answered with "don't know" would be nearer to accepting it than to rejecting it. It is noteworthy that the percentage of those who "strongly disagree" is very low, being between a mere 5% and 10%.

As we explained in foregoing pages, in order to formulate the questions of our questionnaire, we studied about 600 essays on religion written by freshmen at Sophia University. The phrases in these reports, which express the same idea as that given in this first statement of our questionnaire, are most numerous. We have chosen the ten phrases most frequently repeated. Here is how those students themselves expressed their versions of the same idea.[12]

[10] TR=Total results; GA=Group A; GB= Group B; SU=Sophia University; SA=Strongly agree; A=Agree; TA=Total agree; SD= Strongly disagree; D=Disagree; TD=Total disagree; DK=Don't know. We must indicate that the order of the questions in chapter 2 and 3 differs from the order followed in the questionnaire given to the students.

[11] Refer to Appendix III on the Standard Error of the Estimated Percentages.

[12] From here onwards, all the statements which we quote have been taken from these 600 reports written by Sophia University students. Considering the fact that the results from the male population of Sophia University are homogeneous with the results from the male population of the other 44 universities, and taking into account the fact that we are dealing with*

1 The man who relies on religion is a weak man. A strong man does not need religion. I would even go so far as to say that religion makes man weak.

2 I think that religion is unnecessary for those who are living strongly; it becomes a powerful saving God for the weakling.

3 If man has a strong will, it can be said that religion is a useless thing.

4 Religion is unnecessary for a man of strong will.

5 Don't those people who depend on religion do so because they lack self-confidence? At least I want myself to become a strong personality.

6 Isn't a believer somehow weak as a human being?

7 If somebody is determined to develop his own self, that is enough even if he does not believe at all.

8 For a man who in a relentless self-scrutiny advances toward the future, there is no objection for him not to have religion.

9 Even without religion I think that a man can be happy if he goes forward with a strong will.

10 When a man is self-confident, he is an atheist; when he is dispirited he is a believer.

From the religious psychological viewpoint, the content of the above phrases shows not only a negative attitude toward religion but also the presence of an almost insurmountable barrier that prevents the young man's heart from approaching the religious problem without bias. Many of the students who wrote these phrases would say, however, that religion is almost necessary; further, in their very sincerity, they might go to the extent of admitting that, quite frequently, they tend to feel a certain amount of jealousy of those who believe, of those who have some religion. And the reason is quite clear; as they say, such a strong man, such a man with complete self-assurance is a rarity. The weak ones predominate, and for these religion is necessary.[13]

These same young men openly admit that they themselves do not feel sufficiently self-confident to do away with religion altogether. But deep down in their hearts lies a powerful aversion to accepting some religion. To

*freshmen who have not been as yet influenced by the institutions they have chosen, we believe that these statements are truly representative of the general student population. These statements, almost in their entirety, come from the male students, and not the female sector.

[13] In the Japanese magazine *Toki* 時, May 1966, we find the results of a religious survey carried out by Professor Nieda Rokusaburō 仁戸田六三郎, of Waseda University, among 2,000 university and high school students. Only three questions make up the study. The first asked the respondent if he believed that religion was nec-

essary, and to explain his affirmative or negative answer. A preponderant majority of those who replied in the affirmative gave as their explanation the reason that man is weak—*yowai ningen* 弱い人間 and thus needs to lean against something, requires a support for his heart. Those who replied in the negative offered the opposite reason, explaining that the strong man should search for the solution to his difficulties trusting to his own strength and personal resources instead of leaning, in a cowardly way, we might say, upon religion or on that which is called God. *Toki*, May 1966, pp. 264-278.

them the psychological and sociological implications of accepting some faith, of joining some religion, are the equivalent of a public admission of their weakness. It is difficult, at any age, to make one's weakness known; it is even more so at the stage of youthful idealism in which these freshmen now find themselves. In many cases, such a confession before their friends and schoolmates is psychologically impossible. In more than 200 interviews with young university students, we had the personal experience of hearing them express a feeling of opposition to the mere possibility of, some day, their coming to believe in God. Offhand, they cannot express the reason for this opposition; but we believe, however, that the reason lies deep in their sub-conscious attitude toward religion as being proper only for the weak and those lacking self-reliance.

As in many other questions included in the survey, in this one there appears unequivocally the purely subjective aspect of religion, the only aspect accepted by a great majority of the students.

TABLE 3B

Girls:	TR(1,002)	GA(620)	GB(87)	SU(495)
	%	%	%	%
SA:	18.8	20.5	16.1	16.8
A:	29.9	25.6	36.8	21.0
TA	48.7	46.1	52.9	37.8
SD:	14.8	14.7	14.9	23.8
D:	25.0	24.8	25.3	28.5
TD:	39.8	39.5	40.2	52.3
DK:	11.5	14.4	6.9	9.9

How did the female subjects respond? Here, too, the total results are very close to the partial results from the different groups. But there is a divergence of more than 10% between the results among the young ladies and those among the young men. Only about 50% of the women have given a positive reply to our statement.

In the group B results above, we notice a slight increase in affirmative replies. This same change was observed among the boys of Group B. Such a slight increment in those who "agree" with the thesis was expectable, since it might be supposed that those who did not reply to the first letter and had to be cajoled into responding by a second letter, an additional telegram and even by a personal call, would generally tend to have an attitude more unfavorable to religion than that of those who responded to the first letter with the questionnaire.

The general observation that the girls showed a lower percentage of agreement with the thesis than the boys could be due to the feminine psychology which makes consciousness about self-confidence less pronounced among the girls than among the boys. We might express this better by stating that the problem of having or not having self-confidence is less pressing on the females than among the males.

An interesting observation which must be pointed out here is the fact that the results from the girls of Sophia University differ patently from the general results, underscoring a divergence of these girls from the general student population in this respect. We attribute this difference to the fact that a great number of the women students at Sophia University had come from religious schools prior to their entry into this university. We shall go deeper into this problem when we analyze the results of the survey according to the schools from which the subjects had come.

2 *For a person who is satisfied with his life, religion is not really necessary*

MORE than 55% of the male student subjects gave their agreement to this second statement about religion. Religion is taken as a life tool which helps to counteract or balance one's frustrations and pains. Therefore, it is logically concluded that a person who is happy, satisfied and contented has no need for religion; and the greater this contentment and the more pleasant life is, the less need there is for religion. On the other hand, the greater the frustrations a man has, the more acute will be his need for religion. Here we see the inverse of the proportion we observed in the relation of religion to self-confidence.

There is, however, a noticeable difference between the two theses already presented. To have self-confidence, to depend solely on oneself in the overcoming of difficulties which are encountered in life, shows a positive aspect of an individual's character. Such a trait tends to remain with the man who has it till the end of his days. After all, personality characteristics are not easily changed. On the other hand, to live a life full of frustrations, even to lead a life over-accented with sad experiences, does not lessen an individual's personal worth. It is not a negative aspect of his character or of his personality

TABLE 4A

Boys:	TR (5,178)	GA (3,066)	GB (480)	SU (1,120)
	%	%	%	%
SA:	29.5	28.1	30.4	22.6
A:	26.1	26.5	25.9	27.5
TA:	55.6	54.6	56.3	50.1
SD:	8.8	9.2	8.5	13.0
D:	22.6	22.5	22.7	24.2
TD:	31.4	31.7	31.2	37.2
DK:	13.0	13.7	12.4	12.7

TABLE 4B

Girls:	TR (1,002)	GA (620)	GB (87)	SU (495)
	%	%	%	%
SA:	18.1	17.2	18.7	10.7
A:	26.8	27.6	26.3	20.8
TA:	44.9	44.8	45.0	31.5
SD:	13.2	12.6	13.5	26.3
D:	26.2	26.4	26.1	31.5
TD:	39.4	39.0	39.6	57.8
DK:	15.6	16.1	15.3	10.7

to happen to have a life unusually marked with lamentable afflictions. These circumstances of living are beyond man's will.

In this sense, the attitude of acceptance of the second thesis on religion is not as insuperable a barrier, psychologically, as the postulate that religion is only for the weak. To be thought of as weak will always be a minus sign in one's personality; but to admit to being frustrated in life, to acknowledge being the victim of life's unsavory accidents, to confess to suffering a sad fate, has no connection with one's personality, not directly at least.

A group of 20 students, who gave positive answers to the first statement and negative ones to the second, were asked to give their reasons for the difference expressed in their opinions on these two theses. Their answers were to the effect that they believed those who feel satisfied with their lives, in many cases, attribute it mainly to their leaning upon religion. Hence, for these, religion was not only necessary but it was the means relied upon to attain a life that is adequately peaceful and happy. These students added another interesting aspect of their thinking on the topic when they expressed the further opinion that only those with low ambition, and, therefore, only those with poor personality, are the ones who often claim to feel satisfied with life. Perhaps this is the way of thinking of the 10% of students who gave different answers to the two questions which we have thus far been studying.

But a full 55% of the male students very clearly defend the claim that religion is absolutely useless to those who feel happy and contented with life.

As in the case of the first thesis question, there is a slight increase in the percentage of those who "agree" among those in Group B, while a slight decrease among Sophia University students is noticeable. It is to be noted, too, that those subjects who displayed some doubts in their answers or who were inclined to neither accept nor reject the thesis proposed, showed by their very hesitation a rather unfavorable attitude toward religion. The percentage of those who "strongly disagree" remains very small throughout, ranging from 8% to 13% only.

The percentage among the girls is a little smaller here than that obtained for the first question.

The above results exhibit the same characteristics noted in the analysis of replies to the first question.

Let us now quote some of the most frequently used statements by the students in their essays, to show their manner of thinking relative to religion and its relation to satisfaction in life.

1 When we are happy, we think of religion as something which represents weaklings, or as something that has absolutely nothing to do with us, and to a certain degree we even scorn it.

2 For us young people, burning as we are with hope and resolutely marching toward our goals, religion is not necessary, since we don't feel any unrest or dissatisfaction.

3 At present I cannot help feeling that religion is very far away from me. The reason is that, far from being unhappy, I am living in a blessed milieu.

4 Religion is not necessary for a person who is healthy, content with life and has a strong will.

5 If I had financial troubles and as a consequence started worrying spiritually and ended up by being driven to the wall, I guess I could be led to faith as a support for my heart.

6 If you have no distress in your heart or anything like that, there is no reason why you should cling to God.

7 If I fall into trouble or lose confidence in myself, I may also join a religion, but right now religion has nothing to do with me.

8 I think that only the sick and the poor believe in such things as religion.

9 In this present stable world there is no need for such a thing as religion. Why? Because in daily life there are neither anxieties nor any particular worries.

10 It is desirable to eliminate the need for religion by raising the material and spiritual level of society.

Aside from their obvious contents, the above phrases are indicative of the inordinate optimism of the subjects' mentality, as phrases 9 and 10 demonstrate, which makes them dream of someday being able to eliminate completely all the anxieties and worries from this world. It is likewise noteworthy that some of them should state categorically, without the least embarrassment, that they, too, have recourse to religion in moments of illness or frustration. No such openness was evident in these students when they talked or wrote about self-confidence. Notable, too, is how some students combine in a single phrase the two ideas: dissatisfaction or unhappiness together with self-confidence or strength of will.

3 *The decision to acknowledge religion or not depends only on man's feelings and moods*

THE great influence which sentiment, feelings and an individual's affective life exert upon his solution to religious problems is an admitted fact in religious psychology. However, it is considered to be a rather primitive state of religiousness when it is dictated by sentiment and feelings alone to the exclusion of ratiocination, tranquil reflection, and serene and logical judgment which constitute, after all, the most intelligent human method man can apply to his decision-making.

In this third postulate presented to the students, the absolute precedence of feelings over reasoning, as far as religious problems were concerned, was underscored, particularly in regard to the fundamental decision of accepting or rejecting a certain religion. Further, reason was not only relegated posterior to sentiment, it was actually excluded from consideration by the purposive use of the word *dake* which means *only*. The question, thus, dealt with the matter of joining a religion, accepting a faith, on the *exclusive* basis of feeling. The given statement, therefore, is daring, expressing as it does an extremist opinion which, it would appear, could be accepted with great difficulty even by those whose concept of religion is merely subjective.

Among the male subjects, 47.8% indicated their approval of the opinion. The nearly identical percentages of the different groups included in the survey is highly significant. Those who answered "don't know" reached more than 20%. There appeared no great difference, for statistically practical purposes, in the positive answers given by Sophia University students, and by the students from the other 46 universities.

TABLE 5A

Boys:	TR (5,178)	GA (3,066)	GB (480)	SU (1,120)
	%	%	%	%
SA:	22.8	23.8	21.3	20.2
A:	25.0	24.1	26.3	26.1
TA:	47.8	47.9	47.6	46.3
SD:	11.0	11.1	10.8	15.1
D:	19.9	21.1	18.1	21.7
TD:	30.9	32.1	28.9	36.8
DK:	21.3	20.0	23.5	16.9

The phrases used by the students in expressing themselves relative to the phenomenon of religion's being purely sentimental and dependent upon mood were numerous, and they reflect the subjective nature of religion in all its extremes: that religion belongs exclusively to the sphere of sentiment and feeling which should dictate whether religion is necessary or not; it is senseless to speak of, much less discuss, the existence of God for, after all, no one can say that he has discovered His existence; to have faith is nothing but the attitude of a man who, impelled by his feelings, decides that it is more convenient, and better, to believe in God; man should not bother trying to decide whether this or that religion is good or bad, so long as he finds in that faith a feeling of well-being and satisfaction—such are the attitudes displayed by the young men in their essays on religion.

1 Religion is necessary, depending upon a man's feelings and moods.

2 I know that there are many people who follow God. As they see it, He is someone who watches them and encourages them. But I think that it all depends upon a man's emotional makeup.

3 Japanese people accept religion in an intuitive and sensible way, and are deficient in believing religion on a rational basis.

4 Religion is something in the realm of emotion, in the realm of relief from anxiety.

5 Well, as for this question about what I think about faith, really, since I don't have any religious faith, I'll be able to give an objective answer. I think of a church as a very solemn place which can help you to compose yourself. As for why I think this, well I have been in a church about two or three times, and this was my first impression. I got the impression that this was the sort of place where you could pray undisturbed and somehow, without realizing it, become alone with God and come to a state in which you would clear away the tangle of things in your heart. To put it simply, isn't faith a sort of self-induced hypnosis?

6 For the man who believes in God, it is not a matter of knowing God's existence; but rather the point is that he recognizes God in relation to himself; that is, he thinks of God as existing because He is a help to his personal happiness.

7 From beginning to end, religion is an emotional thing.

8 Religion is something that enables you when you are in distress to go to a Shintoist or Buddhist temple or to a church and talk about your troubles. Just by doing that, I think you are helped out and put back into good spirits.

9 When someone really believes in a religion, one should not put the question as to whether this is good or bad. If the man himself is satisfied, then his believing is a good thing.

10 Rather than being intellectual, religion is a phenomenon of emotion. The choice of a religion is not based on an intellectual understanding.

To this thesis we should have expected a larger, or at least an equal, percentage of positive replies from the girls. One of the basic principles of feminine psychology is the predominance of feelings and affectiveness in their lives, which is one of the reasons why woman's religious world is usually more emotional than that of man. However, the female sector of our survey sample that thinks of religion as merely a product of human feelings is less by about 6% than the corresponding male sector; and in the case of Sophia University girls, it is less by about 15%. All that proves that the girls have a more favorable attitude toward religion than the boys.

TABLE 5B

Girls:	TR (1,002)	GA (620)	GB (87)	SU (495)
	%	%	%	%
SA:	18.9	18.4	19.2	11.3
A:	22.5	21.8	22.9	19.8
TA:	41.4	40.2	42.1	31.1
SD:	14.4	13.8	14.8	22.6
D:	21.8	24.1	20.3	31.7
TD:	36.2	37.9	35.1	54.3
DK:	22.4	21.8	22.8	14.6

We are of the opinion that, among both the girls and the boys, the percentage of positive replies would have been greater if the proposition had not been stated so succinctly and in such a clear-cut way, and if we had omitted the use of the adverb "only." This belief is borne out by the answers given to another statement, which we shall forthwith examine.

4 *There are many kinds of religion, and their viewpoints differ. Therefore, it is all right if people choose that religion which suits their own taste*

IN the above statement, there is no direct mention of feelings; neither are other human factors which can influence the choice of a religion clearly excluded. But in a general—even ambiguous—way, the fundamental criterion in the choice of a religion is determinate; this criterion is no other than the phrase "it suits my taste." In other words, the choice of one religion over another, even the choice of a religion or none at all, is made to appear like a matter of taste. Left out is the question of individual liberty which each person, following his conscience, is supposed to exercise in relation to his religious beliefs; rather, only the criterion is dealt with, which every person should establish in the choice of one religion or another, and such a standard would seem to be a yardstick which does not take into account any judgment of truth or falsity. In the final analysis, it is none other than whether it suits my taste or not.

It is evident that, in this criterion, feelings are bound to play a decisive role when the moment of decision comes. Whether it is this or that faith that we are talking about is of no import; what counts and has weight is that "it suits me fine." Presented in such a manner, the postulate elicited affirmative replies from more than 70% of both the girls and the boys.

At this point, we must make clear some outstanding aspects of the above results. Running counter to what ordinarily might be expected, a larger number of positive answers were obtained from the subjects in Group A than from Group B. The reason lies in the ambiguity of our postulate, as we acknowledged from the start. The statement, as further explained above, deals with the criterion for choosing a religion; thus students with a very negative attitude toward religion gave a negative reply, in numerous instances, not because they denied the contents or the idea expressed in the text of the postulate but because they denied the presumption, which they thought they found in the phraseology of this postulate, which is that one ought to have some religion. We received responses to the question which clearly stated, "There is no need to choose any religion," or "I believe that there is no need to choose some religion; hence I answer in the negative." However, since the number of boys who had this interpretation were too few in contrast

TABLE 6

Boys:	TR (5,178)	GA (3,066)	GB (480)	SU (1,120)
	%	%	%	%
SA:	42.7	45.4	38.8	47.3
A:	30.0	29.1	31.3	26.3
TA:	72.7	74.5	70.1	73.6
SD:	5.5	5.4	5.6	6.2
D:	6.0	5.5	6.7	6.7
TD:	11.5	10.9	12.3	12.9
DK:	15.8	14.5	17.6	13.5

Girls:	TR (1,002)	GA (620)	GB (87)	SU (495)
	%	%	%	%
SA:	43.8	45.3	41.4	37.4
A:	29.0	29.2	28.7	26.7
TA:	72.8	74.5	70.1	64.1
SD:	4.5	4.5	4.6	7.5
D:	8.0	6.6	10.3	12.9
TD:	12.5	11.1	14.9	20.4
DK:	14.6	14.4	15.0	15.5

with the total respondents, we prescinded from this slight ambiguity which is at the root of the abnormality we noted in the responses of subjects in both Group A and B. As noticed in the previous questions, the girls from Sophia University had the least number of positive replies.

Following are some of the numerous phrases written by the boys which make clear to us their frame of mind relative to the theme of the fourth proposed axiom:

1 Personally I think that religion is a way of thinking. So, for me, the problem of the existence or non-existence of God is without meaning. Since it is a matter of one's own thought, if this way of thinking strikes a responsive chord in me, I believe; if it doesn't, I don't believe.

2 The final choice of one among the various religions depends upon one's taste.

3 Religion is not the goal of life, but rather a means or a way. Therefore, it seems only natural that there should be all sorts of ways.

4 I think it is a good thing for people to have faith, but since tastes vary according to persons, the choice should always be free.

5 I think that religion is the support of man's heart. Therefore, I don't think there is need to limit God to one definition. In other words, no matter what each individual believes in as the support of his heart—be it God or whatever it is—I think the act itself of believing is religion.

6 I think it is up to man to select any religion at all.

7 For those to whom religion is necessary, it is necessary. For those to whom it is not, it is not.

8 Religion is an individual problem. For the one to whom it is necessary, it is something which he must have. But for the one who has no interest in it, ultimately it will be of no use.

9 Religion is a kind of philosophy for composing a man's spirit. As for me, though, I can take it or leave it.

10 I think that for contemporary man it is irrelevant the religion he may believe, be it either Christianity or Buddhism, or Islam or any other one.

All of the above phrases reveal the most absolute relativism in the religious concepts of university youth. They show that these young men and women will have or will not have an interest in religion, that they will choose one religion or another, according to their feelings, according to their tastes, in relation to their inclinations, depending upon their personal psychological needs; but it will always be with the conviction that it is all something relative for which there cannot be any rule for veracity or falsity.

For every individual who professes a religion, *that* will be the true religion, in the most pragmatic sense of the word "true," the religion which fits his personal inclinations and which can be a support for his life.

5 *Religion is a means to escape from the troubles of the real world*

THE following three questions are closely related to the first four; they take up religion as an "escape from reality," as a "spiritual sedative," and as "recourse to the gods in time of troubles." But there is an important difference; in these three expressions, the words used—*tōhi, chinseizai,* and *kamidanomi*—indicate to the Japanese that we are dealing with a negative attitude relative to religion. On the other hand, in the first four postulates, the core words employed—*jishin, manzoku, kimochi to kanjō,* and *hada ni au* —are words which, to the Japanese way of thinking, do not in themselves have any negative connotation.

The typical Japanese youth is not conscious of having a negative attitude toward religion; many do not consider as antireligious the responses they gave to the first four theses. They think that the cultured man of these times has freed himself from the myth of considering religion as possessing absolute values. But they also believe that an attitude of clear opposition, one that is extremely negative, is an equally erroneous appraisal of their position vis-a-vis religion. Therefore, as the statements which we shall continue to present become progressively, clearly and explicitly negative, we should expect a corresponding decrease in the number of affirmative replies. Naturally, there will always be an extremist group who will voice their approval.

The positive replies to the next three statements will continue to be high. Let us look into the replies to the first of this group of postulates, which sounds the opinion of the subjects on whether religion is a mere escape from reality.

TABLE 7A

Boys:	TR(5,187)	GA(3,066)	GB(480)	SU(1,120)
	%	%	%	%
SA:	11.3	11.3	11.5	7.2
A:	35.0	34.3	36.0	31.6
TA:	46.3	45.6	47.5	38.8
SD:	15.8	16.2	15.0	23.3
D:	24.7	26.2	22.5	28.7
TD:	40.5	42.4	37.5	52.0
DK:	13.2	12.0	15.0	9.2

This is the first time we find a difference that is noteworthy between Sophia University male students and those from the other universities which were surveyed. Henceforth, this distinction will become common in most of the questions. Undoubtedly, this is due to the fact that the young men enrolled in Sophia, known as the Catholic University of Tokyo, tend to be more restrained in their approval of opinions which they think are antireligious. The fact that this difference was not apparent in responses to the first four statements is further proof of what has been pointed out above, i.e., that to the Japanese youth such statements do not imply a consciously negative attitude toward religion.

Following is the tabulation of the girls' answers:

TABLE 7B

Girls:	TR(1,002)	GA(620)	GB(87)	SU(495)
	%	%	%	%
SA:	8.7	7.7	10.3	2.2
A:	32.8	31.1	35.6	26.3
TA:	41.5	38.8	45.9	28.5
SD:	20.8	24.4	14.9	30.1
D:	28.9	26.9	32.2	34.3
TD:	49.7	51.3	47.1	64.4
DK:	8.7	9.8	6.9	7.1

The noticeable differences are normal, as we have explained from the start of the analysis, beginning with the first question.

Following are quotations of some of the phrases used by the young men in commenting on this question:

1 I think that the so-called "believer" is a man running away from real life—very much like a coward would.
2 Religion amounts to nothing more than man's escape from present reality and the problem of conscience.
3 Religion is both a cringing dependence upon something or someone else and a flight from the real world.
4 Religion estranges man from the problems of society, removes him from the present world, and satisfies his longing for an undisturbed life, making for him an ideal, individualistic, little paradise of his own.
5 Shouldn't we define religion as running away from the real world?
6 Even though I may have to face hard times, I'm certainly not going to go running the escape route of faith.
7 It seems to me that it is the weak man, the one whose difficulties are too much for him, who turns from real life and goes into a monastery.
8 The way I see it, the only time a Japanese gets serious about religion is when something has got him down and he is looking for an escape.
9 Nowadays, in the midst of a mechanized society, religion is nothing more than one way of getting away from everyday reality.
10 Religion is but a means of escape. The attitude of "looking to God for salvation" means to stop looking at reality and to give up all personal efforts. And I think that the saying "what is beyond the power of men can be achieved with God's help" is also a form of escapism.

6 *Religion is nothing more than a kind of sedative*

THE meaningful phrase in the above statement is "nothing more." So, religion is used up as it plays the role of "spiritual sedative" in a man's life.

The proportion of the male subjects who give their assent to this opinion is still above 40%.

This is the first time we find a predominance of negative answers over positive replies. The students from Sophia show more or less the same per-

TABLE 8A

Boys:	TR(5,178)	GA(3,066)	GB(480)	SU(1,120)
	%	%	%	%
SA:	10.3	10.2	10.4	9.6
A:	30.9	31.6	30.0	30.4
TA:	41.2	41.8	40.4	40.0
SD:	18.6	20.1	16.5	25.0
D:	28.1	28.2	27.9	28.0
TD:	46.7	48.3	44.4	53.0
DK:	12.1	9.9	15.2	7.0

centage in their affirmative responses, but the number of those rejecting the idea increases significantly. Here, also, we see for the first time more than half of the subjects to be against the postulate. Among those who approved of the thesis, there were a few young men who expressed their opinions cuttingly and vehemently. Below are typical comments:

1 Does not Christianity act like some kind of spiritual tranquillizer?
2 Religion is the object of man's selfish needs and a kind of hypnotism.
3 Religion is like a meaningless charm. Actually, it is just a way of escaping from hard reality.
4 Religion is no more than a personal prop for man. A person has to adapt himself to this evil world in which he finds himself. But for those who cannot endure it, religion becomes a refuge where they can forget themselves, rest and create new feelings.
5 A fervent believer can be compared to a heavy drinker.
6 Religion and such things are no more than a pacifier for the conscience.
7 Religion has some significance in helping men to preserve mental stability.
8 It is all right for us to rest for a time in the shade of religion. But we must realize we cannot remain there for ever. Since we do nothing there, is there not danger of our getting lazy? After resting a while we must get rid of our attachment for shady places. That is, we must not neglect to prepare ourselves for getting over religion.

9 Religion acts as nothing more than a spiritual sedative.
10 Could it be that ordinary people suffer, as a rule, from some kind of spiritual deficiency? I think that some sort of religion becomes necessary to make up for such a deficiency or as a help.

Results from the girls:

TABLE 8B

Girls:	TR(1,002)	GA(620)	GB(87)	SU(495)
	%	%	%	%
SA:	7.9	6.5	10.3	3.0
A:	26.2	26.8	25.3	21.8
TA:	34.1	33.3	35.6	24.8
SD:	27.3	28.5	25.3	29.5
D:	29.4	31.3	26.4	40.4
TD:	56.7	59.8	51.7	69.9
DK:	9.1	6.9	12.6	5.3

7 *Religion is nothing more than calling upon the gods in time of trouble*

As expected, the replies to the above postulate are almost identical to those given to the preceding question. The phrase is actually a translation of a Japanese adage often employed by, and widely known to, Japanese people when speaking of religion. It embodies a deprecatory notion of religion, but there are numerous young men who are not ashamed to admit that they themselves practice what the adage preaches. As we shall later find out, when we come to the question of prayer, there is rarely a young man who has not prayed in time of illness, examinations or difficulties. They do not believe in God, yet they conform to the Japanese saying without feelings of self-contradiction.

Because a well-known adage is involved, numerous young men cited it in their reports on religion. Following are examples of statements either quoting that adage or explaining its meaning:

1 As proverbs such as "the drowning man snatches at a straw," and "call on the gods when trouble comes" illustrate, religion is a thing men resort to in order to struggle through hardships.
2 "Call on the gods when trouble comes" sums up completely my view of religion.
3 "Call on the gods when trouble comes"—that is me exactly! I cannot bring myself to believe in God with heart and soul.
4 When one's own strength utterly fails, for example in times of sickness or in danger of death, one yearns for God's existence and begs his help.
5 When our heart is confronted with suffering, because of its yearning

for the existence of something greater than itself to depend on, it gives birth to God.

6 Those who have incurable diseases, those who are poor, those who are in distress; that is, all those who are troubled in heart seem to cling fast to "call on the gods in time of trouble."

7 As the proverb "in time of trouble appeal to the gods" indicates, when one is pushed to the wall, one gets an inkling of the existence of God.

8 The common characteristic of the various religions consists in the tendency men have, when faced with misfortunes and troubles, of wanting to depend upon something. Following this tendency man gets religion and relying on religion he can face the misfortune.

9 Whenever man is faced with a situation which is beyond him, or a matter he cannot handle, he thinks in terms of getting God's help. But after all, isn't this just because he is weak?

10 When man is healthy and without worries, religion does not exist. But when bodily or spiritual troubles arise, involuntarily God's name comes to his lips. I, myself, in time of health, behave without embarrassment in contradiction to the way I act when I am sick.

TABLE 9

Boys:	TR(5,178)	GA(3,066)	GB(480)	SU(1,120)
	%	%	%	%
SA:	11.5	10.6	12.7	8.5
A:	29.5	28.8	30.4	26.2
TA:	41.0	39.4	43.1	34.7
SD:	20.0	21.8	17.3	26.4
D:	29.0	30.3	27.3	31.9
TD:	49.0	52.1	44.6	58.3
DK:	10.0	8.4	12.3	7.0

Girls:	TR(1,002)	GA(620)	GB(87)	SU(495)
	%	%	%	%
SA:	5.2	5.6	4.6	1.0
A:	28.2	25.0	33.3	20.0
TA:	33.4	30.6	37.9	21.0
SD:	24.4	29.5	16.1	42.2
D:	34.3	32.1	37.9	31.1
TD:	58.7	61.6	54.0	73.3
DK:	7.9	7.7	8.0	5.7

The mental attitude revealed by the above quotations belongs to 41%

of the university young men in our survey, and to 33% of the feminine group.

As we noted from the very start, the feminine group from Sophia University possess unusual characteristics which serve to distingusih them from the other university groups of girls. We also pointed out above the underlying reasons for their more favorable attitude toward religion. We shall go into this further.

8 *Religion is in contradiction to science and reason*

ABOUT 30% of the total university group, including both boys and girls, gave an affirmative reply to the above statement. However, we must point out that this problem of a contradiction does not have the same connotation in Japan that it has for Occidental people. Western man possesses a traditional culture that is predominantly logical and rational. The whole of Greek and Roman culture, together with twenty centuries of Christianity, is expressed in theological and philosophical formulae which are strictly conceptual and logical. This has made Western man acutely conscious of the logical problems of human reason; it has left him keenly sensitive to every nuance of contradiction in any human discourse.

It is a curious fact that such a nation as Japan, with a high degree of culture and famous for her exactness and meticulousness in the sciences, should depart from logical thinking when approaching religious problems. The typical Japanese feels an aversion for ratiocination, for any discourse or debate of a strictly logical nature, when he comes to the field of religion.[14]

One of Meiji Japan's outstanding intellectuals, Nishi Amane (1829–97), who introduced Western philosophies to his countrymen, failed to free his thoughts from their oriental mold when he presented a synthesis of the philosophy based on the three basic elements of "knowledge-feeling-will"— *chi-jō-i*—placing feeling at the core of human psychology. Feeling spills over into the areas of knowledge and will; knowledge, purely theoretical and abstract, has no reason for being; it has to be knowledge infused with feeling. Neither can there be a will that is cold and dry; it has to be a will steeped in affectiveness. All knowledge relative to man's fundamental problems, all knowledge of nature itself, must be a kind of intuition interwoven with feelings by which the individual identifies himself with the object in a certain manner. This distinction between subject and object is not as clear to the Oriental as it is to the Occidental.[15] Western logic and traditional Western conceptual phraseology mean very little to the Japanese soul.[16]

---

[14] This attitude of the Japanese is well explained in the article of Joseph Roggendorf published in *Japan Quarterly*, 1958, v 21–29. Roggendorf writes: "One gains the impression that a nation so highly educated . . . is harming itself by excluding any rational criterion from religion." (p.24)

[15] Nakamura Hajime, *The Ways of Thinking of Eastern Peoples*, Unesco, Tokyo, 1960, pp. 462–515.

[16] A freshman at Sophia University writes: "It is absurd that Orientals should have to ponder the basic problems of man using the philosophy invented by Westerners. Orientals instinc-*

From ages past, the Japanese learned to combine and merge every aspect that he deemed good and proper of Shintoism, Buddhism, Taoism, Confucianism, and of every other religious philosophy. For centuries past, he has been going to his *jinja* or Shinto shrine to render homage to Japanese gods; at the same time, he has made pilgrimages to his *tera* or Buddhist temples to adore Buddha. The new religions in bloom at present are syncretistic to the extreme, embodying as they do Buddhist, Shintoist, Christian, and even Jewish and Mohammedan doctrines.[17]

The Westerner wants clearness of ideas, exactness of expression in the contents of his religion. The Japanese feels no such requirement. The doctrinal contents of his religions are overwhelmingly vague and confusing; his religious psychology forces him to opt for what is unclear and unexplainable; and he remains undisturbed by whatever contradiction results. It is, perhaps, just such contradictions that he feels are more conducive to perceiving the depth of the mysteries of the gods and of nature.

With respect to the relationship between religion and science, the idea that religion contradicts science is not predominant in an explicit manner. Nevertheless, many Japanese think of religion and of science as two distinct matters, so different from each other that it is natural for their conclusions and teachings to be opposed, if an attempt were being made to compare one with the other. But it would be senseless to try to make such a comparison. What is truth in religion could be denied in science, and vice versa. As an illustration, let us cite what a young Japanese says about miracles:

It is only natural to deny all miracles from the scientific viewpoint.

*tively know how to appreciate properly the values of man. Not being Westerners we are unable to reflect on man's basic problems in a Western fashion as it is expected in this report. Of course, it does not mean that superficially we cannot think in a Western way without contradiction, but then the real meaning of reflexion is lost. In a word, in case there are contradictions in what I write, I hope you will understand and see that this is due to my being an Oriental."

（東洋人が，西洋人の考えだした西洋哲学で，人間の根本的な問題を考えるのは不合理である。東洋人は本能的に人間の価値の正しい決め方を知っている。私達はこのレポートの様な人間の根本問題を西洋流に考察するには西洋的でない。もちろん，表面的に矛盾なしに西洋流に考えることも出来ないこともないが，しかしそれでは，本来の意味を持たなくなる。つまり多少矛盾があってもそれは東洋人であるがゆえであると了承してほしいのである。

[17] One of the most interesting books on the historical development of the religions of Japan and their syncretistic nature is the work of Anesaki Masaharu, *History of Japanese Religions,* Kegan Paul, Trubner and Co., Ltd., London, 1930. The mass of literature on the phenomenon of the new religions in Japan also brings out this same spirit of syncretism. See, C. B. Offner and H. van Straelen, S.V.D., *Modern Japanese Religions,* Rupert Enderle, Tokyo, 1963. Official data on the religious situation in Japan as issued by the Ministry of Education and appearing every year in the *Religious Year Book,* show the existence of several hundreds of religious sects. A most unique aspect of the religiosity of the people is the apparent fact that the total of affiliates with the different sects is greater than the total population of the country by some 30%. This phenomenon, more than anything, confirms the syncretistic nature of the religious spirit of the Japanese people which finds no difficulty whatsoever in belonging to two or more sects at the same time.

Therefore the discussions between scientists and theologians about miracles are unnecessary and meaningless. But a person who has faith and as a result of his faith believes in miracles, will be not at all influenced by the fact that miracles are proved to be scientifically impossible. The person who believes in God can possess his world of faith completely different from his world of science.[18]

In other words, a miracle is a falsehood in science, but it is truth in religion. Is there any contradiction? Religion and science are two separate worlds, each with its viewpoint and criteria, and it is absurd to want to compare them. If we were to omit the confrontation, i.e., the comparison of the two truths, the contradiction ceases to be. Here, then, is the problem of the double truth or the problem of the subjective and the relative truth, which we shall touch upon more in the following pages.

After the above brief explanation, we would like to interpret the results of our survey related to this topic. Only 30% answered that religion is in contradiction to reason and science. We are of the opinion that those who replied in this manner are those who would go farther yet to believe that religion is an obstacle to scientific development. But those who answered negatively, or didn't answer, do not mean that there really is no contradiction in what religion says, on the one hand, and what science does, on the other. Rather, as we explained above, many students think that the two, religion and science, are two different worlds, each with its own teachings and its own criteria for truth. What they would imply by their responses is that they do not think religion is really an obstacle to the progress of the sciences. In fact, we didn't meet one student without religion who admitted the possibility of miracles; they affirm that miracles are in clear contradiction to science. But, many of them think that religion is not opposed to the development of science, and that it is natural for believers to admit miracles in their different religious level of truth.

The phrases which we quote below express the idea that religion is something antiscientific, something which is contrary to the development and progress of what is modern in our society.

1 There can be no coexistence between science and religion. Going against science, which is in quest of the true image of man and of nature, religion is something artificial made by man himself.
2 As for the unscientific matter of God's existence or non-existence, I have no interest at all. To argue about God's existence in an era as scientifically advanced as the present one is meaningless.

---

[18] 科学の立場から奇蹟を否定するのは当然である。だから，宗教家が科学者と争って奇蹟を論争しようとするのは必要でもなければ可能でもない，まず，信仰にその結果として奇蹟を信ずるものには，奇蹟が科学的に不可能という事から何の影響も受けないだろう。神を信ずるものには科学と異なる別の信仰の世界をもつ事は出来るからである。

Results:

TABLE 10

Boys:	TR (5,178)	GA (3,066)	GB (480)	SU (1,120)
	%	%	%	%
SA:	9.7	9.4	10.2	7.4
A:	22.5	23.8	20.6	24.9
TA:	32.2	33.2	30.8	32.3
SD:	18.5	18.2	19.0	20.9
D:	28.8	29.2	28.3	29.4
TD:	47.3	47.4	47.3	50.3
DK:	20.4	19.4	21.9	17.4

Girls:	TR (1,002)	GA (620)	GB (87)	SU (495)
	%	%	%	%
SA:	7.9	7.1	9.2	3.5
A:	22.3	21.9	23.0	21.2
TA:	30.2	29.0	32.2	24.7
SD:	25.2	27.3	21.8	31.1
D:	28.1	26.9	29.9	32.7
TD:	53.3	54.2	51.7	63.8
DK:	16.5	16.8	16.1	11.5

3 Someone like me who is studying rational social science cannot bear to believe in something as irrational as religion.

4 Since today religion is looked upon as something unscientific and not in conformity with the age, the average man cannot accept it.

5 Here in Japan we learn from grade school on that science and religion are incompatible.

6 In a scientifically advanced era like the present, is there really in existence a being like God so immensely surpassing man? Rather than doubting about it, one could hardly say otherwise than to think in such a way would be foolish. I think that any man who believes in God is a fool. No, rather than that, I would say that I pity such a person.

7 That religion thwarts the progress of science is an historical fact.

8 I think that religion and science are opposed. Science bit by bit explains the systematic principles which govern nature, their mysteries and their order. The origin of all this (especially the origin of life) no one at all understands yet. So as for myself in the face of all this, I can only bow my head and say, "I don't know." Religion

steps in here and tries to give some sort of explanation, but I can't go along with the type of thinking which postulates the need for some divine Lord of Creation. And the fact that God who had done this world would then turn around and bind man with all sorts of dogmas I find fearful and distasteful.

9 In an era like the present, it is hard to think that people in such a scientifically advanced world who believe in and respect God actually exist.

10 I am studying electrical engineering in the College of Science, and the only absolute which can be an object for me are the phenomena which arise at the present moment. Therefore, it is utterly out of question for me to recognize something as abstract as God.

9 *The case of scientists with religious beliefs reflects an improper attitude from the scientific point of view*

IN the pilot test conducted for our survey, we discovered a very noticeable difference between the answers to the above question and the answers to the preceding one. It seemed to us that there should have been a greater degree of correlation among these answers. In an effort to clarify this divergence, we started a series of interviews with various university groups. Their responses tended to coincide in two or three respects.

The results of the survey completely coincided with the results of the pilot test. Going back for 25 additional interviews to use as a check, we obtained the same responses from this new group.

We must understand, first of all, that we are dealing with the spirit of liberalism and tolerance which characterizes Japanese youth. Everyone, whoever he might be, enjoys full liberty in his beliefs and opinions about religion. If a scientist wants to believe, no one should criticize him for it.

In the second place, the responses of the young men agree with our interpretative analysis of their answers to the preceding question; namely, that religion and science are two distinct spheres, each totally different from the other. The scientist can live in both spheres at the same time, accepting simultaneously the scientific values of one and the religious values of the other. Thus, it was senseless to have added to the postulate the phrase "from the scientific point of view." If he follows a religion, the scientist will not be bothered by recognizing certain tenets of his religion which may be contrary to some scientific truths; he merely takes them on different levels: the first, on the religious plane; the second, on the scientific plane. Let us point out once again that this brings up the theory of double truths. Religion and science pertain to two levels of values and these levels will never coincide. It would be irrational to deny one set for the other.

Finally, the scientist is likely to have the same human problems as everybody else; like everybody else he can seek for their solution in religion. Anyway, it is to be presumed that people of great culture, particularly outstanding scientists, would possess strong personalities and would have a high degree of self-confidence; consequently, they could more easily dispense with God and with religion in their lives. We quote from the students' reports:

1 Rather than look to the power of God for help, I want to believe in my own strength and live my life accordingly. As for educated men, men with personality, I think it would be better if they placed a little more trust in their own resources.

2 I believe that among those who believe in religion, uneducated people make up the greater number. However, I think that this fact, far from being strange, is only natural.

The scientist and all persons with a high degree of culture and a vast store of knowledge, will one day have to cope with the problem of dying. It should be easy at such a moment, for even such people, to find in religion some surcease of their agonies.

3 The professor gave us an example of the Nobel Prize winner, a great scientist who finally cast aside his atheism and embraced the faith. I couldn't help thinking of the Japanese saying "Maybe I would too, if I were near death's door. . . ."

The psychological defense mechanism of trying to escape from the problems of reality is not limited to people of scant education. The scientist also takes such a recourse at times.

4 Why do present-day intellectuals believe in God? They stand head and shoulders above the crowd, but to cope with the loneliness of everyday life, and to divert themselves from their responsibility they believe in God. I think it is just for the sake of escapism or diversion from their cares.

In many cases, the faith of scientists and of those people of much culture and powerful personality can be explained as the result of the atmosphere in which they obtained their education.

5 When I hear that educated people, that people of great personality, "believe," I think that this is to be explained by the environment in which they have found themselves from birth.

Anyway, the fact that scientists themselves do believe in God and lean on religion is nothing but the clearest proof of human weakness.

6 I have heard that outstanding scholars can be found among those who believe in religion. Hearing this, though, makes me feel so disgusted I can hardly stand it. It is really nothing more than propaganda taking advantage of the mental weakness of men.

These young men talk not of the scientist as such but, rather, of men of intellectual attainment. Their general idea may thus be summed up as follows: It is to be expected that men of high educational training, and, perforce, all scientists because they have in greater abundance personal human resources, will not seek in religion the solution to their difficulties as would a person of lesser personality and lower cultural level. However, the fact that there are in the first group those who also profess some religious faith can be attributed to any number of possible reasons. Given the freedom and the spirit of liberal democracy which dominate modern society, nobody should interdict such a fact. Moreover, there is no reason why a scientist, in the name of science, should deny religion at all.

This mentality is the reason, we think, for the extraordinarily low percentage of positive answers to our statement.

TABLE 11

Boys:	TR (5,178)	GA (3,066)	GB (480)	SU (1,120)
	%	%	%	%
SA:	6.4	6.2	6.7	3.7
A:	9.0	8.4	9.8	7.0
TA:	15.4	14.6	16.5	10.7
SD:	38.3	41.7	33.5	44.1
D:	27.9	27.1	29.0	30.9
TD:	66.2	68.8	62.5	75.0
DK:	18.4	16.6	21.0	14.3

Girls:	TR (1,002)	GA (680)	GB (87)	SU (495)
	%	%	%	%
SA:	2.5	3.4	1.1	3.6
A:	7.9	6.5	10.3	5.9
TA:	10.4	9.9	11.4	9.5
SD:	45.8	48.5	41.4	58.2
D:	29.2	26.6	33.3	23.8
TD:	75.0	75.1	74.7	82.0
DK:	14.5	15.0	13.8	8.5

10 *Religion weakens one's individuality and blocks the development of one's personality*

ON analyzing the responses to this question, we were surprised to discover that only 25% of the men surveyed were in agreement with the postulate. Was not the disproportion great when a large majority of them admitted religion to be for the weak, and yet only 25% of them were of the opinion that religion weakens one's personality and stultifies personality development? To clarify the apparent discrepancy in consistency, we interviewed various groups of young students. We think that their explanations helped us find satisfactory interpretation of the seemingly disparate results.

Even those students who had given negative replies to the statement told us that they believed religion to be an obstacle to the development of great personalities. Those with outstanding individuality, who are acutely conscious of their personal autonomy, who have a deep sense of personal liberty, who have high ambitions and possess tremendous human qualities to realize them, suffer a decline in these characteristics from the moment they submit to the ideology and discipline of a religion. But in the case of ordinary persons (which covers the majority of people), religion, quite the contrary, serves as a crutch for their personality. Religion sustains these individuals, comforts and animates them, gives them the strength needed for life's struggles. Further, religion inculcates in them some ideals and converts them into strong people. The common person will not be able to achieve such development of his personality without religion. All these conclusions we shall see confirmed upon analyzing the responses of the same young men who have given us favorable comments on religion.

The outcome of the interviews with the young men was the discovery that our question contained a certain ambiguity. They could not give an answer that was unqualified. The moment they read the statement, there immediately arose within them the problem of the two types of persons we have just described—namely, the people who comprise that select group with strong personalities, for one; and those who make up the plebeian sector, for the other. With respect to the first group, the replies would tend to be affirmative: to them religion is an obstacle, a "minus." With regard to the second group, the answers would veer to the negative: to them religion would be something positive, a "plus." In view of this, we believe that if we had clearly expressed in the postulate that religion stunts the development of the personality when it concerns persons possessed of a strong personality and great human traits, the affirmative responses would have passed the 25% mark to such an extent as to approach the 60 to 65% level in correlation with our first questions. We repeat that, in numerous interviews with the young students who betrayed a more or less favorable attitude toward religion, they always mentioned religion as something that curtails freedom, that impedes full personal autonomy, eradicates outstanding characteristics that set an individual apart from others, and ends up producing a standard personality type that betrays a common mold into which they were all made to fit. Religion, as one of the young students wrote, is for the "quiet" people who "have low human ambitions." These people find the solution to their difficulties in their religion, without which they would end up even lower than the common level.

In our opinion, the 25% who show up in our results belong to the antireligious extremist group who go to the extent of asserting that religion makes men abnormal, and that it is the greatest enemy of youth and is anathema to the healthy development of the total personality. Let us go over some of the expressions of the students, which we quote below:

1 The one who becomes a believer, somehow appears maimed as a man.
2 We should have firm convictions, but I can't help thinking that religion turns you into a weakling dependent upon something outside yourself.
3 The truly beautiful image of man must be shaped by man himself, not by any dependence upon some other, such as God, it seems to me, for in the latter case man's personal identity is lost.
4 I never want to profess any faith, because, as I see it, insofar as you come to believe in religion, you entangle yourself in a prearranged system of thought, and this amounts to the same thing as giving up your individuality.
5 Religion is a cowardly fleeing from one's self. I think that in a way it is the greatest enemy of the development of personality. Why? Well, instead of facing distress and worry head-on, wrestling with fair and square, you try to evade it with prayers and adoration, making no effort to really use your intelligence.
6 I don't recognize the necessity of religion. I place the highest value upon personal autonomy.
7 I feel that insofar as one comes to believe in God, one becomes weak.
8 As far as thinking about religion goes, it seems to be something removed from ordinary life. Then, too, if you study religion deeply and become a believer, not only your daily life, but your thought processes also become extremely constricted, and furthermore, in the eyes of those around you, you become some sort of special being.
9 Religion enervates man and strengthens his feeling of dependency. And I think that this does the greatest harm to the young.
10 I think that [Christian] believers lack personality. They are all stiff-mannered and seem cast in the same mold.

Results:

TABLE 12

Boys:	TR(5,178)	GA(3,066)	GB(480)	SU(1,120)
	%	%	%	%
SA:	7.5	7.0	8.3	5.0
A:	18.4	18.6	18.1	17.9
TA:	25.9	25.6	26.4	22.9
SD:	21.8	23.2	19.8	28.7
D:	33.5	33.6	33.3	35.9
TD:	55.3	56.8	53.1	64.6
DK:	18.8	17.6	20.4	12.5

Girls:	TR(1,002)	GA(620)	GB(87)	SU(495)
	%	%	%	%
SA:	3.2	3.1	3.4	1.2
A:	16.5	16.0	17.2	10.5
TA:	19.7	19.1	20.6	11.7
SD:	31.5	34.0	25.3	33.5
D:	33.8	35.3	33.3	47.5
TD:	65.3	69.3	58.6	81.0
DK:	15.0	11.6	20.7	7.3

We come now to the group of the last eight questions, all of them complete-ly negative toward religion. Religion is a sheer hallucination, a superstition inconceivable in today's world, it is a sheer fabrication of utter human igno-rance, appropriate only for primitive man. Religion becomes the opium of the poor and needy, it is the instrument manipulated by the powerful and leading figures of society to subdue men. To put it briefly, religion is thoroughly in contradiction with our contemporary age. It could be granted or understood that religion might offer some comfort to the aged, to those deprived of any human hope in this life since they are so close to death. For youth, however, religion is totally void of any value or significance.

These are the topics treated in the above-mentioned questions. As we have pointed out before, the percentage of university students with a com-pletely anti-religious attitude, consciously manifested, is a minority. Sum-marily, the percentage of those students who have given an affirmative answer to the eight questions fluctuates between 15% and 25% among boys, and 10% and 18% among girls.

We think it is worthwhile to examine in detail how the students have expressed their anti-religious attitude. Obviously, as we have shown above, such an attitude is not representative of the majority of the student population. It represents only a minority group. Nonetheless, it can never be overlooked or minimized in any serious attempt to study the attitude of contemporary Japanese youth toward religion.

11 *Religion in our present state of advanced civilization is close to superstition*

TABLE 13

Boys:	TR(5,178)	GA(3,066)	GB(480)	SU(1,120)
	%	%	%	%
SA:	6.9	6.8	6.9	3.8
A:	18.1	17.2	19.4	13.2
TA:	25.0	24.0	26.3	17.0
SD:	25.6	27.6	22.7	38.0
D:	38.1	38.8	37.0	38.9
TD:	63.7	66.4	59.7	76.9
DK:	11.3	9.6	14.0	6.1

Girls:	TR(1,002)	GA(620)	GB(87)	SU(495)
	%	%	%	%
SA:	2.1	2.7	1.1	1.4
A:	12.3	12.7	11.5	5.5
TA:	14.4	15.4	12.6	6.9
SD:	36.9	38.4	34.5	35.2
D:	39.7	37.9	42.5	54.9
TD:	76.6	76.3	77.0	90.1
DK:	9.0	8.2	10.3	3.0

1 When I hear the word "religion," the first images that arise in my mind are those of a bonze making his appearance and reading a sutra before an image of Buddha in a dark and gloomy place, that of a crowd of austere, superstition-swallowing people out of touch with the present age, or the feeling that once one becomes a firm believer one becomes deranged.

2 My father prays everyday to the gods and the *hotoke*. Everyday I see and hear this. My father appears in my eyes as a man who, bewitched by some kind of witchcraft, has lost his childlike, honest heart.

3 I think that religion is the same as witchcraft.

4 Because in Japanese society nothing about religion is taught in the schools, the way of thinking which equates religion with magic is unopposed.

5 It is generally thought that faith as a rule is tied up with superstitious elements, and that only people without education and of a low cultural level profess it.

6 Religion tends to be rife with superstitions.

7 I would go so far as to say that religion is extremely superstitious, non-scientific, and therefore unnecessary for life.

8 Doesn't it seem that in all religions unscientific and superstitious doctrines persist?

12 *Religious belief is born from man's ignorance*[19]

TABLE 14

Boys:	TR(5,178)	GA(3,066)	GB(480)	SU(1,120)
	%	%	%	%
SA:	6.8	7.1	6.5	3.9
A:	18.1	17.7	18.8	13.0
TA:	24.9	24.8	25.3	16.9
SD:	25.0	26.8	22.3	32.9
D:	29.2	29.8	28.3	36.6
TD:	54.2	56.6	50.6	69.5
DK:	20.9	18.6	24.1	13.6

Girls:	TR(1,002)	GA(620)	GB(87)	SU(495)
	%	%	%	%
SA:	2.9	3.2	2.3	1.2
A:	13.2	11.5	16.1	7.9
TA:	16.1	14.7	18.4	9.1
SD:	31.7	36.3	24.1	28.7
D:	35.9	33.9	39.1	54.7
TD:	67.6	70.2	63.2	83.4
DK:	16.3	15.1	18.4	7.5

[19] See below p.44 the expressions of the students quoted in analysis of Postulate 13, in which appear commingled the concepts of religion as a product of human ignorance and as something primitive and a relic of the ancestors.

13 *Religion is nothing more than a heritage from primitive ancestors*

TABLE 15

Boys:	TR(5,178)	GA(3,066)	GB(480)	SU(1,120)
	%	%	%	%
SA:	4.3	3.8	5.0	2.7
A:	14.0	13.0	15.4	11.0
TA:	18.3	16.8	20.4	13.7
SD:	33.9	34.4	29.2	34.7
D:	33.8	37.0	33.1	39.5
TD:	67.7	71.4	62.3	74.2
DK:	14.0	11.8	17.3	12.1

Girls:	TR(1,002)	GA(620)	GB(87)	SU(495)
	%	%	%	%
SA:	3.2	2.3	4.6	0.6
A:	11.8	9.8	14.9	5.9
TA:	15.0	12.1	19.5	6.5
SD:	42.1	45.3	36.8	30.9
D:	29.6	30.8	27.6	57.8
TD:	71.7	76.1	64.4	88.7
DK:	13.3	11.8	16.1	4.8

1 Religion was born from primitive man's ignorance of nature. Modern man, in order to show that he has progressed both spiritually and intellectually over ancient man, does not turn back to the things that ancient man believed in (the sun, the moon, the light). He looks to Christianity. But fundamentally there is absolutely no difference between Christianity and ancient religions.

2 If I were asked about religious belief, I would say that it begins when ignorant man thinks he has discovered God or some such thing and applies absoluteness and almighty power to this. This is faith.

3 Religion is a support for the ignorant man who feels insecure in his everyday life.

4 If you look at ancient men from today's viewpoint, they were ignorant in many respects. Because of this they could believe in the fantasies they did. But in today's world of science, if you don't believe in these groundless things, human life will in no way be inconvenienced.

5 Religion is a primitive, historical, traditional phenomenon rooted in man's life.

6 Religion and science cannot coexist. Science is progressive and civi-

lizing and, as such, opposed to religion which is primitive.

7 Whenever I heard the word "God" I felt a very strong opposition. Even now when I hear it, I get an obscure, uneasy feeling. And speaking about Christian believers, the only thing I can think about them is that they are "blind to modern reality."

14 *Religion is now out of date*[20]

TABLE 16

Boys:	TR(5,178)	GA(3,066)	GB(480)	SU(1,120)
	%	%	%	%
SA:	3.9	3.4	4.6	1.6
A:	9.9	9.3	10.8	6.9
TA:	13.8	12.7	15.4	8.5
SD:	36.5	39.7	31.9	32.5
D:	37.1	37.4	36.7	50.6
TD:	73.6	77.1	68.6	83.1
DK:	12.6	10.1	16.0	8.4

Girls:	TR(1,002)	GA(620)	GB(87)	SU(495)
	%	%	%	%
SA:	1.4	0.8	2.3	0.6
A:	4.4	5.6	2.3	2.2
TA:	5.8	6.4	4.6	2.8
SD:	55.4	55.5	55.2	52.1
D:	31.6	30,5	33.3	42.0
TD:	87.0	86.0	88.5	94.1
DK:	7.2	7.6	6.9	3.1

1 Religion turns men's eyes from the wretchedness of reality; it completely robs one of the competence to survey reality scientifically and rationally. Therefore, the fact that at Sophia University we have to study religion, as a required course, is, in my opinion, a step backward and runs counter to the spirit of the times.

2 Isn't it true that religious faith can't cope with new changes? I think

[20] The percentage of affirmative replies to this question decreases somewhat in relation to the two preceding ones, so that it seems that there has to be a greater correlation among the results. The reason given us by various students is that present-day society has not progressed sufficiently to be able to do away with religion; thus, it cannot be said that religion is "out-of-date" today. On the other hand, they easily accept that it is a result of human ignorance and a legacy of the past.

that it is an out-of-date formalism which doesn't add anything to our modern life.

3　The great number of Japanese don't believe in religion. This is very modernistic, I think, and a good thing.

4　Religion cannot flourish much nowadays. Why? Becasue life today depends on science.

5　Today, according to the current trend of thought, there is no God. Today is the era in which we have come to the limits of the course, toward unbelief in God.

6　The ways of thinking about God (an idol dreamt up by man) must always change, and have de facto changed, to allow mankind to make progress. Faith in God is out of date.

7　Religion is considered to be behind the times and to place a high value on truths which don't change. To the men who are trying to press ever forward, religion gives the strong impression of being at cross purposes with the present age.

8　As soon as religion is mentioned I can't help feeling that it runs counter to the present scientific age.

15　*It may be that religion is something fitting for old people, but for young people it is something you may take or leave*

TABLE 17

Boys:	TR (5,178)	GA (3,066)	GB (480)	SU (1,120)
	%	%	%	%
SA:	4.2	4.0	4.4	2.5
A:	10.3	9.8	11.0	7.1
TA:	14.5	13.8	15.4	9.6
SD:	31.8	35.0	27.1	39.5
D:	40.7	39.4	42.5	43.0
TD:	72.5	74.4	69.6	82.5
DK:	13.0	11.8	15.0	7.9

Girls:	TR (1,002)	GA (620)	GB (87)	SU (495)
	%	%	%	%
SA:	1.7	1.3	2.3	0.6
A:	5.3	5.0	5.7	3.2
TA:	7.0	6.3	8.0	3.8
SD:	48.4	51.3	43.7	64.1
D:	36.0	34.8	37.9	29.9
TD:	84.4	86.1	81.6	94.0
DK:	8.6	7.6	10.3	2.2

1 When I hear of religion, I have a feeling of something outdated, something which is approached by old people. It is foolish for us young people to approach it.

2 Religion has no relation at all to the young people of today. Rather than spew words about religion and the like that are of no use to the belly, it seems it would be better to use your spare time some other way.

3 I think it can be said that in Japan religion is something which exists only among people fifty years old or older. That is to say, religion is not modern and has become unnecessary in the present world, and you can lead your life without feeling the least bit hampered.

4 When I am older than I am now, and tossed about in the storms of human life, I think I will feel deeply the need for religion as a way of calming my soul. It seems that one wants to believe in God as he advances in age. But I am still young.

5 My father had no faith or anything of that sort before, but recently I have seen him with both hands clasped worshipping in front of the household altar. "It is because our father is also finally approaching nearer to the next world, isn't it?" my brother and I have sometimes joked.

6 Since I am still young, I believe in neither Jesus or Buddha.

7 I consider religion to be something for old people, who experience uneasiness about that world that they are on the threshold of, or for the incurably ill who are looking for some help. Therefore, as far as we healthy young people are concerned, religion is considered irrelevant.

8 In Japan, has not religion come to be thought of in the minds of young people as a cane for old people?[21]

[21] It surprised us also that only 15% of the students gave their approval to this statement. The number of statements made by them in the reports, in which they affirm that young people should not bother with the problem of religion goes beyond 15%. In a number of interviews with them, we found that some of the young men who had replied in the negative to this postulate did so in the sense that they also believed that religion was not an appropriate problem for the elder people to tackle, either. Both from the analysis of the essays written by the students, and from what was gathered in interviews with them, we believe that the percentage of students actually in favor of proposition No. 15 reaches beyond 20%.

16 *Religion is founded on man's hallucinations*

TABLE 18

Boys:	TR (5,178)	GA (3,066)	GB (480)	SU (1,120)
	%	%	%	%
SA:	5.3	5.7	4.8	4.7
A:	17.7	16.2	19.8	13.6
TA:	23.0	21.9	24.6	18.3
SD:	24.6	26.9	21.3	30.3
D:	27.9	28.0	27.7	35.3
TD:	52.5	54.9	49.0	65.6
DK:	24.5	23.2	26.4	16.1

Girls:	TR (1,022)	GA (620)	GB (87)	SU (495)
	%	%	%	%
SA:	1.7	2.1	1.1	1.6
A:	16.0	13.9	19.5	13.5
TA:	17.7	16.0	20.6	15.1
SD:	29.8	27.6	26.4	49.7
D:	30.6	33.2	33.3	24.5
TD:	60.4	60.8	59.7	74.2
DK:	21.8	23.2	19.6	10.7

1 The real trouble with religion is that when man is looking for a support he comes to believe in hallucinations. It happens that, momentarily or for a while, man experiences hallucinations. But it is inconceivable that countless people believe in and live for these hallucinations from morning till night for an entire lifetime.

2 When I see people praying zealously, I feel funny. I consider them to be pitiful, people of weak will who believe in an illusion to support their heart. The mere thought of belief makes me shudder.

3 In the course of yearning for faith in the idolatrous God of his desires, man falls into the hallucination of thinking that God really exists and believing in God's teachings.

4 When I hear the word "religion," it brings to my mind the scene of a church or temple where people are praying to God and kneeling and worshipping the spirits of the departed. I think that these things are antiquated, unscientific, visionary and mysterious.

5 It is generally admitted that the religious mentality is abnormal or close to it.

6 From the viewpoint of a normal psychological life, the spirit of faith is, of course, an abnormal phenomenon. If you ask what it is, you can explain it as something close to a primitive impulse.

7 I have the feeling that only a man who is able to deceive himself is capable of belief.

8 I cannot understand the psychology of people who are inclined to believe in religion. As for me, I cannot help thinking that religion is a pure fabrication.

17 *Religion is nothing more than a drug which makes man submissive and resigned*

TABLE 19

Boys:	TR (5,178)	GA (3,066)	GB (480)	SU (1,120)
	%	%	%	%
SA:	6.3	5.5	7.5	4.4
A:	16.2	15.3	17.5	13.8
TA:	22.5	20.8	25.0	18.2
SD:	29.3	32.5	24.8	32.7
D:	30.2	30.7	29.6	38.1
TD:	59.5	63.2	54.4	70.8
DK:	17.9	16.0	20.6	11.0

Girls:	TR (1,002)	GA (620)	GB (87)	SU (495)
	%	%	%	%
SA:	2.9	3.2	2.3	1.0
A:	14.2	13.1	16.1	8.1
TA:	17.1	16.3	18.4	9.1
SD:	39.5	41.9	35.6	58.4
D:	31.0	30.3	32.2	26.1
TD:	70.5	72.2	67.8	84.5
DK:	12.3	11.5	13.8	6.4

1 I hear that religion is a drug and I myself am becoming convinced that to a certain degree this is true.

2 Religion is a harmful drug which stands in the way of man's true liberation.

3 To pass through life merely by relying on God is resignation. Certainly by complete resignation all problems are solved. But if we deal with all problems in this way, there is no need to keep on living. This being true, can't we say that people who are believers merit being called "weaklings" or "escapists."

D

4 It is said that religion is the "opium of the people." This also reveals one aspect of the truth.

5 I have sometimes thought of religion as a spiritual support for those in a state of slavery so they can endure it.

18 *Religion is a means of exploitation for the ruling class; it is of no use for ordinary people*[22]

TABLE 20

Boys	TR (5,178)	GA (3,006)	GB (480)	SU (1,120)
	%	%	%	%
SA:	4.6	4.4	4.8	1.7
A:	13.0	11.6	15.2	6.6
TA:	17.6	16.0	20.0	8.3
SD:	33.4	36.1	29.6	50.3
D:	32.1	33.4	30.2	31.3
TD:	65.5	69.5	59.8	81.6
DK:	16.9	14.5	20.2	10.1

Girls	TR (1,002)	GA (620)	GB (87)	SU (495)
	%	%	%	%
SA:	2.5	1.9	3.4	0.2
A:	9.3	7.9	11.5	2.6
TA:	11.8	9.8	14.9	2.8
SD:	41.9	46.5	34.5	69.5
D:	35.7	30.8	43.7	21.6
TD:	77.6	77.3	78.2	91.1
DK:	10.6	12.9	6.9	6.1

1 From the time that man began to be exploited and ruled by man, religion inevitably came into existence.

2 Aside from the founders, religious groups were always joining forces with the ruling class, and have always been conservative. In the instances when religious groups have seized political power, inhuman actions have frequently occurred.

3 In present-day society, the power of religious groups is something

[22] Most of the phrases quoted here, more than expounding an opinion, really tell of historical facts with true bases in the histories of the religions of the world. But the fact that they insist upon this partial and negative aspect of religion could be indicative of an unfavorable attitude towards religion. It is a fact that 17% of the students see nothing in religion except a means of controlling and exploiting used by the high and commanding levels of society.

extraordinary. They are able to stir up a whirlwind even in the political world, and, in the future, religious groups might expand even more.

4 From ancient times it seems that religion in Japan has been armed with a realistic character, and was always useful for sustaining the power of the ruling class.

5 In Japan, religion has been nothing more than one means for a dictator to win the people.

6 Although religion itself is a genuine thing, in the world we live in, it is used for many dishonest purposes, e.g., as a means to collect money, or as a means for rulers seizing political power to pacify those who are ruled, etc.

Upon reading the above quotations, the very first question that comes to mind is: "Where and how did Japanese students learn such ideas about religion?"

At this point we can not give an adequate answer to such question. Professor Anzai Shin is preparing an article, in which he attempts to look into the historical background and development of the different religions in Japan in an effort to discover whether therein lie influences upon the religious mentality of Japanese youth. On the other hand, we ourselves have begun a scrutinizing survey of the textbooks used in middle and high schools and of the literature most read by young boys and girls, with the end in view of analyzing their contents for any reference, direct or indirect, to religious ideas. We likewise attempted a survey among teachers in middle and high schools simultaneously with the survey of the students, to discover some correlation, if any, between the students and the teachers. However, due to the insurmountable difficulties which we encountered, this project had to be abandoned.

We hope, however, that in the not-too-distant future, we shall be able to offer an explanation, with scientifically documented supportive data, to the question we propounded above. However, by way of trying to give an answer now, which will certainly be subject to some amendments later, we shall attempt to make clear in a few lines some of the factors which, we believe, have something to do with the formation of these negative attitudes toward religion.

As mentioned repeatedly, we conducted hundreds of interview with university youth on the topic of religion. It is a curious observation that not a single one of those interviewed had conscious knowledge of his having formed his religious attitudes by some method of apprenticeship. One will not find a more embarrassed freshman than the one who, after expounding on his opinions about religion, is then asked how he has formed such opinions, how he has arrived at such conclusions. They will say that they have not studied anything on religion in school; they will claim that they never, or almost never, talked about religion with their teachers. Rare, indeed, are the young Japanese of today who received some religious instruction in their family circle; and the great majority of them will admit that they never talked about religion with their parents. And if they are asked about their reading, they are apt to answer, in most cases, that they do not remember having read anything specifically dealing with religion. Even among their friends in high school, they almost never touched on the topic of religion in their normal daily conversations. After hearing such answers as these, one's first impulse is to conclude that their religious ideas are inborn in Japanese youth. But, evidently, nowadays nobody accepts the theory of innate concepts. Every idea, opinion and attitude is learned in the course of life experiences and amidst the social intercourse in one's environment.

Following our talks with the young men, we began to come across a series of factors which could enlighten us in our search for the solution. In short, we would say that it is the environment in which the young man grew up which, imperceptibly and with the greatest subtlety, moulded his opinions and gave body to his attitudes toward religion. We shall now proceed, without regard to order of importance, to cite the different factors in such environments as inferred from the remarks of the young men themselves.

First of all, there is a fact of great importance which exerts a tremendous influence upon the young men. They very well know that the teaching of religion in schools is forbidden in the country, and in twelve years of studies, before reaching university level, they have not had a single hour devoted to religion in their classes. On the other hand, the young Japanese knows that his country is one of the most progressive nations in the world; he is conscious of the fact that the cultural level of the Japanese people and their scientific advancement as a people are admired the world over. Thus, their first conclusion, arrived at unconsciously, as far as religion is concerned, is that it cannot be something really important, much less necessary, in the modern world of culture and the sciences. It is impossible, then, that religion could have the importance its proponents claim for it, or that it is as necessary as they affirm it to be.

But this young man lives in a society where he notices that religion continues to be practiced. He knows that weddings and funerals go on being occasions when man has recourse to religion. To this he attributes some routine of historical tradition, in a sense a primitive custom, which Japanese still cling to in the same way that peoples the world over continue to do. Many a young man expressed the belief that Christianity in Europe is equally circumscribed to weddings and funerals. It is impossible, they say, for a nation to rid itself of antiquated customs and traditions.

The young man's experiences related to religion are really abundant. For instance, ordinarily, there would still be an altar to Buddha and an altar to his ancestors in his home. He must have seen his grandparents—and his parents, too, if they are over 50 years of age—pray at these altars with hands folded against their breasts and with heads reverently bowed. Instinctively, therefore, he concludes that religion is for the old generation but alien to the young. He is likely to have noticed, too, that these prayers are lengthier when someone in the family is ill, more varied when the family faces some serious problem. If he should, by chance or for curiosity, happen to have entered a shrine or temple in his neighborhood, he is apt to have seen only old women in prayerful attitudes, never anyone young. And if among his family, or friends of the family, there were some who belonged to any one of the new kinds of religion which blossomed in the country after the war, it is probable that he has witnessed some demonstration of faith healing, smacking suspiciously of superstition.

It is quite a common belief outside of Japan that the new religions, particularly the Sōka-gakkai, also exert a powerful influence in university campuses. This is not accurate. In our survey of 46 universities within the Tokyo area alone, we found a mere 1.21% of the students acknowledged belonging to Sōka-gakkai and the modern "faiths." As a matter of fact, our impression from the aforesaid interviews and from the young men's essays on religion is that their attitude toward such religions is patently negative since they do not even consider them as serious religions. The following is what a young man said about the subject, which numerous others echoed in their own statements:

> Can we say that true religion exists in Japan? However, it seems that at least many things resembling religion do exist. But, among the Japanese who believe in religion, how many believe in it with a real pure heart. I think that Japanese who really have a true religion are very few, a little group among those who profess Buddhism and the majority of those who profess Christianity. People who belong to Sōka-gakkai and the like must not be considered as having a true religion.[23]

It is not our intention to touch on every aspect of the new religions in Japan. We shall simply point out one aspect which the young men refer to most frequently—the goal of material advantages. The new faiths are religions of the messianic type, but of mundane messianism. They offer a salvation which we might call intra-terrestrial, or simply wordly. The goal of such salvation is to obtain the advantages and benefits which can be gained in this life. A large portion of the affiliates of these new "faiths" belong to the poor and lowly strata of Japanese society which make up the neediest groups. A typical characteristic of these new religions is the emphasis they place

---

[23] 日本には一体宗教なんていうものはあるのだろうか，でも一応宗教らしきものはたくさんあるようだ。しかし日本人のうちで，清い心で，宗教を信仰している人は一体どれほどいるだろうか，ほとんど全ての日本人には，宗教がないのではないか，真の宗教をもっているものは，一部の仏教徒と，大部分のキリスト教徒であろう。創価学会等の信者は私達には真の宗教をもっている人たちとは言えないように思われる。

upon the healing of every kind of illness. In his book on the new religions, Professor Takagi states that about 60% of the adherents joined this or that new religion in search of phy sical health.[24] A recent set of statistics from the Ministry of Education shows that 17.4% of the Japanese take to superstitious practices and beliefs in times of illness instead of going to see a physician.[25]

On the other hand, the young Japanese realizes that the Japanese intellectual and the Japanese scientist, as a rule, do not believe in any religion, and he is convinced that the same thing is true in Europe and America.

The young Japanese is mistaken when he avers that he never learned anything of a religious nature in school or college. In the textbooks he uses there are plenty of instances where religious topics appear. In the history of Japan, as well as in the history of the world, the topic of religion is mentioned innumerable times. Everyone knows of the religious wars in Europe, and the influence of these lessons upon Japanese youth, from the viewpoint of religion, is definitely negative. They all know the case of Galileo. They believe that even the modern Church is against the theory of evolution which to them is something as clear as day. They have heard of miracles, and they cannot admit such fables. They also know all the Shintoist myths.

Perhaps these Japanese youths have not really read books dealing specifically with religion, but, being avid readers of books, periodicals and everything that might give them additional information, they surely must have come across some articles in which the religious question was discussed. Such reading material frequently takes up very clearly the purely subjective aspects of religion. Despite the fact that many of the young people had not read the works of the novelists, philosophers and thinkers best known to them, whether these be Japanese or not, they are typical symbols of the purely subjective attitude toward religion.

Even though the youths may not have chatted about the religious problem with their friends with any frequency, surely the majority of them have done so at sometime. This is enough to realize that on this point they are all agreed: that they all have more or less the same fundamental ideas on religion. This is an unconscious and indirect confirmation of the straight-forwardness of their opinion and of their attitude toward religion.

Such, therefore, are the elements of the environment in which the great majority of Japanese youth were reared and educated. They came to form their ideas on religion by osmosis. An extremist group of them, in the small minority, will come to dislike religion and will ascribe it to superstition, to ignorance, to something for the aged alone, to something essentially old-fashioned and antiquated. Such a group would even accept the Marxist philosophy that religion is the opiate for the down-trodden and a political

[24] Takagi Hiroo 高木宏夫, *Nihon no shinkō shūkyō* 日本の新興宗教 (New Religions in Japan), Iwanami shinsho 岩波新書, Tokyo, 1959,

p. 94.
[25] See Offner and van Stralen, pp. 37-38, footnote 17.

tool of the powerful. But still a much greater group, while admitting that such things are true of some religions, will not go to the extreme of consigning all religions to the same radical heap. This sector of the youth is more likely to consider religion purely in its subjective aspect, presumably, seeing in its practice some human weakness. But they will recognize the value of the comfort and support which it affords many people, especially those who are weakest and those who have ineffectual personalities who alone cannot meet the problems of daily existence. Ordinarily, this group will also recognize the great moral values offered by the great religions. We shall go into all of these presently when we comment on the results of the responses which the students gave to our postulates expressing a positive attitude with respect to religion.

We can, therefore, state, in general, that there are many young university students among the subjects of our survey who make clear distinction between what they consider, in a certain sense, to be serious religions and what they truly doubt can be properly called religions. In this second category they place the new religions in Japan. In the first group they certainly place Christianity and Buddhism (traditional). We even have the impression that they think Buddhism is less adaptable to modern society and modern living than Christianity. A number of respondents have gone to the extent of stating, or writing, that if someday they should embrace some faith, it would probably be that of Christianity. There are also quite a number who show interest in *zazen* or meditation, advocated by the Zen sect, as a manner of spiritual exercises and training. There are, too, many suspicions about and objections to Christianity, which to them is as subjective as all the rest of the other religions. But in the majority of cases where the subjects expressed a positive attitude toward religion, they frequently referred to Christiantiy.[26]

---

[26] To prove that students are against the new religions, we cite again the survey made by Nieda Rokusaburō, already mentioned in footnote No. 13. The third and last of his survey questions asked the subjects if they sympathized with the new religions. Of the 2,000 students, 1,704 replied in the negative; 115 answered showing an indifferent attitude; and only 181 gave replies in the affirmative, representing only 9% of the respondents. Even the explanations given as their reason for such answers do not show any great degree of enthusiasm, remarking only that if, after all, these new religions serve as comfort to many people, they see no reason to reject them: *ningen no kokoro no sasae ni nareba yoi* 人間の心の支えになればよい, *Toki,* May 1966, pp. 275-277.

Chapter Three
GENERAL ANALYSIS OF THE RESULTS
(CONTINUED)

A LARGE portion of Japanese youth recognize a series of positive values in religion. Up to this point we have looked into the responses which the young men have given to the statements containing an attitude which was either clearly negative or, at least, had negative traces with respect to religion. It is precisely to avoid a bias in our survey that we have endeavored to present other statements or theses of a favorable shade.

We believe we have not come across any contradictions among the replies given to the two groups of opinions. On the contrary, we believe that they harmonize, and they enable us to know better the entire religious mentality of the university freshmen. If, to the statements that contained an opinion on religion that was negative in the extreme, the young Japanese responded with a more or less definite "no" (with the exception of about 25%), he also responded with a "no" to those statements which more positively presented religions as "something strictly necessary, as the only true way which a man should follow, as the light that directs man to the genuine truth and shows him what is truly good and beautiful! The positive replies to these statements are very few, frequently no more than 11%.

However, there is another series of statements which present religion as a means of securing calm and interior peace, as one solution to the fundamental problems of human loneliness and the feeling of alienation which the modern man of today bears deep in his soul, as a moral ideal which gives direction to his behavior. In brief, the series portrays religion as a prop for the human heart. It is a religion which makes man the center not God.

To these postulates, the positive responses are freqeuntly in the majority and they are not opposed to the mentality of the students as we discovered in the preceding pages: that religion fulfills the purpose of furnishing a support for the human heart in those persons who need it and who will always be in the majority; and that the individual who finds within himself such a support for living will never have any need for religion. These are two mental frames which are not contradictory. Actually, they complement each other.

19 *Religion instills peace in the depths of a man's heart*

THE statement which elicited more affirmative replies is the one stating

TABLE 21

Boys:	TR(5,178)	GA(3,066)	GB(480)	SU(1,120)
	%	%	%	%
SA:	16.5	18.9	12.9	22.6
A:	48.8	50.0	46.9	52.4
TA:	65.3	68.9	59.8	75.0
SD:	4.6	4.1	5.4	2.5
D:	9.1	8.3	10.4	7.6
TD:	13.7	12.4	15.8	10.1
DK:	21.0	18.7	24.4	14.9

Girls:	TR(1,002)	GA(620)	GB(87)	SU(495)
	%	%	%	%
SA:	22.1	23.7	19.5	37.2
A:	52.0	52.9	50.6	48.9
TA:	74.1	76.6	70.1	86.1
SD:	3.6	2.9	4.6	1.6
D:	6.5	6.3	6.9	5.2
TD:	10.1	9.2	11.5	6.8
DK:	15.8	14.2	18.4	7.1

that religion infuses into the deepest recesses of the human heart a certain serenity and peace of soul. It is quite strange to note that, although the percentage of university students who believe in God or profess some faith is most slight, more than 65% of them aver that religion possesses this tranquilizing power upon the hearts of men.

We believe we can find the explanation for such a phenomenon in the fact that there is rarely a man who has not had in his life some religious experiences. Even those who expressed the strongest sentiments against religion had, at difficult moments in their lives, taken recourse to religion and prayer. This is not a mere supposition of ours. In the course of our survey, preceding the 36 questions which we are presently analzying, certain questions are asked, one of which concerns the young man's experience with prayer. Only 11% absolutely deny any experience related to prayer or religious pleading. We shall deal with this subject later on; but at this point what we would like to underscore is that a large majority of these students have undergone such an experience, and it is precisely the peace of soul which they gained in such moments that has left its imprint upon their memory. Let us recall the statement of one of those young men who denies all religion and who declares that it is impossible to believe in God. He adds to his first comments the remark that:

However, there are times when I also cling to some absolute, something like God; and in fact when I did it sometimes in my life, my heart could obtain peace.[27]

On the basis of such personal experiences, the young men gave their assent to this positive value of religion.

Let us listen to the young students themselves explaining their responses which approve of this opinion about religion:

1   By believing in religion, man's heart can obtain peace.
2   By believing in religion you have a feeling of relief and become composed. And this, I think, is both profitable and necessary.
3   Religion puts our hearts at rest and adds greater dimensions to our daily lives.
4   Peace of heart is something extremely important for man's happiness, and I think religion is what aims at this.
5   In order to achieve peace of heart, religion is necessary.
6   Fundamentally, religion is that which gives us peace of heart.
7   Considering human life in all its aspects, you see that, when a man believes, his unrest over his defects is remedied and he gets peace of heart.
8   While one is aware of the severity of the man who believes, it seems nevertheless that faith gives him peace and tranquility.
9   What a man has to do continuously in his life is to keep a balance between internal and external values. Now when he fails in this, he is plunged into a state of uneasiness. Religion exists precisely as a means to give a solution to this problem.
10   I think that religion is just one means of obtaining peace of heart.

As we can see from the above excerpts, the word religion is very closely associated in the minds of the students with the idea of peace of heart, inner calm, serenity (*ochitsuki, yasuragi*). Religion is an instrument, a means of obtaining this state of mind so much sought after by all men.

20   *Religion saves man from his emptiness and loneliness*

THE internal feeling of loneliness is very typical of the university young men of today. The word *sabishii,* or *sabishisa,* punctuates what they say. In moments of close confidence and friendly intimacy when they open up on their inner sufferings, they always wind up on the problem of the solitude of the human heart. They existentially bear this lonesomeness of the heart, this *sabishisa,* which is what will urge them to seek in group living the complement of their so deeply felt solitary life.

---

[27] 私も何か神のような絶対者にすがりたくなることがあり，そして，すがった時 | に何か心に落着きのようなものが得られます。

Those who know about life in the different clubs which thrive in all universities in Japan and who observe the unity that binds the members, those who notice the sacrifices which often have to be borne by the young men for what they deem is the good of the entire group, who eye the value and appreciation they have in belonging to such a group over and above other values, and who realize they feel a greater sense of duty and responsibility toward such a group than toward anything else, will have no doubts about how such group living satisfies many of youth's psychological needs. And among these psychological necessities, we believe that the most pressingly important for Japanese youth is to find a solution to the problem of solitude. We do not deny that numerous other factors are involved in this search which requires the smooth meshing of one's personal life with group living—such as, for example, the desire for acceptance and recognition by others—but we are of the opinion that the most important psychological factor responsible for this attitude in Japanese youth is none other than the factor of aloneness, together with a lack of confidence in themselves.

TABLE 22

Boys:	TR(5,178)	GA(3,066)	GB(480)	SU(1,120)
	%	%	%	%
SA:	10.1	11.4	8.1	10.4
A:	47.5	48.3	46.5	48.8
TA:	57.6	59.7	54.6	59.2
SD:	6.1	7.2	4.6	5.9
D:	12.8	11.8	14.4	12.4
TD:	18.9	19.0	19.0	18.3
DK:	23.4	21.3	26.4	22.5

Girls:	TR(1,002)	GA(620)	GB(87)	SU(495)
	%	%	%	%
SA:	12.3	14.2	9.2	18.4
A:	55.7	53.9	58.6	57.8
TA:	68.0	68.1	67.8	76.2
SD:	4.6	5.3	3.4	4.2
D:	10.0	10.5	9.2	8.7
TD:	14.6	15.8	12.6	12.9
DK:	17.4	16.1	19.5	10.9

What is the relation between religion and this problem of solitude which the human heart feels? Here, too, Japanese youth, in the majority, believe that religion can be a satisfying companion in moments of greatest loneliness.

Our own experiences show that many of the university students who requested Christain instruction were motivated by this sense of solitude. To queries as to why they were seeking instruction in Christianity, they frequently answered that their ultimate reason was their feeling of *sabishisa* and their belief that, perhaps, religion would afford them strength in their feeling of aloneness. We also have knowledge of numerous cases where young students, in moments of overwhelming loneliness, went inside St. Ignatius Church, which is on the Sophia University campus, there to remain for long periods. And these were young students who had no religious beliefs whatsoever. What they did while inside, we do not profess to know; but they admitted that they left the Church of St. Ignatius comforted and with their feelings of loneliness greatly relieved.

Many Japanese university young men readily admit that religion is a good companion in the midst of human solitude, which is another positive value of religion.

In the selection of expressions which we quote below, the young men emphasize almost exclusively the preoccupation with the word "loneliness." Although human contingency, vanity and the transitoriness of human existence are connoted in the word *hakanasa*, which appears in the questionnaire statement, very few students made any comment on these concepts. They will touch on these topics when the problem of death is dealt with, as we shall see later.

1 Isn't it true that we know of God's existence when we recognize that man is loneliness?

2 When man feels his own lack of strength or strong isolation he searches for God or Buddha. Therefore I don't deny religion.

3 Religion is nothing more than a means for man to escape from his own personal loneliness.

4 I consider religion to be something which solves the question of man's isolation.

5 I think the source of religion is man's search for some absolute being on which he can rely to save himself from his fear of death and feeling of loneliness. At this moment man invents God. Therefore I think of religion as one aspect of man's weakness.

6 When we are alone, when we enter into our private world we are overcome with very strong feelings of loneliness. It is then that our state of nothingness reveals itself. To save himself from this thoroughly ominous situation, man looks for an ally. In a word, this ally becomes God.

7 I wonder whether religion in the final analysis does not exist but as a refuge for the lonely heart of man.

8 Man is sometimes overcome with terrible feelings of loneliness. At such times he clings to something having absolute power and under

its protection he wants to secure his safety. In this way religion and faith are born.

9 When man is struck by something, for instance if his mother, his beloved wife, or a close relative die, he becomes lonely. In such situations religion becomes our support and consolation.

10 Human life is empty and lonely. Therefore man tries to find whatever small happiness he can in life. For this reason he invents religion.

21 *Religion is extremely worthwhile as a support for man's heart*

Kokoro no yoridokoro, kokoro no sasae are phrases which appear in almost all of the papers of the students who wrote about religion. Religion affords a support, a brace for the human heart.

The Japanese youth lives in an environment of doubt and personal insecurity. From the first years of his adolescence, he starts to feel the harshness of a society where the spirit of competition prevails; then he realizes the insecurity of his existence. His experiences with the famous entrance examinations in the high schools and the universities bring home to him this insecurity with telling definiteness and special emphasis.[28] In a recent survey involving free response, carried out with groups of students recently registered at Sophia University, we gathered numerous replies in which the freshmen remarked that the greatest joys and sorrows of their lives were connected with entrance examinations given prior to entry into high school and, later, into a university. In his article, entitled "Junior High School Students," Professor Sayama Kisaku quotes the following statement of a young student:

> I want to run away. I want to run away from junior high school where everything seems to depend upon passing the high school entrance examinations. Just because of these examinations everyone has to go to special schools or their parents have to hire private tutors—anything at all to raise grades. Examinations divide people into the good and bad. Why doesn't everyone resent this world where examinations decide everything?[29]

The young man entering the university still lacks great life experiences and, ordinarily, has not gone through any really tragic situations. However, he has seen and felt enough to realize that human existence is a tough proposition replete with sorrows, disillusionments and failures. The young Japanese of today is schooled in an atmosphere of marked egoism, and he does not trust the society in his milieu. He does not believe he could expect

[28] Ezra F. Vogel, "Entrance Examinations and Emotional Disturbances in Japan's New Middle Class," in R. J. Smith and R. K. Beardsley, *Japanese Culture,* Aldine Publishing Company, Chicago, 1962, pp. 140-152.

[29] Sayama Kisaku, "Junior High School Students," *Journal of Social and Political Ideas in Japan*, 1963, I, No. 3, p. 85.

help from his fellow men. He knows that he will have to make his way by wading through the keenest competition. In life's most difficult situations, he would like to have a firm foundation, a supporting base on which to lean. Today he does not find this encouraging help in the family, in society, or in friendship. The young postwar Japanese does not normally harbor any great ideals. Neither outside himself, nor even inside himself, does he find something which will give him support in his daily life, for his life as a whole. He would like to be sufficient unto himself, and he would wish to have this comforting strength within himself; but his intuition tells him that he needs something else if he is to keep from the road to defeat and ruin. And in his subconscious there frequently wells a normal envy for those who profess some religion. More than 55% of the young men believe that religion can offer them these strengthening encouragements for the flagging heart and spirit. The human heart, safely anchored to religion, will not flounder into perdition; held fast by religion, it can weather the storms of life.

In this sense, we daresay that this 55% of Japanese young men not only have a favorable attitude toward religion but even have an inclination toward it. The young man believes in nothing, and in this vacuum of great ideals and beliefs he unconsciously tries to place religion. Psychologically, he feels bent toward religion, toward this brace for the heart. Deep down, he would like to lean on this support, which is why many of the students say, *urayamashiku omou*, when speaking of those who believe in some faith, "I feel envious of them!"

But human psychology is most complex. To this attitude and this inclination, another attitude and another inclination are opposed, which are stronger than the first and which, in a certain sense, nullify them. For how else is it possible for less than 10% to have a religion while a great majority believe that religion is such a comfort and strength for the human heart? Is there any contradiction in these two facts? Yes, there is, if one looks for a logical contradiction; but there is not a psychological contradiction. It is simply that in the sphere of youth there is another belief—the belief that religion is something merely subjective, relative and personal, and marks those who believe in it as weaklings, cowardly, wanting in character and of mediocre personality. Here we are merely repeating what we have explained a number of times further back, especially in the analysis of responses to the first postulate. The Japanese young man would like to lean on religion, but over and above this desire is the inborn tendency of youth to hate admitting being weak and cowardly, which is why he does away with religion in his life. But there are those who will concede it is probable that when they grow more mature and find themselves tossed about by life's tribulations, they will seek religion as a last recourse.

TABLE 23

Boys:	TR(5,178)	GA(3,066)	GB(480)	SU(1,120)
	%	%	%	%
SA:	14.0	15.3	12.2	19.2
A:	43.1	44.2	41.4	47.4
TA:	57.1	59.5	53.6	66.6
SD:	9.2	9.1	9.3	6.8
D:	20.9	19.4	23.1	19.8
TD:	30.1	28.5	32.4	26.6
DK:	12.8	12.0	13.9	6.8

Girls:	TR(1,002)	GA(620)	GB(87)	SU(495)
	%	%	%	%
SA:	16.4	17.3	14.9	24.5
A:	47.4	47.6	47.1	50.3
TA:	63.8	64.9	62.0	74.8
SD:	6.0	6.1	5.7	1.8
D:	19.6	17.6	23.0	15.7
TD:	25.6	23.7	28.7	17.5
DK:	10.6	11.4	9.2	7.7

Quoted below are the 10 most typical remarks of the young men:

1 What with the development of science, the mechanization of man, and man's alienation, society has become one in which mutual confidence is attenuated and the sense of human sympathy and affection doesn't appear. Because of this isn't religion becoming more necessary as a support for man's heart?

2 I think it is a good thing that by relying on God people obtain support and peace of heart.

3 I don't deny religion in all of its aspects, as I acknowledge its value as a spiritual support.

4 I think that religion is important both to steady the heart when it is wavering and also to build man's character.

5 I don't want to deny religion, because it is more convenient for man to create a God he can rely on than to rely on man.

6 If there is someone who can be happy by believing in and relying on God, I think it is a very good thing.

7 All men are weak in some way and are looking for some kind of support. If thereby a man comes to believe in a certain sense it is perfectly all right.

8 The man who is looking for something to rely on becomes predisposed to believe in God. Isn't it a very good thing if by this belief his heart is relieved and a smile appears on his face?

9 At present I acknowledge the existence of God as a support for my heart and the object of my aspirations.

10 Man, facing his existence, finds a support for himself in religion and makes it a place of repose.

A careful scrutiny of the above statements will certainly reveal quite clearly the purely subjective aspect of religion to the responding subjects.

22 *Religion gives meaning to a man's life and clarifies the purpose of his existence*

THIS statement presents religion more or less in a doctrinal aspect. Religion teaches man what his purpose is, enlightens him, gives sense to his life, and elucidates the reason for his existence. In this sense, religion appears to be more directly connected with reason than with human feelings. The students accepting this thesis are fewer in number than those who agree with the premise that religion strengthens the human heart.

It is clear enough that the young Japanese would like to discover why he exists, what he exists for. It is upon entering the university that perhaps he begins to ponder with greater frequency upon fundamental human problems. This is a period of reflection. Ordinarily, however, he is lost in this contemplation. Those who feel such problems more acutely try to find some solution in their reading and their conversation with friends. The books most often sought in these cases are the works of Jean Paul Sartre, Bertrand Russell, and even Nietzsche. They know the translations of Albert Camus, André Gide, Thomas Mann and Ernest Hemingway. But they fail to find any positive solution in such Western literature; as a matter of fact, most of them lack the necessary background to understand the works of Occidental philosophers. Furthermore, Western philosophy is seen by these youths as essentially metaphysical discourses, which is contrary to the intuitive nature of Oriental peoples. The young Japanese will continue admiring the West for its technical and industrial development and progress, but he is likely to feel nothing but distrust, confusion and skepticism about its philosophy. Actually, the young Japanese just entering the university, more often than not, is thoroughly ignorant about Occidental philosophy: yet, even then, he already harbors some suspicions and doubts about it.

The Japanese young man unconsciously feels a certain aversion for anything that spells unconditional adherence to absolute values. He recognizes such faithful attachment as the cause that led the preceding generations to failure and ruin from the last war. These past generations had clung to certain values which they believed to be true and absolute and, on the basis of such tenacious belief, they led the Japanese nation to the tragedy of war.

E

The failure of the last war has led the Japanese youth to assign relative values to what used to be taken as genuine and sacred. On the other hand, the Occident known by these young men appears to them as a completely materialistic and egoistic world. The logical consequence of the resulting confusion is their skeptical attitude toward all problems related to the transcendent, to everything that extends beyond the empirical field of the sciences.

Japanese youth, if asked whether they believe man can know what the true reason in living is, what man's purpose is, would answer, in an overwhelming majority, that that is an impossibility. And, in accordance with the passive resignation to fate that characterizes Japanese psychology, they would add: *shikata ga nai*—there's nothing that can be done about it, that such is man's destiny, to just live without knowing why or for what ends. To discuss such problems is pure *rikutsu*—belaboring human understanding. Any interpretation of what man's purpose is will always be subjective and relative.

However, about 40% of the students accept the premise that religion enlightens man on the reason for his existence and shows him his purpose. There are numerous statements by the subjects that show this opinion.

1 By believing in religion, one can lose his uncertainty and is able to go on with a purpose in life.
2 When I consider the purpose of life or how a man should live, then for the first time I am confronted with religion.
3 Religion in the true meaning of the word is born precisely at the moment man thinks of the meaning and the purpose of human life.
4 If a man sincerely believes in religion, I think his life becomes somehow consistent.

We would be interpreting the above remarks erroneously, however, if we were to consider them to be dealing with the true, objective purpose of man. The four young men who are quoted above are enrolled in the Department of Sciences of Sophia University and are personally known to the author. They not only do not profess any faith but also have a clearly skeptical attitude toward religion. Their own interpretation of their responses is the ordinary one of students. Religion is concerned with man's fundamental problems and all religions speak of the purpose of man and of the reason for his being. Whoever believes in religion and accepts its tenets will have some orientation in his living and will proceed with determination toward a definite goal. What is important is to believe in this purpose; whether the religion be true or not, whether it advocates one or another purpose—these are of the least importance. After all, everything in this respect is always subjective and relative. But the people who cannot find this orientation in life by themselves would be better off looking for it in some religion.

TABLE 24

Boys:	TR(5,178)	GA(3,066)	GB(480)	SU(1,120)
	%	%	%	%
SA:	8.8	9.0	8.5	13.1
A:	32.4	33.2	31.3	37.3
TA:	41.2	42.2	39.8	50.4
SD:	12.8	13.9	11.3	12.0
D:	21.8	20.9	23.1	20.5
TD:	34.6	34.8	34.4	32.5
DK:	24.1	23.0	25.8	17.1

Girls:	TR(1,002)	GA(620)	GB(87)	SU(495)
	%	%	%	%
SA:	14.7	16.6	11.5	27.5
A:	34.1	33.9	34.5	39.3
TA:	48.8	50.5	46.0	66.8
SD:	11.2	11.1	11.5	5.1
D:	19.8	18.5	21,8	16.8
TD:	31.0	29.6	33.3	21.9
DK:	20.2	19.8	20.7	11.3

5 Religion guides all the actions of man to one end. If the religion is true, the life of a man who relies on that religion becomes very consistent. But even if the religion is not true, it does not matter. One who is not able by himself to grasp the purpose of life, does it by religion. By believing in religion one directs the course of his life toward a purpose full of meaning.

We believe that some of the other remarks, which are quoted below, can also be taken in the same sense.

6 I think of religion as something which gives the answers to the problem of human existence.

7 Religion comes into being when man asks himself what is man and what is his purpose in life.

8 Religion is something which constantly gives an interpretation to man's life.

9 Religion outlines the purpose of man's existence.

10 I would like to know the goal of man's development. I firmly believe that some goal exists. If an answer can be given, probably it will be found in religion.

23 *Religion dispels the uneasiness about drifting into nothingness with man's
death*

THE thought of death is intimately woven into the idea of religion. All religions have their special rituals for the hour of death and for the burial. Japanese youth also connect these two ideas in their concepts of religion. In the first form of our questionnaire, the relationship between religion and death was expressed in a different manner. There it was said that religion is born of the fear which man has of death. The affirmative replies wavered between 55% and 60% of the respondents. But we chose to present the theme in a more positive way. In the original postulate, we presented religion, as we did in several other propositions, as something purely subjective, devised by man to defend himself against his fear of death. As revised, the thesis presents not this negative aspect but the positive idea that religion calms human anguish at the prospect of death, at the thought of returning to nothingness.

The affirmative responses to the question, as formulated in this manner, go down to 30%; we believe this difference in the replies to be a natural one. In the first place, the young man just entering the university will very rarely have thought seriously of death; further, numerous young men admit that

TABLE 25

Boys:	TR(5,178)	GA(3,066)	GB(480)	SU(1,120)
	%	%	%	%
SA:	7.1	7.5	6.5	10.6
A:	23.1	24.0	21.7	33.1
TA:	30.2	31.5	28.2	43.7
SD:	15.1	14.9	15.4	11.7
D:	18.1	17.9	18.3	12.8
TD:	33.2	32.8	33.7	24.5
DK:	36.6	35.7	38.1	31.8

Girls:	TR(1,002)	GA(620)	GB(87)	SU(495)
	%	%	%	%
SA:	8.7	9.0	8.0	13.1
A:	33.8	31.9	36.8	46.1
TA:	42.5	40.9	44.8	59.2
SD:	10.0	11.9	6.9	7.7
D:	18.7	16.8	21.8	12.7
TD:	28.7	28.7	28.7	20.4
DK:	28.8	30.3	26.4	20.4

they systematically reject any thought of death which may come to them. Only in cases where they have had to witness the death of someone close have they been forced to think of death. When at times we have had to touch on the subject of death in psychology classes, we felt in the students a reaction of displeasure and annoyance. *Iya da*—it bothers us—has been the remark most frequently repeated by them on such occasions. "Death is not for the young; it is too far removed from us," a group of young men once told us. The majority of the young people solve the problem of death in the most simple and ordinary manner: they simply refuse to think about it.

In the second place, the young Japanese has not had any religious experience connected with death or the idea of death. As we mentioned earlier, the majority of the young men have had some experience of a religious nature related to prayer and to the discovery of peace and comfort during difficult times in their lives; this is why, to questions on such topics, they could give answers of a more positive tenor and with a greater knowledge of the premises. But when he is told that religion soothes fear of death, he is being spoken to of something he has never experienced; never has he attempted to seek in religion the solution to the problem of his having to die someday. Furthermore, he is inclined to view this point with a certain amount of skepticism. When he comes to old age, when the hour of death should approach, it is possible that religion may give him comfort; but normally he does not believe that religion could really be the true solution to the anguish of death.

Their responses are in accord with the interpretation we give to their attitudes. About 30% would be inclined toward accepting the comforting value of religion on the thought of dying; another 33% would be for denying this; and the majority of about 35% would give a doubtful reply, not knowing whether to say yes or no, not having had any experience on which to base some categorical reply and not having really thought seriously about it previously. This last group simply knows that all religions touch on the problem of death and that this is why many older folks come to follow some belief; but they can neither affirm nor deny that religion actually dissipates distress and grief at the prospect of death.

Following are typical statements of young men:

1 To the extent that man is a living being, he seems not to be able to put off death. It is there that there is a reason why man is in search of some absolute, be it God or Buddha.

2 Religion is a mighty force. I think it is the solution in the face of human death. It gives an answer to the riddle of man's death. One who believes in religion is always somehow free from anxiety. He can lead his life accordingly in a composed way.

3 Man's life is a very transitory, short thing. A man so limited yearns for something of immortality in eternity. Isn't this just what religion is?

4 It is said that all living beings must die. And so I think it is because man thinks of death that he discusses religion. Is it not in religion that man seeks a support from this spiritual anxiety?

5 Because man has received life in this world, he must experience death. But man fears death. Any religion at all takes as its point of departure the time when it began to consider human death.

6 Believers in religion believe because they fear the life after death.

7 If there were not such a thing as death for man, religion would probably not have come into existence. Religion, it seems, arose to comfort man a little bit in bearing this transitory fate.

8 When I think of death, a kind of anxiety arises. To divert anxiety in some way I do not think it would be an overstatement to say that man wants to believe in religion with all his heart in an attempt to cling to something.

9 When one faces death squarely or when one feels it, unfailingly fear arises. In an attempt to ease that fear even a little, I think one's heart is attracted to religion.

10 We can think in a very clear cut way about the theory that life is a very fleeting thing which ends in this present world; but this theory is very unsatisfactory and we prefer not to think in that way. Is it not from this attitude that one creates religion and tries to attain satisfaction by giving oneself in belief to it?

24 *Religion offers a solution to man's anxieties*

A BIG majority of the students agree that religion comforts man. While they may have in mind purely subjective comfort, a comfort of man's imagining, or the kind of comfort needed especially by the weak, the young men do not usually deny religion's soothing property. And it is precisely because it affords such a relief that even modern man of today often seeks religion.

The replies that we received do not reflect this attitude of the students, since only 36% answered affirmatively while more than 40% gave negative responses. In the same way that we proceeded where our statement produced answers which seemed contrary to our expectations, we also conducted for this thesis different interviews with numerous students to unearth further details relative to their true opinions. From these talks, we discovered that to the students the postulate has two interpretations. Frequently, students have given it too broad and literal an interpretation, as if religion magically made trials and sorrows disappear so that for a follower of a religion there are no difficulties and pains. It is clear that those who understood the postulate in this manner could not have given a positive response. It is this misunderstanding of the question that makes the negative responses relatively great in number. On the other hand, those who understood it to mean that religion comforts and relieves human suffering, and give strength to endure life's hardships, were inclined toward a positive reply.

TABLE 26

Boys:	TR(5,178)	GA(3,066)	GB(480)	SU(1,120)
	%	%	%	%
SA:	4.1	4.8	3.1	5.6
A:	32.6	33.4	32.3	39.5
TA:	36.7	38.2	35.4	45.1
SD:	18.9	19.0	17.9	17.8
D:	23.9	24.0	23.8	22.5
TD:	42.8	43.0	41.7	40.3
DK:	20.5	18.8	22.9	14.6

Girls:	TR(1,002)	GA(620)	GB(87)	SU(495)
	%	%	%	%
SA:	5.7	5,0	6.9	7.3
A:	35.4	36.0	34.5	43.8
TA:	41.1	41.0	41.4	51.1
SD:	15.2	16.1	13.8	12.3
D:	27.5	26.8	28.7	24.7
TD:	42.7	42.9	42.5	37.0
DK:	16.1	16.1	16.1	11.9

Quoted below are typical remarks of the students:

1　Man is a very weak creature. When he is confronted with all the problems and difficulties inherent in human life, he is able by relying on religion to pull himself through.
2　Religion offers a solution to the various anxieties that a man runs into in the course of his life.
3　Besides the anxieties of present-day man being so excessive, there is virtually no one that he can depend upon. In order to save himself from such a situation, I think that religion is the one thing he can depend on.
4　By relying on religion you can find alleviation for your anxieties and troubles.
5　Man leans on religion to free himself from his worries, weakness and perplexities.
6　Religion harmonizes man's divided heart.
7　In a time like today when the number of people who are anxious because they have no idea what tomorrow may bring is increasing and the variety of human worries is becoming ever more diverse, the need for religion is more intense.

8 Man is a being of spiritual activity and, consequently, he has spiritual anxieties. The direction to be taken in this regard, that is the way which leads to a solution, is that of religion.

9 Religion is something to heal social anxieties and man's internal contradictions.

10 Man tries to alleviate his sufferings and make less heavy the responsibility for his sins by speaking of it to someone outside. And he tries to do it by believing in God or Buddha. In this way these sufferings and this responsibility don't lie hidden inside of him. In this respect, religion helps a lot in ordinary daily life.

All the above expressions show that the young men know that religion does not make human suffering disappear, but that it does help by giving spiritual comfort in such misery. Many of the students speak of human problems, trials and miseries in general terms, but some go to the extent of specifying a few of the more serious difficulties which man today has to face, such as the uncertainty of human life, the insecurity of tomorrow, the complexities of actual social problems, mutual distrust among men and an absolute lack of mutual affection, inner conflicts of emotions, one's own personal limitations, qualms of conscience arising from sin, and others. In all these tribulations, religion intervenes as a faithful friend to be trusted, ever ready to extend a helping hand to aid and comfort.

25 The teaching of religion is morally excellent, and, because it fosters kindred human love, it is quite important for mankind

A NUMBER of Japanese writers have come to say that "the end of the war was the end of Japanese virtue and morality." The very words *dōtoku*, meaning morality, and *shūshin*, for moral training, ceased to be employed; and until recently the English word "moral" was preferred when speaking of ethical problems. Evidently, moral education prior to the war was the most efficacious in inculcating patriotic spirit to the point of fanaticism. Japanese morals, founded upon the nationalistic myth and directed entirely toward the emperor and the country, taken as a family community, found its base crumbling, and the initial natural reaction was loss of direction and ethical anarchy.[30]

The only moral principles which came to fill the postwar ethical gap were the democratic beliefs imposed by America. These tenets raise high the rights of the individual; they exalt equality among men, human liberties, and the freedom to seek one's own happiness. Added to this is the fact of the tragic situation in which Japan found herself after the war: spiritual anguish, material needs in every sphere of living, struggle for self-survival, dearth

---

[30] We find these ideas developed in the article "Atarashii moraru o motomete" 新しいモラルを求めて (In Search of a New Morality), *Chisei* 知性, June 1955, pp. 27-47.

of food and shelter. All these led to an amorality that is definitely hedonistic, selfish and individualistic, which brings about, in a wide swath of the youth, antisocial behavior and an alarming growth of delinquency.[31]

It has been widely discussed, and it is still being debated, whether the traditional Japanese morality was what the moralists and cultural anthropologists call "shame morality" as opposed to "guilt morality." We do not concur with the radical opinion of some writers who consider Japanese morality as a culture which excludes consciousness of sin; but we do believe that the pristine Japanese cultural and educational systems stressed principally "the consciousness of shame before others" more than it did the interior feeling about sin. *Haji no kyōiku* is the apt Japanese phrase for it.[32] What is of special interest to us is that, in the midst of the moral dislocation into which Japanese youth was plunged after the war, according to many Japanese authors, there is emerging a new morality which they refer to as the "morality of common sense," or "practical and utilitarian morality," which in the process of day to day living, goes on teaching us what is good, showing us what is noble, what falls under human nature, and underscores the dignity of man who lives in a society and co-exists with nature.[33] It would appear that in this new morality the personal, inmost element of man, that element which makes him conscious of sin, is receiving increasing accentuation, at the expense of that other feeling of "shame before others." While all are agreed that it is an imperfect morality which lacks the fundamental principles upon which such morality can be based, and that there is still a great need for broader and better moral education in schools, it is tacitly admitted that it is possible such new morality could come to be better than the old principles of Japanese morality, as regards its aspects of greater sincerity toward the self and a clearer individual moral consciousness. We shall come back to these points when we deal with the attitude of Japanese youth toward the problem of morality, in chapter V.

[31] The latest statistics show that juvenile delinquency during 1966 continued to increase. From January 1 to November 30, 1966, the police arrested 174,595 young boys between the ages of fourteen and nineteen years. Excepting 45,178 who are taken in for "violations of the Traffic Law," the rest, 129,427 teenagers, "were charged with atrocious crimes, intellectual offenses, offenses against public morals and theft. Classified according to types of crimes, 6,140 were accused of vicious crimes, and 37,385 for crimes of violence. The number arrested for other crimes was: 81,469 for theft, 2,251 for intellectual crimes, and 2,183 for gambling and immoral offenses." *The Japan Times,* December 22, 1966.

[32] Douglas G. Haring writes: "The Japanese exemplify the anthropological concept of a 'shame culture'; the driving motive of individuals is fear of shame rather than sense of guilt." *Personal Character and Cultural Milieu,* Syracuse University Press, Syracuse, 1964, p. 426. See also Ruth Benedict, *The Chrysanthemum and the Sword,* Houghton Mifflin, Boston, 1946, pp. 195-227.

[33] Hasegawa Nyozekan 長谷川如是閑, "Rinrigaku to dōtoku jijitsu" 倫理学と道徳事実 (Ethics and Moral Reality), in *Gendai rinri* 現代倫理 (Modern Ethics), Chikuma shobō 筑摩書房, Tokyo, 1958, IV, 139-154. See also Alfonso Nebreda, "The Japanese University Students Confront Religion," *Monumenta Nipponica,* 1965, XX, 298-318.

Does religion play any role in this moral readjustment? The topic of the separation or duality which the Japanese have maintained vis-a-vis religion and morals, has likewise been widely written about and discussed. "The Western world," Professor Matsushita Masatoshi tells us, "tends to join Christian faith with morality. While there are exceptions, the countries of the West, in general, place morality upon the foundation of religious beliefs, so that people tend to degenerate morally according to how far distant they separate themselves from religion. The Japanese has a high degree of morality, but his morality is independent from religion."[34]

We agree with Prof. Matsushita's opinion, and we are of the belief that whoever understands the whole moral system by which Japan has been ruled for centuries will likewise concur with him. Furthermore, we believe that even today the great majority of the Japanese people go on living in such duality. However, we are of the opinion that, when considering the younger generation in Japan, particularly university students, there are quite a number of them who look upon religion as a means to moral training. This could be due to the influence of Christianity; but it is certain that those students are in the majority who speak of religion in such a way, and they recognize the moralizing influence of religion. Are they thinking of Christianity when making such statements? Although they speak of religion in broad, general terms, perhaps they refer in a special way to Christianity. We lean to this conjecture because of the fact that while very few really know the doctrinal contents of Christianity, very many of them are congizant of its moral aspects. In numerous talks with these students, we tried to discover up to what point they knew about the subject of Christianity. With almost no exception, they came to mention that famous principle of charity expounded in the bible: "Love thy neighbor as thyself." And upon numerous occasions, we experienced the surprise of hearing from their very lips, even from those who had just entered the university, that they believe this principle is the only true one, and because of it Christianity should be respected.

Let us listen to these young people tell us of the importance of religion in encouraging morality. On this point, our difficulty lay in choosing only 10 typical expressions because of the great many which we were able to single out.

1. Religion is the basic moral principle of life.
2. Religion is necessary to instill human morals in all peoples.
3. I think that the teachings of Christ constitute the true religion which directs human moral life.
4. If the teachings of religion on love, and the religious systems of morali-

---

[34] Quoted in J.J. Spae, *Christian Corridors of Japan*, Oriens Institute for Religious Research, Tokyo, 1965, p. 175. This text is attributed to Prof. Matsushita Masatoshi by Kusanagi Yutaka.

ty did not exist, I wonder whether a man could be called a real man.

5 The heart of religion is said to be love. Religion may become the spiritual support of mankind, and have the role of spiritually binding the human community together.

6 From religion man learns how he must live.

7 Religion's greatest role is love and spiritual joy.

8 Religion's role has been to offer the ideal for human morality.

9 Religion is that which leads man's vague and unfathomable heart in the right direction.

10 Christianity strongly stresses love. If all the people in the world were really bound together by love, there could not be any greater happiness.

TABLE 27

Boys:	TR(5,178)	GA(3,066)	GB(480)	SU(1,120)
	%	%	%	%
SA:	11.8	12.7	10.4	14.8
A:	43.7	43.7	43.5	50.0
TA:	55.5	56.4	53.9	64.8
SD:	7.1	6.8	7.5	5.2
D:	19.3	19.4	19.2	19.8
TD:	26.4	26.2	26.7	25.0
DK:	18.1	17.4	19.4	10.2

Girls:	TR(1,002)	GA(620)	GB(87)	SU(495)
	%	%	%	%
SA:	16.3	18.4	15.0	19.8
A:	45.9	47.1	45.2	49.5
TA:	62.2	65.5	60.2	69.3
SD:	6.4	5.7	6.8	3.2
D:	14.9	12.6	16.2	17.4
TD:	21.3	18.3	23.0	20.6
DK:	16.5	16.1	16.8	10.1

Notice that in some of the statements there is concrete and specific mention of Christianity.

Fifty-five percent of the students answered affirmatively to our question; that is, they consider religion of great importance to man insofar as it teaches high moral doctrines and fosters mutual love among men. However, the second point, about the encouragement of mutual love, has kept, we believe, the percentage of positive replies from being larger. Touching upon it, many young men relate it to the question of religious wars. We all know that, unfortunately, religious wars are not yet things merely of the past for they go on being waged up to the present. Both in their essays and in their conversations, the young men ask the question of how it is possible that social disturbances still persist under religious motivation. They speak of the tremendous conflicts between the Buddhists and the Catholics in Vietnam, which are known to all. And they have heard it said that, in general, those of one religion lambaste those of another religion. To them, all this poses a real paradox: how can it be explained that religions which teach brotherly love have followers who, contradictorily, practice something else between themselves?

26 *Religion gives discipline and moral training to the whole man*

As was to be expected, the positive replies to this postulate were almost exactly the same as those obtained for the preceding question. There is a shade of difference between the two statements: in the former, religion was mentioned in a setting more or less theoretical insofar as it offers man a moral ideal, a moral code of great perfection; in the latter, religion is touched upon in its practical aspect in the sense that it is a means, an effective tool for self-discipline and an instrument of moral exercise. There is a reason why we included this question: the words *tanren*, discipline, and *shūyō*, moral education or spiritual training, are frequently employed by the young people when talking of religion. This convinces us all the more that the young gneration of Japanese do not persist in retaining the duality of the terms "religion" and "moral" as had prevailed in the old Japanese culture. It does not necessarily mean that the young Japanese believe religion is absolutely required for a perfectly moral existence; but it does mean that they believe religion greatly assists many people in attaining the point of putting into practice the great human virtues.

Here are typical expressions used by the subjects relative to the question:

1 For me religion is nothing more than a means to good moral behavior.
2 Could it be possible to have moral education without a religious foundation?
3 Isn't religion the thing which cultivates man? At least I have this feeling.
4 Religion is a spiritual thing. By relying on religion we improve our moral behavior.
5 Religion supplies moral norms to man.
6 Religion is something for man. It fosters in him a more perfect spiritual life.
7 In today's world with its many strong stimulations I think it is good to be educated in a religious school.

8 By means of the discipline of *zazen* of Zen Buddhism and suchlike things, men are purified in soul and body, they gain an insight into their essence, and achieve peace of heart. I think the making of such men is a good thing.

9 I don't have any faith but I am of the opinion that man should have some interest in religion because, from the moral point of view, it has many good points.

10 Because many of religion's concepts are morally good for us, in order to progress in life we must clearly understand this religion and then act according to it. Those with faith can live a better life than those without faith.

TABLE 28

Boys:	TR(5,178)	GA(3,066)	GB(480)	SU(1,120)
	%	%	%	%
SA:	10.8	11.7	9.4	13.6
A:	44.2	45.4	42.5	50.5
TA:	55.0	57.1	51.9	64.1
SD:	8.3	8.2	8.3	5.1
D:	15.9	15.9	16.0	14.9
TD:	24.2	24.1	24.3	20.0
DK:	20.8	18.8	23.8	15.9

Girls:	TR(1,002)	GA(620)	GB(87)	SU(495)
	%	%	%	%
SA:	11.2	12.4	9.2	18.2
A:	50.8	47.4	56.3	55.0
TA:	62.0	59.8	65.5	73.2
SD:	5.3	6.5	3.4	3.2
D:	15.5	15.2	16.1	11.1
TD:	20.8	21.7	19.5	14.3
DK:	17.2	18.5	14.9	12.5

27 *Religion unceasingly stirs up in man aspirations for his self-improvement*

RELIGION is a dynamic, spiritual, internal force which makes man always want to better himself, to perfect himself. This is the meaning of our postulate here. But the bettering and the perfecting are understood by the students not only to mean improvement in virtues and perfecting in a moral sense but also in the broader sense of man's total perfection including his personality and other human qualities. It is interesting to note that the word *kōjō*—elevation or uplift—which many students used when speaking of the effects religion has on man, is almost always connected with the word *jinkaku*, as in *jinkaku no kōjō*—elevation of the personality.

1 Religion has as its aim the elevation of man's personality.
2 Religion must contribute to the uplift of human personality.
3 The true teachings of religion do not pertain to such things as personal gain here and now, consultation about one's personal affairs, or ancestor worship; but rather to the elevation of oneself and the enjoyment of happiness with other people.
4 In order to live in such a way as to develop to a higher degree one's potentialities for growth, religion is necessary.
5 If one believes in God, one is lifted above oneself, and with courage and self-confidence one is able to move ahead and to cope with difficulties.
6 True religion must be such as to make up for the defects or human nature and to elevate all men to the level of true men.

In this sense, religion is something more than a mere guide to the solution of moral problems; it is more than a means affording a chance to practice virtues. Those who responded affirmatively to this statement are the very

TABLE 29

Boys:	TR(5,178)	GA(3,066)	GB(480)	SU(1,120)
	%	%	%	%
SA:	6.7	8.1	4.6	10.3
A:	27.8	27.3	28.5	31.3
TA:	34.5	35.4	33.1	41.6
SD:	11.0	10.8	11.2	10.0
D:	20.7	22.0	11.8	22.0
TD:	31.7	32.8	30.0	32.0
DK:	33.8	31.8	36.9	26.4

Girls:	TR(1,002)	GA(620)	GB(87)	SU(495)
	%	%	%	%
SA:	12.8	14.4	10.3	23.0
A:	35.0	33.9	36.8	37.0
TA:	47.8	48.3	47.1	60.0
SD:	7.9	7.1	9.2	5.6
D:	18.8	18.4	19.5	16.2
TD:	26.7	25.5	28.7	21.8
DK:	25.5	26.2	24.1	18.2

same ones who replied negatively to statement No. 10 where it was said that religion inhibits personality development. Their answers here, therefore, could only mean that religion does help in personality development and growth. Expectedly, the affirmative replies decrease proportionately in relation to the previous ones; despite the percentage descent, the ratio is still a considerable 34%. It is noteworthy that those who answered "Don't know," 33.9%, are more numerous than the ones who denied the proposition a mere 31.7%.

28 *Religion can make a great contribution to the realization of peace among mankind*

ABOUT 50% of the students recognize some social values in religion. Specifically, they believe that religion can be a very important factor in the establishment of the ideals of peace among men. It is interesting to note that when the subjects cite this idea, they do not come out directly with a statement to the effect that religion contributes to the peace of the world; rather, they say that religion should have among its most important ends the establishment of this peace. They are of the belief that every religion should have as the ultimate objective of all its activities the internal and external peace among nations. As we noted in commentaries on other postulates, one of the most profound shocks which religion produces in students is the historical fact that in various past instances religion was the prime factor in international discord and even war. However, these students come finally to understand that these conflicts run direclty counter to the very essence of what religion should stand for. If not all of them think in this manner, at least half of them do.

It is possible that such a mental attitude could have been produced by the frequent mention in the newspapers of the appeals for peace of the last several Popes, of the peace movements and world-girdling travels organized by the Buddhist associations of Japan. As a matter of fact, there is hardly any society or religious group anywhere which has not made, in the past few years, some call for peace and the end of all wars, in one way or another. If all the religions of the world were to labor indefatigably for peace in every country, religion would emerge as a tremendous moral force which will exert great influence toward the achievement of such a peace.

1 For all men to live equally and peacefully in present-day society, together with self-reflection, mutual confidence and supplication, it is necessary to build a progressive society. For this end, religions such as Buddhism, Christianity, etc., are necessary.

2 If one were to specify the purpose of religion, I think it is peace and happiness for mankind.

3 At the present time one cannot talk about religion and ignore the social community. That is to say, I believe that religion and society are

mutually related, and should contribute to the happiness of mankind.

4 In a world like the present one, I think that religion must greatly contribute to world peace.

5 Since contemporary civilization has become rather advanced, I think that if we follow religion (true religion), we can hold in check contemporary dangers too.

6 If men could develop a world view based on a single way of expression (e.g. believing in a world religion), would not peace be present in this world to a great extent?

TABLE 30

Boys:	TR(5,178)	GA(3,066)	GB(480)	SU(1,120)
	%	%	%	%
SA:	12.0	13.9	9.4	20.1
A:	38.7	39.7	37.3	47.2
TA:	50.7	53.6	46.7	67.3
SD:	12.1	11.0	13.8	5.6
D:	19.5	18.8	20.4	14.6
TD:	31.6	29.8	34.2	20.2
DK:	17.6	16.6	19.1	12.5

Girls:	TR(1,002)	GA(620)	GB(87)	SU(495)
	%	%	%	%
SA:	17.4	18.2	16.1	31.7
A:	39.2	37.9	41.4	44.7
TA:	56.6	56.1	57.5	76.4
SD:	8.5	8.1	9.2	2.6
D:	18.5	18.5	18.4	12.5
TD:	27.0	26.6	27.6	15.1
DK:	16.4	17.3	14.9	8.5

29 *Religion has the power to solve the disorders of society and to overcome personal egoism*

THE difference, in some aspects, between the above statement and the one immediately preceding it is the same one we already noted in other cases. Here it is not averred that religion should help uproot social disorders and their principal cause which is great human egocentricity; if these factors were to disappear, the peace of the world could readily be attained. Instead, it is stated that religion has, in fact, the strength and the power to destroy these enemies of society and of peace.

Confronted with such an optimistic point of view, the young Japanese, naturally, shows himself to be skeptical. Religion should aid in the lessening of people's egoism, in the eradication of society's disorders, in the encouragement of peace among nations, it is true; but that religion should have the power to destroy and eradicate all these ills is something very dubious.

Thus, the affirmative responses to this postulate are down quite a bit.

The following are typical remarks of the students:

1 Religion influences the moral aspect of mankind. Furthermore, it is important for keeping social order.
2 Religion contributes considerably to the cohesion and unity of society.
3 Religion soothes the feelings of men. On the social scene, it helps do away with undesirable thinking among individuals.
4 Religion calms the disordered hearts of men.
5 The essence of religion is self-denial and the service of that collectivity of individuals which is society.
6 The belief in God becomes a force which fosters harmony in social life.

TABLE 31

Boys:	TR(5,178)	GA(3,066)	GB(480)	SU(1,120)
	%	%	%	%
SA:	6.8	6.9	6.7	8.8
A:	30.6	31.8	28.8	43.5
TA:	37.4	38.7	35.5	52.3
SD:	15.6	15.5	15.8	9.8
D:	23.9	24.5	22.9	17.7
TD:	39.5	40.0	38.7	27.5
DK:	23.1	21.2	25.8	20.2

Girls:	TR(1,002)	GA(620)	GB(87)	SU(495)
	%	%	%	%
SA:	8.3	7.7	9.2	11.5
A:	36.2	35.8	36.8	48.5
TA:	44.5	43.5	46.0	60.0
SD:	11.1	11.6	10.3	9.1
D:	25.8	24.0	28.7	18.2
TD:	36.9	35.6	39.0	27.3
DK:	18.6	20.8	14.9	12.7

F

30 *Man must have an attitude of understanding and respect for religion*

THIS statement is taken from the Japanese Constitution. The new postwar Constitution of Japan proclaims full religious liberty and asserts the mutual tolerance which every Japanese must have for whatever beliefs his fellow citizens may profess. No one is to interfere with, much less exert pressure upon, the religious beliefs of the citizens. The majority of today's youth possess this spirit of tolerance in religious matters.

The way the Constitution is worded shows a double attitude: first of all, an understanding of religion, and secondly a respect and reverence for it. The first merely manifests tolerance in religious questions; the second expresses something more positive, which is not mere permissiveness but a positive regard and deference for religion.

In order not to alter the phraseology of the Constitution in our postulate, we lifted it bodily from the text for use in this statement, fully cognizant of the possible influence it may exert upon the responses of the young men, with its double element of tolerance and respect for religion in the back of our minds. As expected, there were quite numerous cases in which the young men answered negatively and indicated explicitly their non-conformity with the element of *sonchō*—esteem. If the question merely mentioned

TABLE 32

Boys:	TR(5,178)	GA(3,066)	GB(480)	SU(1,120)
	%	%	%	%
SA:	15.6	16.3	14.6	21.3
A:	39.1	41.1	36.0	40.4
TA:	54.7	57.4	50.6	61.7
SD:	9.0	9.3	8.5	7.2
D:	20.2	19.7	20.8	19.7
TD:	29.2	29.0	29.3	26.9
DK:	16.1	13.5	20.0	11.4

Girls:	TR(1,002)	GA(620)	GB(87)	SU(495)
	%	%	%	%
SA:	15.9	19.4	10.3	30.3
A:	45.3	39.8	54.0	42.0
TA:	61.2	59.2	64.3	72.3
SD:	5.7	5.6	5.7	3.4
D:	21.4	21.1	21.8	14.2
TD:	27.1	26.7	27.5	17.6
DK:	11.7	14.0	8.2	11.1

tolerance, we believe that the affirmative responses would reach a very high percentage; but with the "respect and deference" concept mixed, this percentage came to about 55% which is what we should expect. This is to say that we have observed in all the preceding questions precisely this very percentage, more or less, of those who accept the positive values indicated in such statements; the young men who admit these values would naturally also reply affirmatively to the question of whether or not religion deserves our respect and deference.

31 *It can be said that a life based on religion deserves respect*

"THE person who leads a life based on religion deserves our respect." Here we are no longer talking of the abstract respect for religion, but of respect and esteem in the concrete, for the individual who professes some religion. It is clear that this postulate differs from the preceding one to a great extent. The percentage of affirmative responses goes down to some 30% among the boys, to 36% among the girls.

The most proximate experiences of our youth are their contacts with Japanese believers, and they are cognizant of the unprecedented increase in the number of adherents of the new religions. They may have some tolerance for them, but certainly few, indeed, are those who would admit that they hold in esteem those who belong to some religion, precisely because they are religionists. Their concept of the followers of Sōka-gakkai, for instance, is surely not one to evoke in them an attitude of respect and deference. Their feelings toward the followers of the other new religions are not any better.[35]

Even the image they currently have of the Japanese bonze is not any too attractive. The traditional bonze of the Japanese Buddhist temples has in general lost a great amount of prestige and respect in the eyes of the young Japanese. If the bonzes in question are old, the young men consider them "out of date," and if they are younger bonzes, the youth are convinced they came to be such only because of the traditional Japanese custom of having sons inherit their father's position as bonze.

We have on hand a survey conducted in 1959 at the University of Ōtani, a Buddhist institution founded in 1665 as a seminary for bonzes of the Shinshū sect. To this day, the university follows the Shinshū tradition and continues to train those who would become Buddhist priests. The study was made among 100 young men enrolled in the university, most of whom were sons of bonzes and many of whom expected to succeed their fathers as priests in the temples of the Buddhist communities. Forty percent of these young men replied that they did not particularly want to become bonzes, but that they had to follow that career since they were obliged to succeed their fathers when the latter died or retired for reasons of age. Only 25.9% answered that they

[35] See Note 26.

positively desired to become bonzes. While a small group remarked that they did not expect to continue in the priestly field, and were not thinking of becoming bonzes, the other 33.4% did not reply to the question. Those who replied that they were forced to follow in their fathers' bonzeic footsteps because of the traditional family obligations, were asked to give their reasons for having such an attitude. The authors of the study did not give us the exact number of replies to this question, but they assured us that there were many who gave *shinkōshin ga nai*—lack of faith—as one of the reasons. Another reason which was given with sufficient frequency was that they felt disdain for the bonze and his work— *sōryo ga kirai*. The authors explained that this last reason might possibly be a coverup for the inferiority complex with which young bonzes are often afflicted.[36]

Numerous, too, were the young men who have talked with us about their experiences with their few Christian friends or acquaintances. Many of them have told us of their respect for these people; but many more have conveyed to us their impression of such persons as quiet, of low ambition, of colorless personality in most cases, and that very few were observed to have leadership qualities.

TABLE 33

Boys:	TR(5,178)	GA(3,066)	GB(480)	SU(1,120)
	%	%	%	%
SA:	6.5	7.4	5.2	8.1
A:	24.3	25.5	22.5	33.8
TA:	30.8	32.9	27.7	41.9
SD:	19.0	19.4	18.5	16.2
D:	29.7	29.1	30.6	29.5
TD:	48.7	48.5	49.1	45.7
DK:	20.4	18.6	23.1	12.4

Girls:	TR(1,002)	GA(620)	GB(87)	SU(495)
	%	%	%	%
SA:	9.2	12.0	4.6	13.9
A:	27.3	30.0	23.0	38.8
TA:	36.5	42.0	27.6	52.7
SD:	13.9	14.7	12.6	7.9
D:	30.6	26.8	36.8	28.1
TD:	44.5	41.5	49.4	36.0
DK:	18.9	16.5	23.0	11.3

[36] Ikeda Yoshisuke and Naka Hisao, "A Sociological Research for the Opinion and At- titude of Buddhist University Students," *The Otani Philosophical Studies*, 1959, VI, 64-78.

All the above reasons underlie the decrease in affirmative responses to the present postulate as compared to the preceding statement.

We have already quoted many remarks by young men in which they talk of the positive values of religion, an indication of an attitude of respect for religion; hence, we believe that we need not repeat similar expressions at this juncture, since this would be merely multiplying such samples. Rather we shall cite assertions of the students which reveal sympathy and respect for people who profess some faith, and which are typical of about 30% of the men. Our quotations cited in connection with postulate No. 10 might be taken as the negative aspect of this question.

1 I consider people who have faith, who pray to God, who avoid evil desires, who lead a modest life, to be great men.

2 I myself do not know what I will believe in the future. Perhaps I will have no faith. Still, I feel that a man who believes in a religion is some sort of a strong person.

3 I am not a Christian, but an ordinary man of the world. I lose my temper at trivial things, and frequently quarrel. But when philosophy class comes around, I am always envious of my teacher (a Catholic priest), and I feel ashamed of myself. If I myself could have a composed heart such as his and love all things as genuinely as he does, how happy I would be. The other day I saw the movie "The Sound of Music." I felt deeply attracted by the beautiful character of the nun of the story. Does a person who has offered his love to God become such a beautiful person? My heart is filled with so delightful a joy. Somehow I feel the existence of God in this world.

4 I see a good number of believers dedicatedly carrying on a life of service and I consider them to be excellent people.

5 I feel envious of a man who can really believe from his heart in a religion, and I myself would like to come to such a state.

6 I have been blessed with the opportunity of speaking with people who believe in religions of various kinds. All of them were men who enjoyed a serene state of mind. Was this created by their faith? When I see men of this type, there are times when I, too, would like to believe.

7 I become envious when I see the cheerful life of believers.

8 When I see people who believe in religion, I become very envious. Why is this? Because they separate themselves from this fickle world and thereby come to posses something which they can trust.

9 Because of the necessity of more level headedness in today's complex society, I think it would be good if man attached more importance to religion.

10 I have a feeling of envy and a lot of respect for a fervent believer and a certain sadness at my own lack thereof.

32 *If religion should ever disappear from this world, it would be a loss to mankind*

THE replies to this question, as expected, range from 50% to 55% in the affirmative. This is the group who see certain positive values in religion both in relation to the individual and in relation to society; both in the psychological, internal and personal aspects of peace, satisfaction, security, etc., and in the moral and civic aspects. Based on these reasons, they will tell us that it would be disastrous if one day religion were to disappear from the world. Both the individual and society in general would be deprived of a powerful spiritual backing.

    1 As for society, if religion disappears from it, it will become more of a mess.

    2 If the religious inspired commandment of love were to disappear, "the might makes right" way of thinking would stifle us, and man would be reduced to an animal.

    3 If we really depended only upon scientific thought to guide our behavior, the truth of the matter is that this world would in one grand burst totally disintegrate. Therefore, upon the basis of religion

TABLE 34

Boys:	TR(5,178)	GA(3,066)	GB(480)	SU(1,120)
	%	%	%	%
SA:	21.5	22.6	20.0	26.5
A:	31.3	31.1	31.5	35.7
TA:	52.8	53.7	51.5	62.2
SD:	6.9	7.4	6.3	5.8
D:	12.8	12.9	12.7	10.8
TD:	19.7	20.3	19.0	16.6
DK:	27.4	25.9	29.5	21.2

Girls:	TR(1,002)	GA(620)	GB(87)	SU(495)
	%	%	%	%
SA:	21.3	24.5	16.1	36.6
A:	33.5	32.9	34.5	34.3
TA:	54.8	57.4	50.6	70.9
SD:	7.3	6.8	8.0	1.8
D:	12.1	9.7	16.1	7.9
TD:	19.4	16.5	24.1	9.7
DK:	25.8	26.1	25.3	19.4

we must firmly establish respect for this earth and for human life.

4 I think that basically religion is a matter of your clearly grasping what you are. Man has a need to expand himself ever outward, ever outward; but at the same time, he must not forget he has a need also to focus himself upon himself. This expansion ever outward is the stuff of science, but this concentration inward is religion. I think that religion will never disappear.

5 The truth is that religion is essential in this world. On the whole you can say that religion fulfills an important role in providing criteria and rules to this world.

6 It seems that society is in a mess (look for instance at all the juvenile crimes). Especially in this sort of world is religion necessary.

7 It goes without saying that the outlook of mankind is tied in with the problem of evaluation. Evaluating a thing has nothing to do with science. Therefore, it seems to me that a man cannot guide his life by science. Science in no way tells us how life is to be lived. And this problem of how to live is more than any other an acute and vital problem, one which cries out to be solved. If in our need to solve this problem we suppose that religion is our salvation, I think that religion will never disappear.

33 *Religion which makes a man grasp the highest truth, beauty and goodness is most important for man*

THIS is the only statement in the entire questionnaire in which the word *shinri*—truth—appears in relation to religion. Religion is what makes it possible for man to discover fundamental truths, the transcendental ones, the most sublime—*saikō no shinri*. Religion, after all, is what illumines the truth.

There are three statements written by the young men in which we discovered this attitude with respect to religion. Of the three responsible for these expressions, one believes in the existence of God but does not belong to any specific religious group. The other two still do not profess any faith, but they believe that religion is, or should be above all, a light that guides toward the real truth. Of the 600 essays we studied, these three are the only ones we found that clearly manifest such an opinion.

1 I search for God not so much as a "support for my heart" but rather because I love truth.

2 Isn't the heart which is searching for truth and kneels down before it touching the essence of religion?

3 Religion must be a signpost which points the way to truth.

It was these phrases which induced us to propound a special postulate that would clearly show the relationship between religion and truth. In some books on religion, written by Japanese authors, there is frequently found the compound phrase *shin-zen-bi*—a condensation of the concepts truth-goodness-beauty linked together—which expresses the values of religion. In other statements of the young men we also discovered the concept of beauty related to religion:

4 Religion comes necessarily into existence when man looks at the beauty of nature and considers all the mysterious phenomena of the universe.

5 Man is in pursuit of an infinite beauty. This pursuit is religion.

TABLE 35

Boys:	TR(5,178)	GA(3,066)	GB(480)	SU(1,120)
	%	%	%	%
SA:	3.0	3.7	2.1	4.9
A:	16.0	15.7	16.5	18.6
TA:	19.0	19.4	18.6	23.5
SD:	32.2	30.7	30.4	30.1
D:	30.2	33.4	29.4	31.9
TD:	62.4	64.1	59.8	62.0
DK:	18.6	16.4	21.6	14.5

Girls:	TR(1,002)	GA(620)	GB(87)	SU(495)
	%	%	%	%
SA:	6.6	7.9	4.6	13.9
A:	20.7	18.5	24.1	22.8
TA:	27.3	26.4	28.7	36.7
SD:	26.0	25.0	27.6	17.0
D:	28.4	28.2	28.7	29.1
TD:	54.4	53.2	56.3	46.1
DK:	18.3	20.3	14.9	17.2

With our question we intended to find out the extent to which students correlate religion with the yearning which every human heart feels for truth, beauty and goodness. Whoever associates religion with these great values in human living will definitely reveal the most favorable attitude toward religion and will consider it as having great importance. Of the young men, 19% replied affirmatively to the question, 63% denied it, and 18% did not know what to say about it.

It is relatively easy for someone to object to any results to this statement because it can be asked how young university students could possibly believe, no matter how small their group might be, that religion leads man to the real truth, beauty and goodness when more than 90% of them do not even profess any religious faith. While it is true that many of the young men who responded affirmatively do not show in their answers any clear and exact knowledge of religion in relation to these great values, they do convey, however, the impression that deep down in their hearts and souls there is a kind of intuitive feeling that seems to tell them there is something in this world which could acutally lead man toward these values, and they suspect this something to be religion or what they think religion must be. We do not deny the possibility that these young men might also be cognizant of the Japanese expression previously cited: *shin-zen-bi no kyōchi*—the sanctuary of truth, goodness and beauty—and that they have been influenced by such an adage. But the very fact of their having been so influenced would be proof of their inner inclination to accept in their hearts these values of religion. We must not believe, either, that this attitude is actually deeply rooted in them; often it is likelier to be a mere passing intuition, or a superficial feeling, which should explain why even among this group of young men there are many who live without any faith and who would not seriously bother to inquire deeper into the problem of religion. But we cannot deny that inside them there is, no matter how unconsciously and vaguely, this great appreciation of religion. As in the majority of previous cases, we observe here a 10% difference between the men and the girls, with the girls constituting the larger number.

34 *Religion is necessary to obtain true happiness*

MAN attains true, genuine happiness through religion. This is the sense of the question presented to the students. Only 18% replied with a "yes." As we have observed before, students who associate religion with inner peace and spiritual tranquility are numerous enough. But, upon talking to them of true and genuine happiness, *shin no kōfuku,* the majority do not know what this would consist of for mortal beings, in the first place. In the second place, this majority think of happiness in terrestial terms. Taking into account their natural skepticism, it becomes logical for them to consider, and be firmly convinced, that true happiness is a mere chimera which is something almost impossible to materialize. From this, we can understand why 82% gave a non-affirmative opinion regarding the postulate. As for the remaining 18% who approved the statement, we could restate what we indicated in the analysis of the preceding question: in most cases, such a positive attitude comes from inner promptings of the human heart which tell them that such inclinations of human beings toward complete happiness will one day be satisfied somehow, and that religion ought to play an important role in man's attainment of this spiritual felicity.

Following are typical remarks of the students in which they associate religion with the concept of happiness:

1 In religion man searches for happiness and peace of heart.

2 I think that religion is something which looks for ways in which man's happiness can be achieved.

3 The purpose of faith is to build up a happy life.

4 Religion harmonizes man's divided heart, enriches his life and makes him happy.

5 Religion's function is to work for man's consolation, tranquility and happiness by making him yearn, worship, and believe in an absolute man-transcending being such as God or Buddha.

6 The true meaning of religion is precisely this:—it tries to fulfill, either in this life or the next, man's infinite yearning for life and happiness by making him rely on the power of an absolute being.

7 In order to obtain happiness, man revere and worships a being he considers to have greater power than himself. Wasn't it because of this that religion came into being?

TABLE 36

Boys:	TR(5,178)	GA(3,066)	GB(480)	SU(1,120)
	%	%	%	%
SA:	3.8	4.3	3.1	7.1
A:	14.2	13.4	15.4	15.1
TA:	18.0	17.7	18.5	22.2
SD:	34.9	35.9	33.3	28.9
D:	28.6	28.1	29.4	31.7
TD:	63.5	64.0	62.7	60.6
DK:	18.5	18.3	18.8	17.2

Girls:	TR(1,002)	GA(620)	GB(87)	SU(495)
	%	%	%	%
SA:	8.6	8.9	8.0	16.2
A:	14.3	13.2	16.1	20.8
TA:	22.9	22.1	24.1	37.0
SD:	26.5	27.3	25.3	18.2
D:	30.9	28.7	34.5	27.7
TD:	57.4	56.0	59.8	45.9
DK:	19.7	21.9	16.1	17.1

35 *Religion is to man a way of incomparable richness, and therefore man must enter upon this way*

As expected, the affirmative responses to this statement do not go beyond 11%. Here we speak of a duty to follow the way of religion which every man must assume. We no longer talk of religion here as a necessity in the psychological sense that it helps and consoles man; rather, we mention it as an obligation. Even from this point of view, we do not mean the word obligation to indicate an imposition by force; we do not contemplate the idea of religion being rammed down man's throat against his will and volition. Instead, we have in mind the moral, personal urging in every man to seek and accept religion beacuse it will show him the way to the fullness of spiritual wealth. Such is the idea propounded to the subjects in this question.

The mere idea of a man's having some obligation with respect to religion is inconceivable to almost all of the students. They even consider such a concept as assailing an individual's freedom. Man is completely free in his behavior with respect to religion. This freedom is construed by them not in the sense that man alone is to decide his position vis-a-vis religion and that nobody could or should force him to accept one or another religion, or to make a choice between being an atheist or a believer. Rather, they interpret it to mean that man has full moral freedom with respect to religion, equating it with his liberty to choose one university or another in which to go on with his studies, or with his freedom to go on a trip abroad or stay at home. In other words, they cannot see the possibility of anybody being obliged by his conscience to accept some kind of religion. The ideas of moral

TABLE 37

Boys:	TR(5,178)	GA(3,066)	GB(480)	SU(1,120)
	%	%	%	%
SA:	2.4	2.6	2.1	3.2
A:	9.5	8.8	10.6	11.8
TA:	11.9	11.4	12.7	15.0
SD:	43.7	46.1	40.2	42.5
D:	32.1	31.9	32.3	34.6
TD:	75.8	78.0	72.5	77.1
DK:	12.3	10.5	14.8	7.9

Girls:	TR(1,002)	GA(620)	GB(87)	SU(495)
	%	%	%	%
SA:	4.1	5.2	2.3	6.5
A:	13.3	12.3	14.9	18.4
TA:	17.4	17.5	17.2	24.9
SD:	37.1	35.8	39.1	31.7
D:	34.8	35.0	34.5	35.3
TD:	71.9	70.8	73.6	67.0
DK:	10.7	11.7	9.2	8.1

liberty and physical freedom, and the difference between these two concepts of liberty, are mixed up in the minds of the students, and very often they confuse one for the other.

Even among those who gave affirmative replies, in reality how many believe that man can be obliged by the dictates of his conscience to accept one faith, to believe in God? We are of the opinion that most of these mean only that they think it would be good and desirable for man to have some area of his life devoted to religion.

We did not come across a single statement by the subjects wherein they declared, or even vaguely implied, that some moral duty might possibly exist relative to religion. We did see, on the contrary, a number of expressions stating that religion is a source of wealth for man. Not rarely do they use the word *yutaka*—full, rich, wealthy—in association with religion and its influence upon man's life. Following are such typical phrases.

1 In some way religion seems to make one's spiritual life richer.
2 I think that religion makes life richer.
3 I think that sound faith makes man a fuller person.
4 Religion makes the heart of man richer and helps to make him generous and open-hearted.
5 I don't mean to make life easier by depending on religion. Rather I want the sort of faith which makes me, no matter in how small a degree, a fuller person.
6 Religion is that effort within us to save us somehow from the emptiness of the world and to make our inner life richer.
7 I think that religion provides consolation to people and makes human life richer.

All the above-quoted excerpts are clearly positive with regard to religion. The expression *yutaka* confers upon religion the character of opulence and plentifulness which only those who openly have a positive attitude toward religion would accept.

36 *It is necessary that at least once in his life man investigate religion*

HERE we do not speak of a necessity born of a moral duty. Religion is a phenomenon rooted in the history of mankind. It is an astonishing marvel of a historical, sociological and psychological nature. Man must pay it the attention it deserves by studying it. In the same way that the sciences and history are studied, religion must be the subject of deep delving and investigation. At least once in his life man should seriously look into what is known as religion since it is so intimately linked with the history of human culture and civilization.

1 Whether you recognize religion or not, as a man you must study it at least once since it is an indispensable field of learning.

2 If you are a man who takes life seriously, I think that at least once
   you should investigate religion because it is so thoroughly connected
   with human existence.

3 I think that it is necessary to study not only one religion but as many
   as possible.

The positive replies to this statement are very numerous. A full 72% of
the students believe that sometime in their lives they should look into the
question of religion. Such a preponderance of this type of answer could
surprise us, but, we believe, it reveals a basic aspect of the attitude of present-
day Japanese youth. With the exception of a small minority with an openly
negative attitude toward religion, comprising about 25% of the male student
population, the rest of the young men, even those who had given affirmative
responses to the negative statements, or, contrariwise, those who had replied
negatively to positively stated postulates, feel deep down in their hearts
a certain uncertainty in their opinions, a certain vacillation in their attitude
toward religion. They are conscious of the dearth of their knowledge
about religion and of the superficiality of that little knowledge. Even unconsciously, they feel a gnawing doubt regarding their present judgment of
religion, realizing that the inseparability which religion has always had from

TABLE 38

Boys:	TR(5,178)	GA(3,066)	GB(480)	SU(1,120)
	%	%	%	%
SA:	35.3	40.4	27.9	56.1
A:	37.0	35.4	39.4	29.2
TA:	72.3	75.8	67.3	85.3
SD:	4.5	4.5	4.4	2.6
D:	8.7	7.5	10.4	6.2
TD:	13.2	12.0	14.8	8.8
DK:	14.5	12.2	17.9	5.9

Girls:	TR(1,002)	GA(620)	GB(87)	SU(495)
	%	%	%	%
SA:	41.1	46.6	32.2	70.5
A:	38.3	31.5	49.4	22.5
TA:	79.4	78.1	81.6	93.0
SD:	2.4	3.2	1.1	0.6
D:	8.9	8.7	9.2	3.0
TD:	11.3	11.9	10.3	3.6
DK:	9.3	10.0	8.0	3.4

the human race should earn it an importance greater than they themselves presently assign to it. Furthermore, as many of these students have admitted to us, Christianity and Buddhism, at least, should be studied if one is to understand the cultures and civilizations of East and West.

This decidedly positive attitude toward religion lends some tint, in a way, to all the negative responses which the students have given about religion. As of today, they think and feel about religion according to their replies in the questionnaire; but their answers must be shaded somewhat. In other words, their answers must not be taken at full face value but, instead, they need to be read with a certain amount of doubt and hesitation in the background, as explained immediately above. They will say repeatedly that religion is only for those who are weak and have poor personalities and lack confidence in themselves; but however much they may reiterate such an opinion, in 72% of them there lurks an inquieting doubt which makes them also aver that every individual, including themselves, should look seriously into the problem of religion at least once in his lifetime. Even if only as a mark of culture, a man must have some knowledge of religion.

It is this attitude of a positive character among the students which makes them more open to the problem of religion than we might have been led to expect from an examination of their responses.

C. FUNDAMENTAL ATTITUDES OF JAPANESE STUDENTS WITH RESPECT TO RELIGION. A BRIEF SYNTHESIS

THIS synthesis is built on the basis of the statistical data which we have presented, of the remarks and commentaries of the students which we have quoted, and of the interpretations which we have already made. We refer particularly to the male student population encompassed in our survey.

Negative Attitudes

1 We can aver that at least 70% of the students who were the subjects of this study consider religion as something purely subjective and relative. Religion is something fully man-instituted to fill the deepest psychological needs of the human heart. The problem of religion is not the question of the fundamental truth or falsity of its doctrines and of the faith on which these are based; rather, it is the problem of the comfort and relief which it can give man.

2 Is it possible, then, to conclude that the remaining 30% view religion as something objective and absolute? Certainly not.

In the first place, we have the datum that only 8% of the entire male student population have admitted to having some faith, be it a religion and faith of a personal and exclusive kind or some existing religious belief. Therefore, it readily appears that the other 22% do not believe in anything that transcends man and nature. They do not have any faith. Thus, it is difficult to suspect that this 22% could possibly think of religion as the purveyor of posi-

tive values which are absolute and true (in the "authentic" sense of this word)
On the other hand, the atmosphere which completely surrounds the student
is an environment which is contrary to this concept of religion. But what we
can say is that, perhaps, the 22% really are greatly bothered by religion and
deeply esconced in their hearts lurks a nagging, questioning doubt about
this phenomenon of sociology known as religion which has existed throughout the ages and in all societies. In the depths of his soul there is constantly
stirring a positive doubt as to whether there is really so much more to religion
than he can seriously imagine at present. He is bothered by the problem of
whether there lies something deeper than a mere affirmation by man that he
believes in God in order to have someone to fall back on. In short, he is intri-
gued by whether religion is something more than pure fabrication by man,
whether it is something which encloses fundamental truths which man can
discover.

3 There now remains an 8% sector (to be precise, it is 7.6%). Of them,
3% are Christians while 4.6% believe in Buddhism, in Shintoism, in the new
religions, or in some private and personal faith without being affiliated with
any formal religious group. As we shall investigate later, the 3% who comprise the Christians, except in a few instances, cling to an objective concept
of religion. The results from those who believe in some Japanese religion,
in some cases, do not differ much from the general results. This leads us to
think that some of the students replying that they followed Buddhism or Shintoism did not really indicate much beyond the fact that such is their family's
religion, without committing themselves as believers of it or not. It is quite
likely, however, that these young men may feel a certain degree of inclination
toward such a faith. We were able to confirm this prior supposition in the
case of students at Sophia University who replied that they believe in Buddhism. In personal interviews, some of these students explained they had answered positively, meaning that such was their families' faith, but that they
themselves did not really profess it.

4 No less than 60% of the young Japanese students are of a mind that
religion is absolutely unnecessary to anyone who has strong confidence in
himself, possesses a powerful personality, and has determined will power.
Religion is more proper for the weak, the unfortunate, those who have little or
no ambition in life, those who feel the need to lean on someone or something
outside themselves. Also, whoever leads a happy and peaceful life does not
need religion. After all, religion is a problem of human sentiments; to choose
one religion or another, to reject all religions or follow one, is nothing but
pure result of feelings and tastes of every individual. The criteria of truth and
objectivity do not enter into the selection of one religion over another.

We are of the opinion that it is quite probable the students believing thus
comprise or even exceed 70% of our chosen samples. While we placed the
portion who do have such attitudes at 60%, upon examination of the responses under "Do not know," and after going over the essays that they had

written on religion, and in view of the remarks they had made during hundreds of personal interviews, we feel inclined to believe that the students of such a mentality would easily reach 70%.

We hasten to add, however, that although the students have these thoughts about religion, they do not necessarily posses a conscious negative attitude toward religion. To them, their attitude is one which any young man of today should have, and to strike such a pose in relation to religion is compatible with the acknowledgement of a series of positive values in life. Further, within this very group there will be those who might show some interest in religion, thinking that someday they might also need it as a life support. It boils down to the simple fact, which to them is self-evident, that the *tsuyoi hito* —strong man—does not need religion and if they were such strong men they, too, would never have need of religion.

It is probable that the remaining 30% consider the problem of religion as independent of the problem of self-confidence. They may recognize in religion a series of spiritual values, particularly with reference to man's moral and spiritual formation, and consider it of sufficient intrinsic value to deserve man's respect independent of all other considerations. This group, when speaking of religion, would surely be referring principally to those faiths which authentically deserve to be called religions, among which Christianity and traditional Buddhism stand out prominently. The Japanese university student does not show any particular respect for the new Japanese religions.

5 Among some 40 to 50% of the students, there is a clear feeling that religion is disreputable, especially when they consider it as just an excape from reality since such an attitude bespeaks open cowardice in the face of the world and life's problems. Religion is nothing but man's psychological gimmick to which he has recourse in times of tribulation—*kurushii toki no kamidanomi.* Religion could be compared with a pill which a man takes to soothe his nerves *chinseizai.*

6 About 30 to 35% of the subjects believe that religion is opposed to, and contradicts, science and reason; consequently, it is for those men of low culture who are ignorant of the fundamentals of science.

It is important to note that the rest—that is, the remaining 65 to 70%— with their negative answers to this question, or even with their "don't know" replies, do not necessarily believe that what religion teaches is in accord with what science preaches. Rather, such replies mean that the respondents, in the majority of these cases, accept the theory of the two truths, consciously and implicitly, separating religious truth from scientific truth.

7 The students who believe that religion is an impediment to personality development constitute more than 25% of the sample. This group thinks that at least religion lessens the vigorous spirit of independence and freedom and is a barrier to the growth of one's originality and other faculties. Religion, they believe, gives rise to a common type of human being who lacks true individuality; it does not tend to favor and cultivate leadership qualities.

8 The statistical results, in the end, tell us of a minority group with an attitude of open disdain for religion, of a frank hostility and negativeness. These comprise between 15 to 25% of our sample. These students think of religion as a relic of the past, a heritage from our primitive ancestors, the fruit of man's crass ignorance. They consider religion as pure hallucination, plain superstition, and absurd in the light of modern civilization. Further, they realize that history has taught that religion was, and still is, the opium of the masses and serves as a tool of control in the hands of the powerful. They cannot conceive of young people, in the full bloom of life, coming to believe in religion.

9 The above synthesis has reference to the male sector of the student population included in our sample. As for the female portion of our study, all we can state is that their negative replies—that is, their opinions expressing a negative attitude toward religion—tend to be from 10 to 15% less than those of the men.

Positive Attitudes

10 Between 55 to 65% of the male sector of our sample recognize some positive values in religion; they see spiritual values which man should accept and appreciate. Religion often brings inner peace to the individual who has it; it is a faithful companion in moments of solitude, giving comfort and assurance in tribulation and suffering. Religion offers great spiritual support during life's most miserable moments and gives meaning to man's life. Religion is usually a good teacher for all problems concerning human moral conduct. Every religion that is a true religion must struggle for peace among all nations and for social order and welfare, while making men try to control their purely selfish instincts. And religion is often one's only consolation at the hour of death.

11 This very same group—this 55 to 65% of our sample—as a logical consequence of their prior attitudes would tell us that man and society in general would stand to lose tremendously if some day religion were to disappear from the face of the earth. Religion deserves the respect of mankind. If the question were merely one of simple tolerance toward religion, or one of tolerance for people who believe in some religion, the percentage of students who would accept the obligation of being tolerant toward the beliefs of others would certainly go well beyond 65%. This is a sacred principle of the modern age, of the age of democracy.

According to previous explanations, given above, the fact that this group accepts the positive values of religion does not mean that they admit them on an objective and absolute plane; most of them would accept them on the subjective, psychological and moral levels. A reading of the remarks of the young men, wherein they express their approval of these opinions, will confirm our interpretation of their positive responses.

12 There is still 30% of the students who show an attitude of great

G

respect for religion, and we believe that, at least unconsciously, there is in them an implicit wish to be a believer some day. They believe that religion, far from being a barrier to the full development of one's personality, is a most effective means to, an almost necessary tool for, man's conquest of himself and his improvement. It is very probable that these young men will continue through life without any religion, but such a denouement will be due to environment and the lack of opportunities to study more deeply the problem of religion, although it could also be brought about by plain laziness and a lack of the proper amount of courage to start along new ways. Even within this group, there is detectable an unconscious fear of the mere idea of turning believer. They desire it, but they know that such a step would be adventurous and would require a radical change in their internal attitude. Up to the present, "self" has been practically the only end and the only angle which the Japanese young man has greatly valued and for which he has struggled so tenaciously. He realizes that, upon turning believer, religion, or more concretely God, has to enjoy primacy in his life, over and above his egoism, ahead of his tremendous egocentrism. The mere thought of having to accept submission to God often becomes the reason why the young man's unconscious desire to become a believer is frustrated and never comes to the surface.

13 Some 18 to 19% go even farther in their approval of religion. They look upon religion as the great teacher who enables man to taste the great fundamental truths about humankind and who leads him to realize the values of beauty and goodness in their most sublime form. They think that only religion can bring man to genuinely real happiness.

Up to what point do the young men of this group hold an objective view of religion? What is the extent of their great valuation of religion? These are questions we find quite difficult to answer. There are facts which seem to indicate that even among these young men there are many who, while admitting and accepting in their minds these values of religion, still do not feel, deep down in their hearts, such appreciation for religion beyond the superficial level. And which are the facts which lead us to think thus? First of all, the number of believers does not go beyond 8%, including all those who profess some faith or another, even those with their individual faiths of a personal nature who are not affiliated with any single religious institution. This figure of 8% is unrealistic, as we noted previously, for it includes those students who answered that they have for religion some sect of Shintoism or Buddhism and who later admitted that by such replies they meant only it was their family's religion and that such replies did not necessarily mean that they themselves professed such a faith. In the second place, if this admitted interest in religion were really deeply felt, they would look into the religious question by one or another means; and yet the majority of them do not care about it. While it is true that if they were spontaneously offered an opportunity for this, they would grasp it; but they themselves, on their own, would not seek such a chance. Finally, the answers to one of the questions, which we shall analyze presently, led us to the same interpretation.

14   Only 11% believe that religion is necessary for every man. We do not speak here of a necessity in the psychological sense but of necessity in a deeper sense, in relation to religion being the best and only way for man to attain the fullness of his manhood. Every man should walk the way of religion. Only 11% accepted this opinion.

15   Finally, we have only the last attitude of the students to discuss. It is the attitude which reveals that, at the bottom of their hearts, in a great majority of cases, there lies a certain interest and some respect for religion, even though their words deny this. Fully 73% of the students replied that at least once in his lifetime every man should study the question of religion. If there really were absolutely no interest in religion, and if religion were considered trivial or of no importance at all, they would not have said that it would be worthwhile for everyone to devote some time, at least once in a lifetime, to an investigation of the problem concerning religion. Therefore, subtracting the 25% who form the group that is in the minority and that has shown a genuinely negative attitude toward religion, the rest would consist of those who are not sure of their religious ideas but who admit their ignorance implicitly, at least, and who have a positive suspicion that religion might actually have more importance than they now feel. Furthermore, these students believe that, if only for cultural purposes and from the viewpoint of history, they must look more seriously and deeply into the question of religion.

16   Let us here repeat what we have remarked regarding the girls in our survey. In general, their positive attitudes exceed by 10 to 15% the corresponding attitudes of the males covered in our study.

Chapter Four
QUALIFIED RESULTS OF THE SURVEY

THE analysis presented in the preceding chapters refers to the general student population. But this student group cannot be considered homogeneous entirely. Although all those included in the survey are Japanese, the cultural, familial and educational backgrounds of each one of them, nay their very individual personalities, could be so distinctly different as to exert an influence upon religious attitude. To understand and measure this influence of such differences upon the students' attitudes toward religion, we started a second analysis. Here we do not take the entire student population in general; rather, we consider them according to various criteria or categories according to which the students may be divided into qualified groups.

We have chosen 10 criteria for dividing the students which we believe could have some significance in the analysis of religious attitudes. Accordingly, the students were divided with respect to:
1 Geographic region of origin;
2 The school attended for secondary education;
3 The social position and work of the head of the family;
4 Their parents' religious attitudes;
5 Whether they went to the university immediately after finishing high school or waited one or two years before enrolling in college;
6 The university they now attend;
7 The department or faculty they belong to;
8 Life ideal of the student;
9 Experience of religious prayer;
10 Profession of faith.
Not all the preceding criteria proved to be of the same value in discriminating the religious attitudes of the students. According to some of the criteria, the results as gleaned from the responses were quite homogeneous; according to others, on the other hand, there were notable and significant differences.

1 *Geographic region of origin*

JAPAN as a nation is divided geographically into eight regions, some of which possess certain characteristics peculiar to them alone. Five of these regions are on the island of Honshū, namely: Tōhoku, Kantō, Chūbu, Kansai and Chūgoku. Each of the other three main islands forms a different region, to wit: Hokkaidō, Shikoku and Kyūshū. The regions where most of the industrial population is to be found are Kantō, which includes Tokyo, Japan's great metropolis, and Kansai which has the cities of Kyoto, Kobe and Osaka. In the region of Chūbu, there is the big industrial center of the city of Nagoya; while in Kyūshū is to be found the Kitakyūshū industrial hub. The internal migratory patterns in Japan lead principally toward the regions of Kantō and Kansai.

TABLE 39

	Tōhoku	Kantō	Chūbu	Kansai	Chūgoku	Shikoku	Kyūshū	Hokkaidō	Total
Total	283	3,139	710	228	220	168	245	128	5,178[37]
Agree:	%	%	%	%	%	%	%	%	%

Questions:

1　Religion is unnecessary for those who have self-confidence.

| 64.1 | 65.9 | 60.8 | 64.9 | 59.0 | 56.3 | 58.2 | 64.1 | 63.8 |

2　For a person who is satisfied with his life, religion is not really necessary.

| 50.4 | 57.4 | 53.2 | 55.1 | 50.0 | 55.3 | 52.9 | 50.4 | 55.6 |

3　The decision to acknowledge religion or not depends merely on a man's feelings and moods.

| 48.0 | 47.6 | 48.9 | 45.2 | 40.6 | 46.1 | 45.5 | 46.2 | 47.8 |

4　There are many kinds of religions, and their viewpoints differ. Therefore, it is all right if people choose that religion which suits their own taste.

| 76.3 | 72.2 | 73.0 | 72.7 | 74.0 | 71.8 | 72.8 | 78.9 | 72.8 |

5　Religion is a means to escape from the troubles of the real world.

| 42.5 | 45.2 | 48.6 | 44.1 | 44.0 | 46.0 | 49.3 | 41.1 | 46.3 |

7　Religion amounts to nothing more than calling upon the gods in time of trouble.

| 40.0 | 41.2 | 43.5 | 37.3 | 42.4 | 40.0 | 41.4 | 42.2 | 41.0 |

8　Religion is in contradiction to science and reason.

| 24.1 | 34.0 | 30.6 | 30.0 | 20.5 | 33.7 | 29.5 | 27.7 | 32.2 |

10　Religion weakens one's individuality and blocks the development of one's personality.

| 20.9 | 27.1 | 26.2 | 23.5 | 24.1 | 26.6 | 20.8 | 20.3 | 25.9 |

[37] The total of 5,178 does not tally exactly with the sum of the eight groups. This is due to the group of 48 students who failed to give their place of origin; consequently they are not included in any of the above-mentioned groups. We often encounter this same phenomenon in other statistical tables with respect to the results of other questions. The total of the bases and the sums of the partial groups will always show a difference due to whatever number did not answer.

It might be expected that young students would differ in their attitudes and mentality relative to religion depending on the region from which they have come. However, the results we have obtained show no significant variation. The results obtained in the general analysis repeat themselves in each one of the eight geographic regions when the subjects were divided according to the area from which they had come.

We shall show, for each one of these groups, only the percentage of the positive answers to the most basic questions in our survey form. We limited our study to the male student population only, the reason being that the percentage of young girls studying in Tokyo from other regions is too small to be of practical value in our investigation. Of the 1,002 young girls in our sample, 715 are from Kantō district; the rest—the remaining 287—are

TABLE 40

	Tōhoku	Kantō	Chūbu	Kansai	Chūgoku	Shikoku	Kyūshū	Hokkaidō	Total
Total Agree:	%	%	%	%	%	%	%	%	%

Questions:

19 Religion instills peace in the depths of man's heart.

	Tōhoku	Kantō	Chūbu	Kansai	Chūgoku	Shikoku	Kyūshū	Hokkaidō	Total
	66.4	64.1	64.0	63.0	74.0	71.9	73.1	66.3	65.3

20 Religion saves man from his emptiness and loneliness.

	Tōhoku	Kantō	Chūbu	Kansai	Chūgoku	Shikoku	Kyūshū	Hokkaidō	Total
	59.1	56.2	58.4	56.0	59.0	58.7	65.2	64.6	57.6

21 Religion is extremely worthwhile as a support for man's heart.

	Tōhoku	Kantō	Chūbu	Kansai	Chūgoku	Shikoku	Kyūshū	Hokkaidō	Total
	64.2	53.6	58.0	58.3	53.5	62.2	63.4	55.4	57.1

25 Religion in its moral teachings is excellent, and because it fosters kindred human love it is quite important to mankind.

	Tōhoku	Kantō	Chūbu	Kansai	Chūgoku	Shikoku	Kyūshū	Hokkaidō	Total
	64.7	53.2	56.6	50.7	63.6	58.6	61.6	60.4	55.5

28 Religion can make a great contribution to the realization of peace among mankind.

	Tōhoku	Kantō	Chūbu	Kansai	Chūgoku	Shikoku	Kyūshū	Hokkaidō	Total
	50.0	49.0	53.9	52.7	54.8	49.0	53.2	55.3	50.7

32 If religion should disappear from this world, it would be a loss to mankind.

	Tōhoku	Kantō	Chūbu	Kansai	Chūgoku	Shikoku	Kyūshū	Hokkaidō	Total
	54.9	51.0	56.3	53.9	55.2	56.5	57.0	54.9	52.8

35 Religion is to man as a way of incomparable richness, and therefore man must enter upon this way.

	Tōhoku	Kantō	Chūbu	Kansai	Chūgoku	Shikoku	Kyūshū	Hokkaidō	Total
	12.3	7.5	11.3	6.0	17.8	12.7	15.4	14.6	11.9

36 It is necessary, at least once in life, for man to investigate the problem of religion.

	Tōhoku	Kantō	Chūbu	Kansai	Chūgoku	Shikoku	Kyūshū	Hokkaidō	Total
	70.0	71.9	73.8	72.5	74.8	65.5	74.7	75.3	72.3

divided among the other regions, but not a single region has more than one hundred.

Examining these percentages we find that the general median of each group does not vary substantially from the general median of all the students. This, of course, is further confirmation of the correctness of the statistical values obtained in the general analysis, considering the fact that these groupings differ greatly in number from one another and that in such instances it is easy to come upon greatly disparate results.

If we wanted to draw fine shades of difference among the various groups, we would say that, in general, the results from the region of Kantō tend to be somewhat more negative; on the other hand, the results from the districts of Shikoku, Kyūshū and Tōhoku tend to be somewhat more positive.

With respect to the other questions which express opinions of an extraordinarily negative shading, the affirmative replies do not go beyond 25% in any group, varying from 10 to 25%, and more or less following the paradigm of the results of the general analysis.

Let us look at the results of the responses to the statements of a positive nature. (see Table 40)

We cannot categorically affirm that the differences to be noted above are statistically significant. But here, again, we see the Kantō group showing a positive attitude slightly lower than the general median, while the opposite tendency continues observable in the other three districts already cited above. The replies to the other nine postulates of an affirmative character which we have not quoted show even smaller margins of difference.

As a result of this analysis, we can state that today in Japan the geographic regional element is not a factor which needs to be taken into account as a possible influencing circumstance relating to the attitude of students toward religion, at least not as a cause that could produce differences of representative statistical importance.[38]

2 *School attended during secondary education*

THE young men who form the male sector of our sample and who received their secondary education in public institutions number 3,273; those who finished this education in private, non-sectarian colleges are 1,481. The

---

[38] The objection could be offered that we questioned only young people from Tokyo or who had come to Tokyo to continue their university studies, and that this student population could be different from the student populations who preferred to stay in their own native prefectures or who chose to go to places other than Tokyo for their college studies. We cannot answer with certainty that such a difference does not exist, but neither are there reasons to believe that there is such a difference. At any rate, even if there were to be such a disparity, we believe it would be minimal considering the constancy and uniformity of the results obtained, and taking into account the fact that the criterion for distinguishing the two student populations does not seem to have in any manner any notable influence in the religious attitude of the young men.

TABLE 41
Negative Attitudes

	Catholic Schools	Protestant Schools	Buddhist Schools	General Total
	85	159	138	5,178
Total agree:	%	%	%	%
Questions:				
1	43.6	40.3	45.5	63.8
2	41.8	37.3	44.2	55.6
3	20.8	38.3	41.9	47.8
4	58.1	75.7	76.1	72.8
5	24.5	32.3	35.2	46.3
6	20.8	22.1	27.2	41.2
7	18.5	24.6	26.3	41.0
8	11.6	16.2	24.9	32.2
9	4.6	12.0	14.6	15.4
10	13.9	17.1	13.5	25.9
11	13.9	16.1	14.7	25.0
12	13.6	19.1	24.9	24.9
13	11.6	12.1	13.6	18.3
14	2.3	9.0	6.7	13.8
15	2.3	7.9	12.4	14.5
16	9.3	11.1	13.5	23.0
17	4.6	7.0	11.3	22.5
18	4.6	6.0	11.8	17.6

results obtained in the two groups are so similar that there is almost total coincidence and it is difficult to detect the slightest aspects of difference between them that might contrast their respective religious attitudes.

There is another group of 424 young men who had come from colleges of religious institutions—that is, Christian colleges, Buddhist and Shintoist colleges, and schools founded by the new religious sects. The men who received their high school training at these institutions do not generally follow the religion of their schools. Furthermore, religious training is not obligatory even in such institutions. However, the education given by these schools would ordinarily be oriented according to the pedagogical principles of each one of these religions. Thus, it is to be expected that the men trained at these educational centers would have been subjected to some special influence which, in turn, could influence their religious outlook.

Let us now compare the results gathered from the men trained in Catholic, Buddhist and Protestant schools. Those educated in the schools of other religious groups are a mere 42, a small number that is insufficient to establish

Positive Attitudes

	Catholic Schools	Protestant Schools	Buddhist Schools	General Total
Total agree:	%	%	%	%
Questions:				
19	86.0	82.8	77.2	65.3
20	72.6	72.8	68.1	57.6
21	79.6	74.6	71.5	57.1
22	74.4	70.6	55.6	41.2
23	48.7	43.4	37.5	30.2
24	46.5	52.4	49.9	36.7
25	81.3	75.7	67.0	55.5
26	72.8	61.6	74.9	55.0
27	60.4	52.5	48.8	34.5
28	69.7	71.7	66.9	50.7
29	48.8	52.5	47.7	37.4
30	74.3	69.6	69.2	54.7
31	65.0	51.4	45.3	30.8
32	72.4	67.6	64.7	52.8
33	34.8	31.2	37.4	19.0
34	39.3	26.2	36.3	18.0
35	28.0	19.1	19.2	11.9
36	90.6	80.8	81.8	72.3

valid percentage comparison bases. We shall compare these results with the total results from our entire sample.

We cannot doubt that the differences between these three groups and the rest of the majority group of 4,754 young men are statistically significant. These differences, which often vary from 15 to 20% and at times even reach 30%, underscore the degree of positiveness of the attitudes toward religion of young men trained in religious institutions. It then becomes undeniable that these youths—a great percentage of them—were, indeed, influenced positively relative to religion in those educational centers.

There are also differences within these three groups themselves. In general, the percentage most favorable toward religion centered on the young men from the Christian schools.

Inside these three groups, there are responses with such conspicuous variations that we would like to point them out. For example, the fourth question concerns the criterion in the choice of a religion, and states in effect that one should choose that religion which best suits his "tastes"—a criterion implicitly based on purely subjective and relativistic reasons. The affirmative replies to this statement given by the students of Catholic schools were only 58.1%, while similar answers from students of the Protestant and Buddhist schools reached 75.7% and 76.1%, respectively. In like manner, the statement that religion is something purely sentimental in nature received approval from just 20.8% of the group from Catholic schools, while the two other groups registered 38.3% and 41.9%, respectively, of affirmative replies.

In a similar manner, the percentage of the young men from Catholic schools, replying that people whose lives and attitudes are based upon religion deserve every respect, is 65%, superior to the 51.4% of the Protestant group and to the 45.3% of the Buddhist group.

Replies eliciting a differential of approximately 10% really indicate a distinct attitude variation with regard to religion and are not due to mere statistical chance. Also, even smaller differences, when they constantly appear in the answers to almost all of the questions, can also be indicative of really different attitudes.

We observed the same phenomenon among the girls in our survey sample. There is, for all practical purposes, no difference between the group of girls trained in private, non-sectarian institutions (290 girls) and that educated in public schools (546 girls). But the girls (142 in all) coming from Catholic schools (73 girls) and Protestant schools (69 girls) show an attitude toward religion that is definitely more positive than that of the other two groups. This difference is even more pronounced among the girls than it is among the boys. Outstanding as a group are the girls trained in the schools of Catholic nuns. The percentage of these girls who state that religion gives sense and direction to living and makes clear the purpose of man, that it is the source of encouragement for the human heart, that it teaches sublime morals, and is of tremendous transcendence in the life of man, is always around 80%. On the other hand, the group of girls who think that religion is only for the weak and for those who are dissatisfied comprises a mere 20% of them. However, we have to make clear that since the number of these girls polled is a small one, numbering only 73, we cannot know for certain to what extent these percentages are truly representative of the total female population educated in such colleges. We did not include in our study the girls trained in Buddhist and Shintoist schools because they were a scant 23 in all.

Using another criterion, we also studied the results from boys coming from distinct classes of schools, namely those located in cities and those situated in small towns. The atmosphere in cities and the environment in small towns usually differ noticeably, and quite frequently we find the man from the city having opinions and attitudes divergent from those of the country-bred cousin. We encounter serious problems, however, in making such an analysis in Japan because during the past years many neighboring townships have been merged into cities administratively. Many of such new urban units, as a result, still retain their rustic character and would, thus, fail to have any metropolitan characteristics. In spite of this, and keeping it in mind, we tried anyway to study separately the results from boys educated in cities and those from young men trained in small-town schools.

As is only natural, the number of students in the universities within the Tokyo area who finished their pre-college studies in cities is much greater than that of those who finished their high school education in towns. Of the 5,178, only 389 belong to the latter group, while 4,750 are in the first.

Did the difference in atmosphere between cities and small towns influence the religious attitudes of the young men? We cannot speak of any marked difference; however, we do believe the results obtained indicate that, although to a small extent, there is a more positive degree in the thinking of small-town boys than in that of city boys. The variations almost never go beyond 5%, but when we consider that this difference persists in the answers to almost all the 36 statements, we are convinced that there is a certain representative statistical value to such constancy in the figures.

As for the female population, it was not possible for us to establish any basis for comparision since only 51 of the girls in our study had come from small-town schools while 949 had received their school education in rather big cities.

3 *Social position and work of the head of the family*

TABLE 42: Negative Attitudes

	White-Collar	Self-Employed	Directors, Etc.	Farmers
	2,942	1,540	132	356
Total agree:	%	%	%	%
Questions:				
1	65.4	63.7	59.6	55.2
2	58.3	53.2	53.1	48.2
3	49.2	46.8	42.0	48.2
4	73.6	71.0	73.6	72.6
5	48.1	43.4	49.0	44.8
6	39.4	42.0	35.2	31.8
7	41.6	39.6	35.9	49.4
8	33.3	30.2	38.5	34.2
9	16.7	14.6	9.8	12.7
10	25.9	25.6	25.8	26.5
11	26.0	23.0	20.1	25.8
12	25.4	24.2	31.4	20.9
13	18.6	18.1	14.7	18.1
14	14.0	12.4	21.8	17.0
15	14.9	13.2	14.0	16.9
16	23.5	21.6	25.6	21.6
17	24.0	20.6	18.5	21.9
18	17.5	17.7	15.2	17.7

Positive Attitudes

	White-Collar	Self-Employed	Directors, Etc.	Farmers
Total agree:	%	%	%	%
Questions:				
19	62.9	68.6	71.2	66.8
20	56.3	58.6	75.7	56.1
21	53.6	59.2	54.3	59.6
22	38.6	43.7	46.3	46.9
23	28.9	32.2	32.8	33.4
24	35.2	37.4	48.5	42.0
25	53.5	57.5	56.9	60.5
26	51.6	60.2	63.3	56.7
27	32.1	37.9	34.0	36.7
28	49.7	53.6	54.0	53.6
29	36.7	37.9	40.4	44.1
30	53.1	56.8	60.7	56.8
31	28.2	35.5	40.7	29.2
32	50.6	55.4	55.8	57.9
33	17.1	21.3	18.5	25.3
34	15.4	21.4	23.7	21.8
35	11.1	13.2	13.2	15.1
36	71.3	74.4	83.0	67.3

WE divided the "employment status" of the parents of our students into five categories. The big bulk belong to the "white-collar" group; after all, such employees constitute the big nucleus of Japanese middle-class society, particularly of the middle class in the city. There are 2,942 boys whose parents come under this heading. The second category is made up of the "self-employed," people "who own and operate their own business, trade or professional enterprise, with or without one or more paid employees."[39] To this class belong the parents of 1,540 boys. Next come the sons of corporate directors, big merchants, bankers, high dignitaries, etc., who number 132 in all. The fourth class, the farmers, has a representation of 356 young men, while the last, the worker class, has only 12 students. The remaining 195 boys either did not answer the question about their parents' employment or explained that their fathers had no employment at the moment for reasons of illness or something else, or named a type of work that is difficult to place under any of our five category groups.

[39] We give the definition of the term "self-employed," following the Japanese National Census for the year 1965.

Among the girls' fathers, the distribution into the five classes of our subdivision is as follows: white collar: 554; self-employed: 266; corporate directors, bankers, etc.: 107; farmers: 25; workers: 1 only.

Due to the scantiness of the figure for students who have worker-class families, we have decided to analyze the responses of those in the other four groups only.

We did not meet any remarkable differences in any of the four groups. It would seem that the religious attitudes of the young men are not particularly influenced by the scale of living, social strata or employment types of their families. We made the same discovery as far as the girls are concerned. Even when the results of some groups are different from those of other groups with respect to some questions, say more affirmative or positive, they switch to the other side with respect to other statement-questions. Over all, we believe that it is difficult to discover any statistically representative variations using this measuring stick of social level and employment type.

4 *Parents' religious attitudes*

PARENTS' own religious attitudes usually exert a strong influence on the religious attitudes of their children. In postwar Japan, however, this influence seems to have dwindled to the minimum in a large number of families. Of the 5,178 men in our sample, 2,841 answered that their parents were believers. Of these, 2,750 said their families professed the faith of the Japanese religions; only 91 boys are of Christian parentage divided between Catholics and Protestants.[40]

From the entire group of young men in our survey, 1,962 admitted having parents without any religion whatsoever, while 375 failed to answer our question about their parents' religion. If we were to consider only two groups of students—namely, the group whose families are non-believers, and the other whose families believe in some religion outside of the Christian faith—there is a constant difference, with the positive sign toward religion in favor of the second group. This difference is actually small; in the responses to the negative statements, it hovers around 5%; in the answers to the affirmative statements, it inclines toward 10%.

Such a small variation should not really be surprising. The end of the last war saw practically the total disappearance of religious instruction in Japan. As we noted earlier, not only did religious education and instruction cease in all schools, but even in families of believers there remain very few parents who talk to their children about religion and teach them the faith which they

---

[40] We cannot give further details on the religious beliefs of the 2,751 families who profess Japanese faiths. Very many students did not indicate the particular sect of their parents' religion, and there were quite a number who answered that they did not know the sect to which their families belonged. We cannot, therefore, know how many of these families belong to the traditional sects of Buddhism and Shintoism, and how many are affiliated with the New Religions.

themselves are affiliated with and practice. The feeling that religion is largely an exclusive personal problem which every individual must solve for himself alone has grown enormously, so that nobody feels he should interfere with another's religious quandary. It is now considered a transgression of the spirit of democracy to induce children to follow one religion or another, or to educate them in some religious faith. When the child grows up, then he might look into the question of religion and make up his mind about it, decide to follow one religion or none at all, to believe in one or in another. It would also seem that the parents themselves have lost the self-confidence necessary to orient their offspring in matters touching on religion. As a matter of fact, it appears that they have even lost some trust in the very faith, they themselves profess, which robs them of the capacity to lead their children in religious ways.

When the 2,750 students who had replied that their parents were believers

TABLE 43
Negative Attitudes

	Boys of Christian Families	Boys of non-Christian Believing Families (With some religious education)	Boys of non-Christian Believing Families (Without any religious education)	Boys of Non-believing Families
	91	436	2,314	1,962
Total agree:	%	%	%	%
Questions:				
1	42.8	52.0	63.2	66.0
2	40.6	41.7	56.4	58.3
3	34.2	39.1	49.1	47.8
4	60.4	71.3	73.2	72.8
5	28.6	27.5	45.5	50.6
6	14.4	29.3	40.1	45.0
7	18.2	31.2	38.6	46.3
8	23.7	27.5	31.2	33.1
9	7.7	10.8	14.1	18.9
10	19.3	21.8	23.5	29.5
11	5.5	13.9	24.0	28.3
12	11.1	17.9	24.3	28.0
13	8.8	11.0	17.8	19.4
14	8.2	5.9	13.3	17.0
15	7.7	11.6	15.0	14.2
16	9.4	14.6	22.6	25.5
17	8.8	15.6	20.9	25.9
18	4.4	15.4	15.2	20.2

in the Japanese religions were later asked if in their families they had received some instruction or practical education in religion, only 15.8% (436 of them) answered in the affirmative. We looked with great interest into the results from this group, since the differences between this group and the rest were held as more meaningful. In the majority of the responses, there is a variation of between 10 and 20%. We thus see that the mere fact of a family's being followers of some faith does not, in Japan today, exert any significant influence on the religion of the children. Only when these children have received some religious education from the family, no matter how slight, do they frequently come to have a more positive attitude toward religion.

We now have the group of 91 students who come from Christian families remaining to be investigated. In most of these instances, the boys received a relatively greater amount of religious teaching. Consequently, the results of their responses show a more favorable attitude toward religion. Here we have the results of the different groups of boys:

Positive Attitudes

	Boys of Christian Families	Boys of non-Christian Believing Families (With some religious education)	Boys of non-Christian Believing Families (Without any religious education)	Boys of Non-believing Families
Total agree:	%	%	%	%
Questions:				
19	91.5	73.1	68.5	57.7
20	71.7	64.5	59.0	52.6
21	78.5	68.1	60.6	45.7
22	64.6	53.5	40.6	37.0
23	46.4	41.3	30.1	25.2
24	55.5	49.1	37.1	32.0
25	72.8	69.7	59.4	45.7
26	79.1	68.1	57.2	48.0
27	57.3	49.8	34.8	26.6
28	63.7	59.4	53.0	43.6
29	40.4	46.5	40.0	30.8
30	79.1	67.4	58.7	47.2
31	63.9	44.5	30.2	26.3
32	74.6	61.5	50.3	46.7
33	35.5	30.1	19.1	15.2
34	36.6	35.9	17.4	13.1
35	34.8	22.9	11.2	9.5
36	82.2	80.5	68.9	68.7

Among the girls in our sample, 510 come from families professing Buddhism, Shintoism or one of the new Japanese religions, and 39 come from number 439, while 14 did not answer the question. Of the first group, 97 Christian families. Those who admit the absence of religion in their families admit having received some religious teaching in the family circle; this makes them 19% of the group, which is higher than the 15.8% in the boys' counterpart group.

In the girls' groups, we noticed the same differences already commented upon in the explanation of the results from the men.

5 *Whether they enrolled in the university as gen'eki or rōnin*

ENTRANCE into any university in Japan is possible only after a rigorous examination, and the number of those who fail the entrance tests the first time they submit to them after completing secondary education is on the increase. Those who succeed in their initial attempt are called *gen'eki* which means literally "those who are in active service"; the ones who have to wait one, two, or more years before being admitted into the university are known as the *rōnin*, a word taken from the language of the samurai, meaning a samurai without a lord and master to serve and waiting to find one.

As we explained at the start of this work, our purpose was to investigate the mental attitude of the youth toward religion at the end of their high school course. Hence, our desire to look into possible differences in them when they start their university careers as *gen'eki* and when they wait one or more years as *rōnin* prior to their university start.

Among the young men in our sample, 3,800 are *gen'eki* and 1,378 are *rōnin*, of whom 1,122, a majority, are one-year *rōnin*. Among the girls, the *rōnin* do not reach one hundred, numbering just 98.

The results from both groups do not show any appreciable difference, especially if we compare only the *gen'eki* group with the one-year *rōnin* group. The first year of *rōnin* is usually taken by hard work and study in preparation for the admission examinations, and it is hardly a time for the youth to bother about the question of religion. Thus, their religious outlook upon finishing high school is not usually modified during this year.

6 *The university they now attend*

WE divided the universities into three groups, namely: the official state universities; the private, non-sectarian universities; and the private sectarian universities.

In the case of the young men, we cannot say that we found any basic, fundamental difference which could clearly distinguish the religious attitudes of the three university groups. The median percentages of the groups from the state universities and the private, non-sectarian universities are completely homogeneous. In the case of the private, sectarian universities affiliated with some Christian religion, we noted the same tendency we observed and remarked upon in the general analysis of the young men from Sophia University. Many of the responses of the young men from these

H

universities would be about 5% to 10% more favorable to religion. The results obtained from students of the Buddhist University of Komazawa and from those enrolled in the Shintoist University of Kokugakuin come near the general median for the entire university group.

We should not wonder at the slight difference observed between the results from students in non-sectarian universities and those from sectarian institutions. The Christian universities in Tokyo which took part in our survey enjoy a good reputation. In the nationwide atmosphere of fierce competition in the examinations for admission to some university, the first—and almost the only—purpose of every young man is to gain entry into any university; the better the institution's reputation, the better his chances of landing a job afterwards. That the university is a Christian one does not usually deter an aspiring young man from taking his entrance examination there. Thus the big majority of those who come to these centers of learning do not do so precisely because such universities are Christian institutions but because such schools properly fill these students' requirements for the "right" university from which to graduate eventually. Thus, it is but natural that the student's attitude toward religion at the time of his initial enrollment in a Christian university is the same as that of the ordinary Japanese young man. That this attitude may become favorably influenced toward religion during his four-year stay there is quite probable.[41]

Of course, there are in these universities some other small groups of students who enrolled precisely because the schools were Christian universities. Such groups include students who themselves are Christians and so chose such a university, those who had been educated in Christian schools and wanted to continue their studies in an institution similarly Christian, as well as those who had some particular interest in Christianity and enrolled to study and understand it. These groups are always very small compared with the total number of young men who register. It is to these groups that we attribute the higher general median for students in these universities favoring religion.

It seems to us more interesting to publish separately the results of the young men from the principal universities, instead of giving the general results according to the three categories of universities into which we had divided them as explained earlier. We pick from among the universities participating in our study those with the greatest number of students and which are either among the best known or the largest in the entire country. Among the Christian universities, only three participated with more than

---

[41] We do not know of any survey made to determine any change of religious attitude of young men during their four-year stay in a university. As a sequel to this work, we propose to conduct such a survey, particulary among the students enrolled in universities directed by confessional groups.

TABLE 44
Negative Attitudes

Public Univ.	Private non-sectarian Univ.					Christian Universities			Buddh. Univ.
Tokyo U.	Waseda	Keiō	Chūō	Nihon	Kana-gawa	Rikkyō	Kantō G.	Sophia	Koma-zawa
155	377	379	481	506	332	207	103	1,120	191

Total
agree: %   %   %   %   %   %   %   %   %   %

Questions:

1 Religion is unnecessary for those who have self-confidence.

67.8 66.7 65.3 67.0 70.1 63.2 56.8 58.3 60.2 62.4

2 For a person who is satisfied with his life, religion is not really necessary.

55.4 58.0 60.6 54.1 62.2 56.5 45.0 49.8 50.1 52.7

3 The decision to acknowledge religion or not, depends merely on a man's feelings and moods.

44.2 42.2 41.0 46.6 55.5 45.9 49.2 48.9 46.3 47.2

4 There are many kinds of religions, and their viewpoints differ. Therefore, it is all right if people choose that religion which suits their own taste.

73.9 76.2 76.7 71.3 68.9 76.4 79.3 73.6 73.6 76.9

5 Religion is a means to escape from the troubles of the real world.

43.1 48.6 42.9 47.8 48.8 51.5 40.0 40.7 38.8 38.5

7 Religion amounts to nothing more than calling upon the gods in time of trouble.

38.2 34.0 30.7 40.0 47.2 47.3 32.9 33.2 34.7 39.6

8 Religion is in contradiction to science and reason.

30.3 31.2 35.9 34.7 37.9 26.6 32.9 25.0 32.3 28.1

10 Religion weakens one's individuality and blocks the development of one's personality.

24.9 27.6 20.6 27.5 21.2 25.3 19.6 22.5 22.9 19.9

100 students in our sample, namely: St. Paul University, Kantō Gakuin University and Sophia University.

We chose the replies to some of the more fundamental questions in the survey.

Because we deal with the specific and particular medians of each of these universities, we sometimes come across notable differences.

It is curious to note, however, that in the case of some questions the difference is very small. For instance, to the statements that religion belongs

Positive Attitudes

Public Univ.	Private non-sectarian Univ.					Christian Universities			Buddh. Univ.
Tokyo U.	Waseda	Keiō	Chūō	Nihon	Kana-gawa	Rikkyō	Kantō G.	Sophia	Koma-zawa
155	377	379	481	506	332	207	103	1,120	191

Total agree: % | % | % | % | % | % | % | % | % | %

Questions:

19 Religion instills peace in the depths of man's heart.

| 67.8 | 66.9 | 68.8 | 70.6 | 57.0 | 65.0 | 75.0 | 73.6 | 75.0 | 69.7 |

20 Religion saves man from his emptiness and loneliness.

| 61.8 | 66.9 | 59.2 | 59.4 | 50.9 | 57.0 | 63.2 | 58.9 | 59.2 | 57.8 |

21 Religion is extremely worthwhile as a support for man's heart.

| 50.7 | 59.2 | 59.0 | 61.3 | 52.8 | 45.6 | 70.8 | 71.5 | 66.6 | 63.8 |

25 Religion in its moral teachings is excellent, and because it fosters human love it is quite important to mankind.

| 50.0 | 56.6 | 59.4 | 57.4 | 50.7 | 53.1 | 61.8 | 64.3 | 64.8 | 65.0 |

28 Religion can make a great contribution to the realization of peace among mankind.

| 53.3 | 57.9 | 58.2 | 49.3 | 46.4 | 52.7 | 67.5 | 67.4 | 67.3 | 64.5 |

33 Religion which makes man grasp the highest truth, beauty and goodness is most important for man.

| 12.1 | 18.4 | 16.4 | 14.6 | 15.8 | 18.5 | 17.1 | 21.1 | 23.5 | 18.5 |

35 Religion is to man as a way of incomparable richness, and therefore man must enter upon this way.

| 8.5 | 14.3 | 10.3 | 9.4 | 9.8 | 10.5 | 12.6 | 12.0 | 15.0 | 13.7 |

only to the sphere of feelings, that the criterion for choosing one religion or another is whether that religion suits my tastes and interests, that religion is opposed to and contradicts science, and that religion is a barrier to the full development of one's personality, the responses to these statement among the three university groups are very homogeneous.

In the same manner, to the statements of a more positive tone toward religion, which postulate that religion leads man to the more genuine and sublime truths and that it is imperative that man follow the path of religion, the responses are similar and the positive answers are really few.

Among the girls we find a noticeable enough difference between the young ladies from the state and private non-sectarian universities, on the one hand, and those in Christian universities, on the other. The reason for this disparity lies in the fact that a big percentage of these girls come from high schools which are either Protestant or Catholic. The extreme case is that of the University of Seishin which is run by the Sisters of the Sacred Heart: of the small group from it of 43 girls which took part in our survey, 29 had come from Christian schools. A similar pattern is observable among the girls from Sophia University where 169 of the girls included in our sample of 495 girls had completed their secondary education in some Christian school; and this held true, in more or less the same proportion, among the girls from the Protestant universities of Rikkyō, Kantō Gakuin and Aoyama. As previously remarked, the girls who come from such high schools tend to show a more favorable attitude toward religion than the rest of the female sample members. Thus it is but natural that the female population of the Christian universities should show in their responses the same favorable opinion toward religion.

7 The department or faculty they belong to

WE separated the various university departments into eight categories as follows:

1 Department of Sciences and Engineering
   (1,219 boys; 29 girls)
2 Departments of Political Sciences and Economics
   (Commerce) (2,134 boys; 82 girls)
3 Department of Law (555 boys; 33 girls)
4 Department of Medicine (149 boys; 75 girls)
5 Departments of Letters and Foreign Languages
   (232 boys; 284 girls)
6 Departments of Education and Pedagogy
   (299 boys; 152 girls)
7 Departments of Agriculture and Agronomy
   (334 boys; 17 girls)
8 Other Departments (Physical Education, Fine Arts, etc.)
   (254 boys; 325 girls)

The answers to the first four postulates show such small differences that these can be considered meaningless. The percentages obtained for the replies, completely homogeneous among all the groups, agree with the general median of the entire university group. However, we noticed an interesting variation in the responses to the rest of the statements between the group belonging to the Departments of Letters and Foreign Languages, who showed a more favorable attitude toward religion, and those of the group belonging to the Departments of Sciences and Medicine who demonstrated a more unfavorable attitude.

Below we present the comparative results of the responses to those other questions wherein this divergence is more noticeable:

TABLE 45

	Sciences 1,219 %	Medicine 149 %	Letters and Languages 232 %
Total agree: Questions:			

5 Religion is a means to escape from the troubles of the real world.

	49.1	50.2	35.8

7 Religion amounts to nothing more than calling upon the gods in time of trouble.

	46.7	43.2	26.2

8 Religion is in contradiction to science and reason.

	39.1	44.9	19.1

10 Religion weakens one's individuality and blocks the development of one's personality.

	43.4	24.5	19.1

11 Religion in our present state of advanced civilization is close to superstition.

	29.7	23.2	15.3

30 Man must have an attitude of understanding and respect for religion.

	49.6	57.8	66.6

32 If religion should ever disappear from this world, it would be a loss to mankind.

	48.4	51.2	62.5

34 Religion is necessary to obtain true happiness.

	12.0	14.1	28.2

35 Religion is to man a way of incomparable richness, and therefore man must enter upon this way.

	8.0	11.7	17.0

36 It is necessary that, at least once in his life, man investigate the problem of religion.

	68.0	72.1	79.3

The above figures indicate that, within the university group, the young students who are inclined toward the exact sciences and the concrete and experimental studies find less attraction in religion, which they tend to look upon as something purely abstract and with no scientific foundation whatsoever. Thus their attitude toward religion is more negative than that of the students involved in humanistic studies. These latter are ordinarily more open-minded about the religious phenomenon. We found the same differences among the students in these departments at Sophia University.

We cannot make comparisons among the female sector, since their only groups numerous enough belong to the Departments of Letters and Education, and the results from both are most uniform.

8 *Life ideal*

WITH increasing frequency in the innumerable surveys presently being conducted among the youth in Japan, there is usually one or more questions directed to students relating to their life ideals. These studies guided us in formulating five life ideals or goals; from these, the subjects were asked to select one preference. Should one of the five not satisfy them, there were simply to indicate this fact.
The five ways of life proposed to the students are as follows:

1 To live a life according to my likes and interests;
2 To seek after a good social position, wealth and fame;
3 To exert myself for the good of men and society;
4 Without any special aims, to try and live satisfied and in harmony with the environment and the circumstances which surround me;
5 To live a clean and honest life.

Of the above, 32% of the young men chose the first as their goal in life; 22% preferred the last; 16% would exert themselves for the good of society; 10% would try to satisfy their ambitions for wealth, fame and prestige; 3% would be content to lead their lives as circumstances would let them; and the remaining 17% admit having ideals which do not agree with any of the five proposed.

Among the girls, the greatest portion, 34.5%, chose as their life aspirations the moral ideal of a pure and honest life. The second largest group, 28.6% of them, would try to live according to their desires and interests; while 14.5% are swayed toward working for the good of society. A small sector, 3.3%, would take a passive attitude toward life, and only 1.2% would fight for riches and social prestige. Those whose ideals of living are not among any of the five mentioned comprise the remainder, 17.9%.

It is clear that the responses given by the students are not mutually exclusive; whoever accepts one ideal does not necessarily reject the other ones. Their replies, therefore, merely indicate what to them would be the most important element in living, what human value they would give priority to, what life ideal attracts them most, and, consequently, what will guide and direct their future attitudes and conduct.

The percentages we obtained of the answers to these various ideals in life agree with the results obtained in other surveys conducted after the war among Japanese youth. In all of them prevails the tendency to seek a life that would satisfy their personal inclinations and individual desires, leaving as a poor second choice all that has to do with high human ideals.[42]

We sought to discover the relationship that might possibly exist between these ideals of living, on the one hand, and religious attitudes, on the other. It is an interesting fact worthy of note that, among both men and women who preferred as their ideal the exertion for the good of society, we find an attitude toward religion that is more favorable than that which is held by those who chose the first, second and fourth ways of life. Those who placed greater emphasis on the moral aspects of life, seeking as their primary goal honesty of conduct, are very close in their religious view-point to the altruistic group.

To simplify our remarks in the above findings, we shall designate these five groups with the following qualifiers: Altruist Group (3rd way of living), Moral Group (5th way of living), Egoist Group (1st way of living), Ambitious Group (2nd way of living), and Passive Group (4th way of living).

The first difference we notice is that 65% of the students of the altruist group replies that they have a positive interest in religion. The percentage with some religious interest among the egoist group is only 44% and, among the passive group, a mere 32.4%. In between are the ambitious group with a 48.1% and the moral group with a 51.3%. The difference between the altruist group and all the others, varying from 14 to 32%, is certainly very significant.

In the answers to the 36 basic questions of the survey, we frequently find a difference of 10% more in favor of religion in the altruist group compared with the egoist, ambitious and passive groups. The moral group shows a mental pattern very similar to that of the altruist group in their responses. It is to be noted, too, that these differences are observable even in the answers to the first four questions where, ordinarily, the variations are too slight and negligible. Let us look at some of the differences in these results. The results of Table 46 show us that students in whom moral ideals are prevalent and who are strongly motivated by altruism more readily recognize religious values than any other of the boys' groups; however, this does not mean

---

[42] See "Seishōnen no kachikan ni kansuru kenkyū" 青少年の価値観に関する研究 (Youth's Views on Values), *Tōkyō kokuritsu kyōiku kenkyūkai shiryō* 東京国立教育研究会資料, 1964, pp. 158-159 and 202. "8,000-nin no moraru to bijon" *8,000 人のモラルとヴィジョン* (Morals of Eight Thousand Young Men), *Kinrō seishōnen no zenkoku soshiki, shikō-kai shiryō* 勤労青少年の全国組織思考会資料, 1964, No. 6, pp. 20-21. Matsushita Keiichi 松下圭一, "Sengo sedai no seikatsu to shisō" 戦後世代の生活と思想 (Life and Thought of the Postwar Generation), *Shisō* 思想, 1959, No. 424, pp. 84-106. "Seishōnen no seikatsu to kangaekata" 青少年の生活と考え方 (Life and Ways of Thinking of Youth), *Yoron chōsa shiryō* 世論調査資料, Mainichi shimbunsha 毎日新聞社, 1964, No. 12, pp. 26-27. "Seishōnen no kankyō to kōdō" 青少年の環境と行動 (Environment and Behavior of Youth), *Tōkyōto seishōnen mondai kyōgikai shiryō* 東京都青少年問題協議会資料, 1963, pp. 49-51.

TABLE 46

Negative Attitudes

	Altruist Group	Moral Group	Egoist Group	Ambitious Group	Passive Group
Boys:	832	1,138	1,647	483	163
Girls:	145	346	287	12	34
Total:	977	1,484	1,934	495	197
Total Agree:	%	%	%	%	%

Questions:

1 Religion is unnecessary for those who have self-confidence.

55.0	57.0	66.0	70.0	63.6

2 For a person who is satisfied with his life, religion is not really necessary.

49.4	49.1	61.3	61.3	50.2

3 The decision to acknowledge religion or not depends merely on a man's feelings and moods.

44.7	43.6	53.4	49.4	55.9

4 There are many kinds of religions, and their viewpoints differ. Therefore, it is all right if people choose that religion which suits their own taste.

69.7	73.4	77.4	72.9	80.1

5 Religion is a means to escape from the troubles of the real world.

42.0	41.9	49.6	50.8	49.1

6 Religion is nothing more than a kind of sedative.

35.6	37.1	43.4	47.3	53.3

7 Religion amounts to nothing more than calling upon the gods in time of trouble.

33.9	37.7	44.2	51.5	48.0

9 Religion is in contradiction to science and reason.

30.2	30.1	34.3	37.3	35.0

10 Religion weakens one's individuality and blocks the development of one's personality.

21.2	21.7	26.8	31.8	26.5

that they are not sharing the general thinking on religion prevailing among Japanese youth.

9 *Experience of religious prayer*

OF the males included in our survey sample, 7% declared that they pray and worship with great frequency. This group is practically identical with

Positive Attitudes

19 Religion instills peace in the depths of man's heart.

      71.6   68.7   65.4   67.2   53.3

20 Religion saves man from his emptiness and loneliness.

      64.6   63.3   58.4   57.6   51.4

21 Religion is extremely worthwhile as a support for man's heart.

      66.3   58.7   55.5   58.9   46.5

22 Religion gives meaning to a man's life and clarifies the purpose of his existence.

      52.9   42.2   39.3   42.2   29.3

25 Religion in its moral teachings is excellent, and because it fosters kindred human love it is quite important to mankind.

      69.2   59.4   53.7   57.9   47.9

28 Religion can make a great contribution to the realization of peace among mankind.

      56.6   54.9   48.8   53.1   39.4

30 Man must have an attitude of understanding and respect for religion.

      64.1   56.1   51.9   53.9   46.6

33 Religion which makes man grasp the highest truth, beauty and goodness is most important for man.

      25.0   24.9   16.0   20.0   14.6

34 Religion is necessary to obtain true happiness.

      23.7   19.8   15.6   18.3   17.1

35 Religion is to man a way of incomparable richness, and therefore man must enter upon this way.

      21.9   14.8   7.9   11.7   12.8

the 7.6% sector which professes some religious faith. It is natural that their religious point of view should be vastly different from that of the group of non-believers, as we shall see later.

But there has been another, more numerous group of 2,211 young men who, while denying having any faith, still admitted in their answers that sometimes in their past life, in moments of great difficulty, they have prayed and have had that experience of religious pleading. This group comprises 43% of the male sector of our survey sample.

When we explained the results of postulate number 19 in our general analysis in Chapter III, we remarked on this fact of the religious experience of a great number of students. It might sound absurd that young men without any religious faith can have such an experience. But while on purely logical grounds it may not be easy to explain, on a human, psychological basis it is easier to clarify. The boys tell us of an innate kind of instinct which urges man to pray in times of crisis. Human experience confirms this explanation of the young men. They just give such an explanation without stopping to think that there could be some contradiction between the fact of a prayer or a reverent plea, on the one hand, and the absence of a Being superior to man who could listen to that prayer, on the other. Furthermore, if any were to discover such a contradiction, it would not disquiet them. What is important is that, during such difficult times in human existence, the experience of some prayerful thoughts gives comfort and peace to the soul.

We would like to quote here a few of the many remarks of the boys which we gathered while reading their essays on religion. All the phrases chosen were taken from compositions of young men who have denied all religious faith. Nevertheless, they presume that every person, no matter how atheistic, has moments in his life during which he worships and prays, as if it were the most natural thing on earth, as if it were an instinctive human recourse.

1 At one time I had an appendix operation. On account of the great pain, I prayed in my heart, "God, please make it not be painful any more," and during the operation I also prayed that the operation would be successful.

2 Once when I caught a cold and ran a fever of almost 40° C., I thought I would die, and at that time I prayed to God.

3 At times I was in trouble—for instance, at the time of the entrance examinations or when I became sick—it is a fact that there were times when I felt like relying on God.

4 In such cases as when I can't do anything by my own power, or when something suddenly happens, I often think of God. For me to do this is a real contradiction.

5 When I don't have any problems at all I don't have the least thought about religion. But when an emergency arises, of course I think of God.

6 I have never met God. And yet, even though I can't explain how, I place a lot of confidence in the proverb, "In adverse times, pray to God."

7 When in trouble everybody will ask for God's help.

8 Even a man without any faith, when in trouble, will feel like crying: "Oh God."

All the above quoted excerpts show us that the young men, in the difficult times they have experienced in life—which at their age almost always mean examinations in school and illness—have tried to lighten their worries and lessen their sufferings by means of prayer. As they themselves say, it is purely subjective prayer, without any foundation in any religious faith; but, after all, those are moments of religious experience.

TABLE 47
Students Without Any Faith
Their Experience of Prayer

	Sometimes	Almost Never	Never
	2,211	2,023	589
Total agree:	%	%	%
	A. Negative Attitudes		
Questions:			
1	57.7	70.4	76.8
2	51.0	60.0	70.9
3	46.2	49.0	49.8
4	75.1	73.5	62.3
5	41.9	51.0	56.1
6	35.2	37.3	54.4
7	36.5	44.8	54.4
8	27.6	34.6	46.7
9	12.4	16.8	25.9
10	21.5	27.6	41.9
11	20.5	27.9	41.1
12	27.6	34.6	46.7
13	14.5	20.3	30.9
14	10.3	15.5	26.1
15	10.9	16.3	16.7
16	18.2	25.3	28.5
17	16.4	26.3	40.0
18	13.6	20.1	30.3

An extraordinarily interesting fact we have discovered is that this group of 2,211 young men who have admitted this prayer experience even without any religious faith, have shown a religious attitude that is more favorable than that of the group of students who said that they had almost never prayed (2,023 students, 39% of the male population); and, a fortiori, their attitude was much more favorable than that of the group of students who do not remember ever having prayed in their lives (589 students, 11% of the male population). The answers of these three groups of students to the 36 questions in the survey are in almost perfect correlation with their experience of prayer; namely, their religious attitudes are more positive in direct proportion to their previous experience of prayer.

The brief experience of a religious nature consisting of a few haphazardly strewn-about prayer-thoughts among the lives of these young men has left its mark upon their souls, imprinting a memory of inner peace of mind which explains why their attitudes toward religion are frequently more positive by 15 to 20% than those of their fellow students who had never had such

B. Positive Attitudes

19	73.0	59.1	44.2
20	65.6	51.7	38.4
21	64.2	48.2	35.0
22	46.1	35.5	26.5
23	35.4	25.5	18.3
24	40.6	32.0	26.2
25	63.1	48.6	36.5
26	61.9	50.4	36.4
27	39.6	28.8	21.2
28	52.1	46.6	30.3
29	42.0	32.5	21.4
30	61.0	47.9	40.0
31	34.7	24.7	21.4
32	69.4	46.4	37.2
33	23.0	12.7	10.8
34	20.9	13.1	9.4
35	12.9	8.2	6.6
36	75.5	69.6	64.3

an experience. This is an interesting phenomenon in religious psychology.

We have found this same extraordinary fact among the university girls. The group of those who worship and pray frequently reaches 19%, which is larger than the group of actual believers. Those who had had, from time to time, some prayer experience in their lives number 495, which represents 49.5% of the total female portion of our sample; the ones who had almost never prayed are 265, or 26.5% of the entire female subjects; while only 50 admit never having prayed at all. The difference between these three groups is equally remarkable for maintaining the parallel proportions observed among the boys' groups.

10 *Profession of faith*

WE now come to the most critical criterion in the determination and differentiation of the religious attitudes of our subjects. It is obvious that those who profess some religious faith will have a more favorable attitude toward religion than those who do not believe in any religion at all.

The percentage of young men who confess to some religious belief is indeed small, being only 7.6%, which means that of the total 5,178 young men in our survey sample, a mere 397 of them follow some religion as part of their way of life. This number includes even those whose religious convictions are purely personal and are not in accordance with any of the formally established religious groups. Explicitly denying all religious belief are 4,670 young men who constitute 90.2% of our male sample, while 111, or 2.1% of the whole male sector, did not reply at all.

The percentage of the girls who have some religious belief is slightly higher; it is 12.9% of the female sector of the entire sample. Those who admit to no faith at all are 86.4% of the total girls. Those who failed to respond to the question comprise 0.7%.

Which are these religions professed by 7.6% of the boys and 12.9% of

TABLE 48

	Men 397		Girls 130	
	Number	%	Number	%
Catholics	29	0.56	26	2.59
Protestants	130	2.51	59	5.88
Buddhism				
No sect specified	34	0.65	13	1.29
Jōdoshinshū 浄土真宗	21	0.40	1	0.10
Jōdoshū 浄土宗	13	0.25	1	0.10
Zenshū 禅宗	31	0.59	1	0.10
Nichirenshū 日蓮宗	22	0.42	1	0.10
Shingonshū 真言宗	10	0.19	4	0.39
Other sects	9	0.17	0	0.00
Shintoism	17	0.32	6	0.59
New Religions				
(a) Buddhists				
Sōka gakkai [Nichiren Shōshū]				
創価学会〔日蓮正宗〕	39	0.75	13	1.29
Risshokōseikai				
立正佼正会	6	0.11	0	0.00
(b) Shintoist				
Tenrikyō 天理教	7	0.13	0	0.00
Konkōkyō 金光教	2	0.03	0	0.00
(c) Independent				
Seichō no ie 生長の家	4	0.07	2	0.19
P. L. Kyōdan P.L.教団	5	0.09	1	0.10
Personal Religion	18	0.34	2	0.19
Totals:				
Christians	159	3.07	85	8.48
Buddhists	140	2.70	21	2.09
Shintoists	17	0.32	6	0.59
New Religions	63	1.21	16	1.59
Personal Religion	18	0.34	2	0.19
Total:	397	7.66	130	12.96

TABLE 49

Catholics[43]		Protestants		Other Religions		Non-Believers	
Boys:	76	Boys:	162	Boys:	312	Boys:	4,670
Girls:	78	Girls:	86	Girls:	76	Girls:	865
Total:	154	Total:	248	Total:	388	Total:	5.535

Total agree: % % % %

Questions:

11 Religion in our present state of advanced civilization is close to superstition.

| 1.2 | 4.4 | 9.0 | 25.0 |

12 Religious belief is born of man's ignorance.

| 2.5 | 5.2 | 11.9 | 24.6 |

13 Religion is nothing more than a heritage from primitive ancestors.

| 2.5 | 6.0 | 10.4 | 18.5 |

14 Religion is now out of date.

| 2.5 | 0.8 | 4.6 | 13.5 |

15 It may be that religion is something fitting for old people, but for young people it is something you may take or leave.

| 0.0 | 1.6 | 5.1 | 14.2 |

17 Religion is nothing but a drug which makes man submissive and resigned.

| 0.6 | 1.6 | 9.0 | 23.4 |

18 Religion is a means of exploitation for the ruling class; it is of no use for ordinary people.

| 0.6 | 4.4 | 7.8 | 17.7 |

16 Religion is founded on man's hallucination.

| 3.1 | 6.4 | 7.8 | 23.7 |

9 In cases where scientists have religious beliefs, these are attitudes which are not fitting from the point of view of science.

| 0.6 | 6.4 | 10.1 | 15.4 |

[43] As we remarked regarding the group of believers, we included the believers from Sophia University. Among the 1,120 young men and 495 coeds in their freshman year in this university who responded to our questionnaire, there are 99 Catholics (47 young men and 52 coeds), 59 Protestants (32 young men and 29 coeds), and 105 who profess some Japanes religion (74 young men and 31 coeds). Because Sophia University is the only coeducational Catholic University in Tokyo and in the entire Kanto region, it is natural that the percentage of Catholic young men be unusually high in comparison with that of other universities. In Sophia University, this percentage is 4.1% for the men, and 10.5% for the ladies.

the girls? In the graph that follows, we show in detail the distribution of student believers according to the religion they follow. We would like it to be on record that the numbers we give for Catholics and Protestants do not tally with actual figures. We have included among the Catholics only those students who have explicitly replied that they believe in Catholicism, and we put down as Protestants all those who, in a more general way, said that they believe in Christianity, so that among the indicated Protestants it is probable that a number of them actually follow Catholicism. While we definitely know the total number of Christians, we have no accurate knowledge as to just how many of these are Catholics and how many are Protestants We have also avoided mentioning specific Protestant sects; in most cases, the students failed to name the exact communion to which they belong.

What is remarkable in the above figures is the percentage of Christians. For the entire population of Japan, the percentage is a mere 0.7%, approximately; that is, about 700,000 Christians in the entire nation, made up of Catholics and Protestants. However, among the university students in our sample, there are 3.07% of the males and 8.48% of the girls who call themselves Christians. Equally surprising is the relatively tiny group who follow the new Japanese religions which include the Sōka-gakkai with an affiliation of several million Japanese families. These data are a confirmation of what we have remarked in the second chapter of this report concerning the young men's responses to the effect that there is no noticeable interest in the new religions among them, and that these students, when thinking of some religion, tend to think of either Christianity or Buddhism which they consider as genuine and serious religions.

Which are the religious attitudes of the different groups of believers? We already remarked that, when it comes to the students who are believers, the attitudes of the girls do not vary fundamentally from those of the boys. Thus, in our analysis, we have taken the boys and the girls into account jointly. We likewise included in our analysis the believers from Sophia University, Christians as well as Buddhists. The religious views of these believers from Sophia University do not differ, for all practical purposes of this study, from those of believers enrolled in other universities. We divided the religions into three groups, namely the Catholic group, the Protestant group, and all non-Christian groups. With the exception of Buddhism, all the other religions of a non-Christian type have too few adherents for us to consider them separately; so to the third group we have assigned followers of Buddhism, Shintoism, the new religions, and personal religious faiths.

To the statements of a more negative nature, the percentage of those who agree and strongly agree among the Catholics fluctuates from 0% to 2.5%; among the Protestant groups, it varies from 0% to 6%; while in the Buddhist group it ranges from 4% to 11%. (cf. Table 49)

There are five other questions of a negative character, although not as negative as the ones appearing in the tabulation above, which postulate that religion is a human, psychological recourse to escape from the miseries and trials of life. It is further stated in them that religion is against the sciences and acts as a barrier to the development of a strong personality. The percentage of affirmative replies to these questions rises a bit in the various groups: for the Catholics, it goes from 5% to 10%; for the Protestants, from 8% to 16%; and the others from 10% to 20%. (cf. Table 50)

Finally, the responses remaining to be analyzed are those to the first four questions in the survey form. As explained in their general analysis, the young Japanese do not read into the approval of these statements any clearly negative attitude. To them, the postulates are only indicative of the purely subjective aspect of religion, and do not contain or contemplate any definitely negative aspects. Religion is for the weak and those dissatisfied with life, and it is not based upon reason but on mere human feelings. The selection of one or another religion is a matter of personal tastes. Japanese believers feel the impact of such thinking vis-a-vis religion in the environment. Between 10% and 20% of university young men who are Christians think of religion also as something that is purely subjective and relative. These youths might be those with insufficient Christian upbringing; they could be those who were baptized as small children but without subsequent religious instruction, they might be those who were directly influenced by what they had read or what they had talked about with their friends. Given whatever explanation for their being so, the fact remains that this group believes and affirms, in the same manner as the non-believers, that religion

TABLE 50

	Catholics	Protestants	Other Religions	Non-Believers
Total agree:	%	%	%	%

Questions:

10 Religion weakens one's individuality and blocks the development of one's personality.

	Catholics	Protestants	Other Religions	Non-Believers
	5.1	12.8	14.2	26.1

8 Religion is in contradiction to science and reason.

	5.7	18.9	18.0	33.4

7 Religion amounts to nothing more than calling upon the gods in time of trouble.

	4.5	8.0	16.3	42.7

6 Religion is nothing more than a kind of sedative.

	5.8	8.8	19.5	42.8

5 Religion is a means to escape from the troubles of the real world.

	9.7	16.7	20.6	48.1

I

is unnecessary for those who have sufficient self-confidence to depend upon their own selves, come whatever difficulty in life. Their percentage among the Catholics is smaller than the precentage in the other two groups.

TABLE 51

	Catholics	Protestants	Other Religions	Non-Believers
Total agree:	%	%	%	%

Questions:

1 Religion is unnecessary for those who have self-confidence.

12.3	20.2	38.1	64.3

2 For a person who is satisfied with his life religion is not really necessary.

11.6	15.6	34.6	58.6

3 The decision to acknowledge religion or not depends merely on a man's feelings and moods.

14.2	20.9	35.2	48.7

In the figures above we notice higher percentages for the non-Christian religious groups; that is, in the groups including Buddhism, Shintoism and the new religions. We are not too surprised by such data; the phenomenon can be understood in the light of the relativism and the syncretism that have always been predominant characteristics of all Japanese religions.

We must take note of another important factor. In the previous postulates, the percentage of Catholics and Protestants who answered with a "Don't know" is most insignificant; however, this percentage increases in the case of these three questions. To the first statement, 3.7% of the Catholics and 7.3% of the Protestants replied that they do not know whether religion is necessary for the one who has confidence in himself. To the second postulate, those who replied they do not know are 7.2% and 9.7%, respectively; and to the third question, these ratios for those who are not sure rise to 19.0% and 20.2%, respectively.[44] The mere fact that they are in doubt about what to say or think relative to these statements clearly shows to what extent the subjective and relative concept of religion has pierced the thinking of a considerable portion of the Christian youth.

The answers to the fourth postulate are the most difficult ones to interpret. Let us restate the question once more:

4 There are many kinds of religions, and their viewpoints differ. Therefore, it is all right if people choose that religion which suits their own taste.

Of the Catholics, 43.2% gave their approval to this opinion; of the Protes-

[44] Appendix VI gives the complete statistical tables of the groups of believers, pp. 168–70.

tants, 50.3% did; those who believe in some other religion not Christian scored 66.1%; and of the non-believers, 74.0% agreed with it.

Among all the questions in the survey, this one has produced the least reliable responses, but we decided that there is enough reliability to justify our keeping it among the definitive ones in our questionnaire.

It has been called to our attention that this statement is ambiguous so that both those who profess some faith and have a favorable religious attitude, and those without any religion who have a negative religious attitude, can give their assent to it.

We repeat at this point something we stated in the opening chapter. It is likely that people with a sufficiently broad religious background, by intense effort at interpreting this phrase, might understand it to refer merely to religious tolerance. But the young Japanese university student who is a non-believer gives it a meaning not only in this sense of plain religious tolerance but also in the fully relative sense that, basically, all religions are the same, at least the great religions which presently exist in the world; that the important thing for an individual who would like to follow some religion is to accept what pleases him, suits his psychology, fits his social environment, and harmonizes with his tradition. If there was some specific point, which urged us to carry out numerous interviews with the students, it was this. Personally, we cannot doubt that this is the general interpretation of the Japanese young men.

But how should the affirmative replies to this phrase by the believers among the students be interpreted, particularly those answers given by Protestants and Catholics. In the first place, we would like to state here that the difference between the positive responses of this Catholic-Protestant group and that of the non-believers lies between 30% and 24%. Such a magnitude is statistically significant so that this difference can be deemed reliable in distinguishing between the religious attitudes of the two groups.

The percentage of Catholics and Protestants who gave an affirmative reply to this proposal is most high, being more than twice the percentage obtained in the answers to any other of the statements of a negative nature. Does this 43.2% of the Catholics, and this 50.3% of the Protestants, think in the same way as the non-believers who think that, basically, all religions are the same, be the religion Christianity, Buddhism or Mohammedanism? Do these Catholics and Protestants also think that the only important thing is to follow a faith that best suits one's tastes and preferences, so that it becomes of secondary importance whether the religion so chosen is the true one or not?

In the case of those with some faith, especially in the case of the Christians, we believe that what predominates in their affirmative replies to our postulate is the sense of religious tolerance; however, in most cases their interpretation of the idea of tolerance embraces the subjectiveness of religion. We also conducted many interviews with Catholic students. Discounting the few who manifested a concept of complete subjectiveness relative to the Christian religion, the majority of them, fundamentally, are of the belief that Christianity is the only true religion; quite frequently, however, they do not attach any particular value to this criterion as far as the religious question is concerned. Whether a person believes in a religion that is genuine or in one which is not the true one, is a problem of secondary importance to them; actually, it is of little or no importance, to their way of thinking. Furthermore, the majority of these young men interpret religious freedom not in the sense that every man, following the dictates of his conscience, should select that religion which he considers the truly genuine one, but, rather, in the sense that everyone is morally free to choose one or another religion, or none at all. In other words, there are relatively few of these young men in the group which we investigated who conceive of the idea of a personal, moral obligation for a man to follow some faith in conscience.

Opposed to this group is the 50% of Catholics and the 44% of Protestants who gave negative responses and demonstrated a clearly objective concept of religion. They established as a criterion in the choice of a religion, not that it fit one's tastes or that it suit one's inclinations, but the fundamental standard of truth.

This interpretation just stated is further confirmed by the replies to the statements of a positive character. Postulates numbered 33 and 35 are the key ones to help clear up this point. Statement number 33 says that religion is what leads a man to the knowledge of the most fundamental and sublime "truths" as well as to the recognition of supreme goodness and beauty. Statement number 35 says that every man shoud follow the way of religion. Let us look at the answers to these two postulates (Table 52).

Between 20 and 30% of the Catholics, and between 30 and 50% of the Protestants do not agree that religion is necessary to man; neither do they consider religion important as the source of genuine and fundamental truths. It is natural for these young men to give their affirmation to the negative

TABLE 52

	Catholics	Protestants	Other Religions	Non-Believers
Total agree:	%	%	%	%

Questions:

33 Religion which makes man grasp the highest truth, beauty and goodness is most important for man.

	Catholics	Protestants	Other Religions	Non-Believers
	78.1	68.3	49.5	16.6

35 Religion is to man a way of incomparable richness, and therefore man must enter upon this way.

	Catholics	Protestants	Other Religions	Non-Believers
	71.4	52.0	42.2	9.2

question. In other statements favorable to religion, the percentage of positive answers usually goes beyond 80%, and even 90% at times. (cf. Table 53)

TABLE 53

	Catholics	Protestants	Other Religions	Non-Believers
Total agree: %	%	%	%	%

Questions:

36 It is necessary that at least once in his life man investigate the problem of religion.

95.4	86.2	88.6	72.1

19 Religion instills peace in the depths of man's heart.

93.5	92.0	88.3	54.3

30 Man must have an attitude of understanding and respect for religion.

92.8	85.0	81.0	53.1

22 Religion gives meaning to a man's life and clarifies the purpose of his existence.

94.1	89.0	64.0	39.1

32 If religion should disappear from this world, it would be a loss to mankind.

89.2	73.1	72.2	50.9

31 It can be said that a life based on religion deserves respect.

81.1	77.7	64.3	28.1

21 Religion is extremely worthwhile as a support for man's heart.

86.3	89.5	80.0	54.2

20 Religion saves man from his emptiness and loneliness.

87.9	87.9	74.6	57.4

25 Religion in its moral teachings is excellent, and because it fosters kindred human love it is quite important to mankind.

87.0	86.6	79.8	53.5

26 Religion gives discipline and moral training to the whole man.

83.7	75.7	74.3	53.9

27 Religion unceasingly stirs up in man aspirations for his self-improvement.

83.6	79.0	58.3	33.3

28 Religion can make a great contribution to the realization of peace among mankind.

90.1	88.6	72.0	49.1

To four other questions, the affirmative responses are not as numerous. In most cases, the ones who did not give their approval did not answer negatively, either; rather, they replied that they "Don't know." And these "Don't know" answers, we believe, should not be in this case interpreted in a depreciatory sense but, instead, in the sense that the respondents had not had sufficient experience with religion to be able to give their assent to what was being asked of them. The statements we refer to are those that say religion brings true happiness to man, solves his pains and miseries, above all removes the painful anxiety about death. The last of these queries says that religion has in itself the strength with which every man can overcome his personal selfishness and, thus, cause to disappear the disorders which we witness in society everyday.

TABLE 54

	Catholics	Protestants	Other Religions	Non-Believers
Total agree:	%	%	%	%

Questions:

24 Religion offers a solution to man's anxieties.

Catholics	Protestants	Other Religions	Non-Believers
67.4	70.4	58.3	35.0

23 Religion dispels the uneasiness about drifting into nothingness with man's death.

Catholics	Protestants	Other Religions	Non-Believers
72.6	57.6	41.9	30.1

34 Religion is necessary to obtain true happiness.

Catholics	Protestants	Other Religions	Non-Believers
76.0	65.2	44.8	15.0

29 Religion has the power to solve the disorders of society and to overcome personal egoism.

Catholics	Protestants	Other Religions	Non-Believers
70.2	73.2	60.2	35.7

As a final remark, we would like to come forward with an explanation of the notable difference in percentage between the Christian believers and non-Christian believers on many questions. We attribute this difference, partly, to the fact that we doubt whether those who admitted to being Buddhists or Shintoists, without specifying the particular sect of their faith, actually believe those faiths. As was explained in Chapter III in many cases, their responses merely indicate the religion of their families. It is a fact that the religious attitudes of this group are always less favorable than the attitudes of those who specified in their answers the particular sect of the religion they professed.

Chapter Five
COMPLEMENTARY PILOT SURVEYS ON
OTHER THEMES

THERE are other themes of prime importance which it will be proper to analyze in relation to a survey of the religious attitude of university students. We, therefore, conducted a number of studies of a limited scope among some groups of students at Sophia University in order to find out what their concept of God is, what their beliefs are of life in the hereafter, and to what extent their idea of morality is personal and to what degree this morality is conscience-prompted.

These minor surveys do not have the representative value of the general survey which we have been analyzing up to this point; we were merely engaged in some pilot studies. However, the results we obtained seem interesting and we believe that they can lead us into a better understanding of the problems we are investigating. On the other hand, we want to state that the results we obtained in the preliminary studies of religion among the Sophia University students did not appreciably differ from those obtained in the general survey. We can, therefore, suppose that the results obtained in these pilot investigations would not differ much from the results which would be gathered in another general and definitive survey on the same problems.

1 *Survey about the existence and idea of God*

IN attempting to look into the thinking of the university students about their belief in God, we stumbled across the same difficulties which we encountered in our efforts to study their fundamental attitudes concerning religion. If the word "religion" seemed to us ambiguous, in the same manner the term "God"—*kami*—is also subject to numerous interpretations.

In the Western world, to the atheist as well as to the man with a faith, the concept of God is fundamentally the same. Some deny God, while others recognize Him; but the two groups concur in the idea of just what or who God is. They share a common idea of the meaning of "God."

In Japan, the word *kami* has a meaning that is most vague and at the same time confusing. When a Japanese says that he denies or that he accepts God, it is difficult to know exactly in what sense such acceptance or denial is made. This confusion, we find, stems from Shintoist mythology and from Buddhist doctrines in which there is no clear distinction between God, Nature and Man. Shintoism, the native Japanese religion, is a religion of the animistic type. The primitive Japanese saw in every phenomenon of nature forces superior to man which, therefore, deserved his most profound adoration and deepest respect. The world was to him inhabited by innumerable powerful spirits whom he called *kami.*

The real meaning of the word *kami* is everything that "is on top," everything that "is superior." Thus the word *kami* was even used in referring to the authorities, to one's own superiors. Men of outstanding qualities were also called *kami* by the people.

Then there are the titular *kami* of a family, which were identified with the spirits of their ancestors. Further, every town, every region, the mountains, the valleys, the rivers, the forests had their guardian *kami.* Finally, there are the *kami* who created Japan, considered as national gods, whose descendants are the Emperors. As writers on Shintoism say, there are thousands upon thousands of *kami* in the Japanese nation.

In his book on Shintoism, Professor Ono Sokyo tells us that all things can be called gods or can be considered as potential gods. Shintoism, adds Professor Ono, teaches that even men can be venerated as gods. In fact, in recent postwar years, many of the founders of the new religions have given themselves the title of *kami.*[45]

Buddhism, introduced in Japan during the sixth century, did not carry with it any clearer concept of what God is or who He is. In this religion, there have been, and there still are, numerous discussions about the concept of God. The word *kami* does not enter into the metaphysics or the rituals of the Buddhists. There are enough Buddhist authorities who see in their faith a kind of pantheism. In the more popular type of Buddhism, there is the belief in a god, Amida, which could be the nearest idea to a personal God. In Buddhism there is likewise the worship of ancestors whose spirits are believed to have been transformed into "Buddha." These are the famous *hotoke* which are the object of rituals and veneration by the Japanese people.[46]

Because of this vagueness in Japanese thinking about God of the typical Japanese, we attempted to propound to the young university men a series of simple definitions so that they might accept that image, or those images, which were closest to the mental picture created in their minds upon hearing the word "God." The first two questions asked them clearly about their beliefs in the existence or non-existence of God. In order to understand just what God they were accepting or rejecting in their replies, we added those other questions which analyzed the idea of God. We warned the young men that in their replies to these last queries they were to forget completely whether or not they accepted the existence of God, since we were only attempting to discover the most dominant idea they had of God. It was further made clear to them that we wanted to find out which is the God they believe could exist

---

[45] D.C. Holtom, "The Meaning of Kami," *Monumenta Nipponica*, 1940, III, 1-27 and 392-413; 1941, IV, 350-394.

Ono Sokyo, in collaboration with William P. Woodard, *Shinto: The Kami Way*, International Institute for the Study of Religions, Tokyo, 1960.

[46] D.T. Suzuki, *The Essence of Buddhism*, Hōzōkan, Kyoto, 1948. H. de Lubac. *Amida*, Editions du Seuil, Paris, 1955.

in case there really is a God. It is important to note that in Japanese, the word *kami* is the same whether in the singular or in the plural, so that our questions did not presuppose the idea of only one God.

We conducted this study with 111 first-year students in the Faculty of Law and the Faculty of Sciences (49 from Law, 62 from Sciences) of Sophia University during the first days of May, 1965, two weeks after the beginning of the school year. It was carried out during their weekly period in religion.

The first two questions were of a fundamental character to discover their thinking with respect to belief in the existence of God. These are:

1   God did not create man; man created God.
2   God does not merely exist as an idea in man's thoughts;
    He has a real existence.

To the first statement, 82 young men gave their approval, which is 73.8% of the respondents; 13 replied in the negative, which makes them 11.6% of the group; while 16, or 14.5%, answered "don't know." The answers to the second question show insignificant variation. Only 10 (9.0%) students answered affirmatively; 80 (72%) denied the statement; and 21 (18.9%) said they "don't know."

Their answers confirm, in the first place, the statistical data gathered in the general survey as to the number of believers and non-believers. It should be noted, despite the slight difference, that in the case of answers to the negative question, that is the statement that man created God, the percentage of those who deny it is 2.6% more than the percentage of those who state positively that they believe in the existence of God.

Those who clearly deny the existence of God comprise between 72% and 74% of the students. Of those who doubt God's existence, 19% approximately, we think there are many who, despite their inability to affirm that God exists, see reasons for, and the possibility of the existence of God. This group, together with the group of believers, about 9%, correlates with the group of students in the general survey who show a decidedly positive and favorable attitude toward religion.

As to the majority group of young men who fully deny the existence of God do they reject it fully convinced? We would like to venture to say that, in the majority of these cases, we are dealing with an affective convinction. We mean that they are bothered by the mere idea of God's existence. We believe that, in his subconscious mind, the Japanese young man harbors a kind of rebellion against God. The overwhelming majority of the young students have made of themselves a God whom they adore and they dislike any other God. It is the phenomenon of an extraordinary egocentricity where the self is the center and the end of every thought and activity. The mere thought of accepting a God who is above man and before whom they have to bow their heads, is an idea that frightens them. It is *osoroshii* (terrible) as some of them put it. Many of them believe that the moment they accept God they would be deprived of freedom and initiative. The acceptance of God is an incurable wound to their pride and to their autonomy.

We have to add to this complicated psychological analysis of their mental frame the idea, which we have repeated a number of times in the preceding pages that belief in God, dependence upon God, is only for the weak, just for people with colorless personalities.

We quote some of the expressions of these young students in which they definitely deny the existence of God. We selected those phrases which state in a clearcut manner that man created God, that God is a fabrication of man.

1 The problem of whether God exists or not I think is very foolish. For me, to demand from God liberation from suffering is indeed both stupid and worthless.

2 Religion is something thoroughly artificial. I want to deny the existence of God. All the talk about God is fiction. They say that God created man; yet, as a matter of fact, it was not God who created man, but man who created God.

3 God is just an illusionary notion.

4 Man started by inventing God and then went on to obey and adore him.

5 Man seeks something absolute to rely on. Such is the man who invented what we call God.

6 Since God is something spiritual within the heart, if one feels that he exists, he does exist; if one thinks he does not exist, he doesn't.

7 Man cannot help feeling restless. He wants to rely on something. Thus he fabricates an absolute, almighty God and leans on him in faith.

8 I think that what people call God is the conscience within man's heart.

9 Man in his search for consolation, relief and happiness, gives birth within his heart to God.

10 Religion, God and the like are a purely mental notion, a problem of man's heart. Yet, man as a rule, cannot rely exculsively on his heart. That is why he builds up the idol of God.

Let us now see what these students have for an image of God. They gave affirmative replies to the different ideas or concepts they were given of God which most nearly approximated what was in their minds.

The present-day young university student not only does not believe or admit Shintoist mythology but also, in the great majority of instances, does not have as his image of God the mythical gods of Japanese history. There are, likewise, a counted few who connect the idea of God with the spirits of their ancestors or with the souls of great men in history. Three of our postulates were related to these concepts:

3 God, after all, can be identified with the ancestors of all peoples.

    4 God can be identified with the spirits of great men now dead.
    5 God means the world of gods.

Identification of God with the spirits of ancestors got the approval of 17.2% of the respondents; 5% identified God principally with the spirits of great men in history; while 13% think of the mythological world of gods upon hearing the word "God."

In opposition to these ideas about God, the concept of God as a being that is One, Absolute, the Apex of all truth, beauty and goodness, greater than man and nature, is the statement that got the greatest number of affirmative replies.

    6 God is the absolute being which transcends man and nature.
    7 There is only one God and He is the greatest being.
    8 God is a holy being, the supreme culmination of truth, goodness and beauty.

More or less the same group of students accepted these ideas of God. To the 6th statement, 42.5% gave their assent; to the 7th, 44.6% did; while 38.4% approved the 8th.

Another large group equates God with nature or considers God the great energizing force of the world, although more in the material, physical sense of energy.

    9 God can be identified with Nature.
   10 God seems to be a huge complex of energy.

A full 31% answered affirmative to question number 9, and only 25.9% gave their approval to number 10.

But there is another definition of God, taken literally from one of the young men's reports on religion; it obtained the biggest number of affirmative replies.

   11 God is, after all, nothing more than the idealization of your own heart.

This idea of God was overwhelmingly chosen by 69% of the young men. Most of those who approved questions numbered 6, 7 and 8, also approved the above statement. Note that these are not contradictory postulates. They merely place on a radically subjective level what was previously averred; this is but natural considering that 90% of the students deny the existence of God. The human heart is inclined toward what is true, what is beautiful, what is good; the human heart veers toward perfect happiness, toward immortality; the human heart tries to evade death, avoid what is fleeting and relative, seeks indefatigably what is absolute. The human heart creates this absolute and this truth, and this goodness, and this supreme beauty, as the composite idealization of its aspirations and desires. This absolute being is a clear fabrication of man's; it is the ideal toward which he drives, which does not exist in reality, but which can guide and inspire him.

With two other statements we intended to find out also if in their concept of God the students associated certain relationships of God toward man. We limited ourselves to only two aspects of such relations, namely: whether the figure of God represented the image of a just and avenging God, or whether God represented a kind and lovable being who listened to the prayers of men.

12 God is the fearful being who wreaks vengeance on man.
13 God is an understanding and warm being whose ears are open to man's prayers.

Those who prefer God to be a being who listens to men's pleadings comprise 48.5% of the respondents; in 16.5% of them the notion of a just and avenging figure prevails.

The answers to all these questions reveal that about 45% of the students seem to have a concept and ideas about God very similar to the God of Christianity, which is a God who is One, Absolute and Personal. But most of these young men would not accept this idea as representative of a being that really exists but only as the projection of an idealization of the human heart's greatest ambition. But in case these young men should some day come to accept the existence of God, it will be this God and no other, whom they will recognize. One of them expresses it thus:

> If there is a true religion, the object of such a faith is not the type of vague god which most Japanese have in mind, but the God of Christianity.[47]

Another group of about 30% of the respondents equates God with nature, with nature's mysterious forces and energies, or with the ironclad, fixed laws that govern all the visible world. Let us quote the remark of just one of the young men on this subject.

> As for me, I try to think of the so-called absolute being as the law of nature, the phenomenon of nature, the power of nature.[48]

About 15% associate God with the spirits of ancestors; another 10%, approximately, connect God mainly with the pluralistic concept of the gods of mythology.

2 *Survey about the afterlife*

WE conducted this survey among 109 university students from the Department of Economics and the Department of Law of Sophia University.

In the Japanese language there are certain words which have meanings that betray the existence of a life hereafter, but these words are closely associated

---

[47] 真の宗教があるとするならば，その信仰の対象は日本人一般のいだいている漠然とした神ではなく，キリスト教の言う神である。

[48] 私の場合には，言われている絶対的なものとは，これを自然の法則，自然の現象，自然の力として考えてみようと思う。

with certain definite concepts, and it is entirely possible that they could influence, to a great extent, the responses which the young men may give to questions presented to them. We have noticed that the words "heaven" and "hell" (*tengoku–jigoku*) are rejected by almost all students, although their denial of the existence of a heaven and a hell does not necessarily show their denial of all life hereafter. In the same manner, "immortality of the soul" is not a proper expression for translation into their language. The word *tama-shii*, which comes to be the equivalent of our word "soul," is linked in the minds of many of the students with superstitious ideas, with the appearance of ghosts and the like, and to admit of the existence of the soul is, to their way of thinking, most unscientific. Their word *ano yo*, which refers to life after death, is frequently associated with mythological conceptions of what lies much farther beyond. To say that man continues to live for eternity, even after his physical death is, to them, to mean that man leaves upon this world

TABLE 55

	Agree %	Disagree %	Don't Know %
1 The afterlife is nothing more than a fable created by man's imagination.			
	65.1	18.3	16.6
2 Actually, there is no such thing as an afterlife, but becasue people want an afterlife, they believe in it.			
	70.5	16.5	13.0
3 As the saying goes "once dead, you stay dead." And really, for man death is the end of everything.			
	66.0	20.2	13.8
4 Since nobody having seen the afterlife has come back to tell us about it, the belief in such things is completely unreliable.			
	68.8	20.2	11.0

the good deeds he has achieved in life, that his descendants remain in his place, and that his memory lives on, and even that the piece of ground in which he is buried is still there.

As a result of the above potential sources of misunderstanding which might unduly influence the students' replies to our questions, we tried to employ words and phrases which, to our minds, would offer the least possible bias to their manner of answering. In some questions, we used the word *raise*, in others *shigo no sekai*; and in still others we attempted to convey the meaning we wanted by using expressions which they were likely to interpret, from context, in the manner we desired as to the existence of life hereafter and with regard to the notion that death is not the end of everything.

We presented the idea of life and of eternal perduration from the personal angle.

Four postulates were presented which very clearly present the theme denying all life after death. (cf. Table 55)

From the above tabulation it can be clearly seen that from 65 to 70% of the young men completely deny all belief in life after death. Even under the assumption that 93% of the university students do not profess any religious belief, the percentage of 70% still seems small to us. It is interesting to note that among numerous students the problem of the existence of God and that of the question of life after death are topics of an independent nature, dissociated from each other.

The other statements present faith in the life hereafter as a belief that depends principally upon the character and temperament of the person who follows that faith. In other words, to believe or not to believe in a life after death depends to a large extent upon the psychology of each individual. This would be almost tantamount to stating that the only thing of importance, especially in the life of the youth, is to think of life in the present and how to live it most fully. To think of life in the hereafter does not have much sense. These two postulates do not explicitly deny the existence of life after death; but they do aver implicitly that such a belief is entirely subjective and is not proper to persons of a young age.

TABLE 56

	Agree %	Disagree %	Don't Know %
5 There are people who believe in an afterlife and people who deny it—this belief depends on a person's character and temperament.			
	65.2	23.8	11.0
6 It is good enough for a young person in the springtime of his life to think only about living his life to the fullest—to think about things like the afterlife is completely unnecessary.			
	56.0	31.2	12.8

The 65% of affirmative answers to the fifth question is in harmony with the percentages of the other four statements. On the other hand, the percentage of respondents who deny that the problem of life in the hereafter does not concern them is quite a bit higher than the percentage of answers of a negative tenor to the other postulates. Thirty-two percent do not accept the problem as irrelevant to a person's period of youth, and 12.8% have at least some positive doubt about whether this problem concerns them, too, despite their being in the full bloom of youth.

The remaining postulates are positively expressed. In some way or another they aver belief in a life after the present one. It is most noteworthy that only 6.4% answered affirmatively the statements which present life after death as a life of happiness, of complete satisfaction of the most profound human ambitions and aspirations. In the same surprising manner, only 8.2% accepted the thesis that life hereafter is either a prize and payment to the good or a just punishment for the bad, while 78.1% deny it. The main explanation for these answers, as gleaned from various personal interviews conducted afterwards, is that for them to think of life after death as an existence replete with happiness, or in terms of a reward for good work or a penalty for evil done, is but to make use of a psychological mechanism by which man seeks a false soothing relief during times of suffering and trial in the present life, and that such a belief is only a childish solution to the problem of moral evil in this world.

TABLE 57

	Agree %	Disagree %	Dont' Know %
7 The world in which man will be punished or rewarded with perfect justice for his deeds in this world begins after death.			
	8.2	78.1	13.7
8 By nature man seeks unlimited happiness and this aspiration will be perfectly fulfilled in the afterlife.			
	6.4	70.0	23.6

The number of students who categorically affirm the existence of the afterlife is a small 9.1%; but the number of those who are inclined to accept this belief is much larger, about 26.6%.

TABLE 58

	Agree %	Disagree %	Don't Know %
9 I don't know for certain if there is an afterlife or not, but I have a feeling that there is.			
	26.6	47.7	25.7
10 Regardless of how much people deny the afterlife, there certainly is life after death.			
	9.1	73.3	17.6

There is some difficulty with question number 9. Of course, some few who firmly believe in life after death may have given a negative response, so it is probable that the number of students who either believe in, or feel inclined toward vaguely admitting a kind of human immortality that would be something of a life hereafter, could easily reach 30%. In sum, we can state that 70% clearly deny this belief, 9% agree with it fully, and 21%, allowing themselves to be carried away by their hearts' impulses without knowing exactly why, have a definite suspicion that death is not man's last end but that there must be another life after it which is better and which does not come to any end.

Finally, we would like to make note of the fact that we came across two students, among the 109 subjects, who believe in the transmigration of the soul. Following is a reproduction of one of these boys' responses:

> "When a man dies, his soul does not die but it comes again to be born anew. I think it is something which traces a cycle, entering within a man of the following generation, and when he dies passes on to the next man."[49]

3 *Survey about morality*

IN this survey we did not attempt to investigate the moral judgement by the students of definite human acts, such as suicide, divorce, abortion (which is legally allowed in Japan), personal shame, and others. The objective we set was to find out the extent of the personal, internal concept of morality and sin which the new Japanese generations have.

In the remarks made on statement number 25 in our general survey, we briefly noted the problem that arises every time the traditional morality of the Japanese was mentioned; there is always an ambiguity about whether we were dealing with the true morality of personal sin and internal conscience, or with just a morality of shame and embarrassment due to the loss of reputation before others.

It seems that according to the traditional Japanese morality, virtue is considered more of a relationship among men. Examples would be familial relationhips; relationships of loyalty toward the fedual lord, which, since the Meiji Restoration, have been transmuted into an absolute fidelity to the Emperor; relationships arising from service to the community; relationships of external gratitude with all those to whom some favor is owed, which is usually taken as a heavy and bothersome burden. The principal force that impels observance of all the obligations arising from the above-cited relationships comes from the famous *giri*. One way to define *giri* is to say that it is "the moral duty to always so behave oneself as never to elicit the criticism of others." Put in another way, *giri* is the "moral obligation to keep one's reputation ever unsullied in front of others." All other obligations take second place to *giri*.[50]

---

[49] 一人の人が死ぬと，その人の魂というものは，死なずに再び新たに生まれくる。次の時代の人の中に入っていき，又その人が死ぬと次の人へと，順次移っていくようなものであると思う。

[50] Since Ruth Benedict published her famous book, *The Chrysanthemum and the Sword*, Houghton Mifflin Company, Boston, 1946, an enormous amount of discussion has taken place on the true meaning of the word *giri* and to*

Many of seemingly contradictory modes of behavior that we are apt to encounter in Japanese history and legends can be explained by *giri*. In numerous instances in the past, duties arising from filial piety, obligations of loyalty due to the feudal lord, reverence owed the Emperor, and other obligations arising from various relationships, were either contradictory or incompatible. In such situations, there was nothing to do to solve the quandary but to determine which duty, according to Japanese code, came closest to *giri*. But since fulfilling one chosen duty was accompanied by failure to comply with the others, the same *giri* principles required that some reparation be made to the parties to whom an obligation was owed but not fulfilled. In most cases this reparation took the form of the *seppuku*—the suicide of honor.

It is said that, in a sense, such a concept of morality brought the Japanese to an ethics which in modern terms we might call situational ethics. The only absolute principle would be *giri*; all else would be relative, and all human conduct would be good or bad depending upon the circumstances. We shall attempt to explain briefly what is meant here by this situational ethics.

The austerity of the Japanese spirit and the control which the Japanese usually exercises over his passions are well known to everybody. These facts, however, could mislead us into believing that the Japanese is puritanical and

---

*what extent this *giri* represents one of the most typical and essential values in the Japanese culture and morality. It is not our purpose to take part in these discussions, much less to try to give still another theory on the *giri* theme. Letting aside all debatable points we can safely assert as something generally admitted by cultural anthropologists, that "to be affraid of loosing one's reputation" is a distinctive characteristic of the Japanese culture, and one which conditions in a large measure Japanese patterns of behavior. Weston La Barre writes: "The Japanese have a highly developed 'touchy' sense of self, and even as children learn early to fear ridicule. Japanese 'face' is obsessed with the current public status of the self. Behind this is always lurking a fear of ridicule and ostracism, and adult Japanese are always scrupulous to conduct themselves in such a way as to avoid the sting of ridicule. The success of 'thought control' in Japanese life is largely due to this fact. To be ridiculed is to lose one's precarious dignity and self-respect, that is, to 'lose face.' Japanese timidity in what I have called their 'committee behavior' is also part of this" (Weston La Barre, "Some Observations on Character Structure in the Orient," in *Japanese Character and Culture*, edited by Bernard S. Silberman, The University of Arizona Press, Arizona, 1962, p. 344) And writing about this

fear of "loosing face' Geoffrey Gorer sees in it the real cause why the Japanese are so ceremonious and ritualist and given to conformity: "Since there is so much emphasis on behavior suitable to a given situation, the drive to adapt to any new situation is very strong, since the sanction for non-adaptation are among the most terrifying the average Japanese experiences. The Japanese are bound by a conservative ritualism in the Japanese environment" (Geoffrey Gorer, "Themes in Japanese Culture" in *Japanese Character and Culture*, edited by Bernard S. Silberman, The University of Arizona Press, Arizona, 1962, p. 318). The definition of *giri* we have presented is the one given by Ruth Benedict. It stresses this characteristic of the Japanese psychology. Ruth Benedict makes a distinction between the "*giri*-to-the-world" and the "*giri*-to-one's-name"; the latter is defined in these terms: "One's duty to clear one's reputation of insult or imputation of failure, i.e., the duty of feuding or vendetta. One's duty to admit no professional failure or ignorance. One's duty to fulfill the Japanese proprieties, e.g., observing all respect behavior, not living above one's station in life, curbing all displays of emotion on inappropriate occasions, etc. . . . I shall call *giri* to one's name the duty of keeping one's name and reputation unspotted by any imputation." (Benedict, p. 116 and p. 134)

K

ascetic. His self-discipline is directed toward the precise observance of the Japanese code of morality which is based on *giri*; but with the *giri* satisfied, he allows himself to be carried away by his natural inclinations. The Japanese is no puritan; he is a naturalist. He lives with and in nature, and does not let himself get too far from it. It is not nature that needs to be conquered by man; rather, it is man who should adapt himself to nature. The law of nature is a law based on hierarchism: hierarchy in the social structure, hierarchy in the individual's conduct, hierarchy in natural facts and phenomena. To break this law is to go against nature; when it is not violated, all will come out well. It will be against nature to submit to sensual pleasures when higher duties require their renunciation; but when there is no conflict of obligations, it is good and in accord with nature to seek the most sybaritic refinements in every aspect of sensual living.[51]

The same principle of *giri* brings about another kind of relativism to all other principles of conduct and morality. A typical example of this is the famous legend of the 47 samurai who avenged their master even though they had to violate all other kinds of obligations and to go against their familial duties, and against their reverential obligation to the Shogun himself in order to do it. They went to the extent of offering their wives as prostitutes to obtain the financial means for carrying out their plan of vengeance. But the principle of *giri* forced them to carry out the vindication, and the Japanese people expected them to make such a retaliation. And this they did.[52]

[51] The first three chapters of Minami Hiroshi's well known book *Nihonjin no shinri* 南博 「日本人の心理」 (The Psychology of the Japanese), Tokyo, Iwanami Shinsho, 14th. ed., 1962, give us a deep view of the pshychology of the Japanese relying on a hierarchical structure which is considered as a fundamental law of nature. Chapters 9 and 10 of Ruth Benedict's book contain a deep insight into the patterns of naturalistic behavior of the Japanese.

[52] Another controversial subject and a very difficult one to elucidate is the meaning of sin in Japanese culture and morality. It is classic the text of Sir George Sansom on Japanese morals and their concept of sin: "Its code is not ethical, but customary and ceremonial. It reprobates as sins only such acts as are visibly or immediately repulsive...The concept of sin, as distinct from uncleanness, is wanting or rudimentary, and throughout their history the Japanese seem to have maintained in some measure this incapacity to discern, or this reluctance to grapple with, the problem of Evil" (G.B. Sansom, *Japan, A Short Cultural History*, New York, 1943, p. 54). Cultural anthropologist have been repeating the same idea and once more they find the concept of sin and shame intimately connected. The text we quote next has a special value, having been written by the Japanese author Tada Michitarō: " 'People will laugh at you' and other such expressions are repeatedly used to correct the conduct of even small children. In other words, the opinion of others becomes, whether consciously or not, the norm according to which our acts are judged. The reaction of others to our behavior, therefore, becomes the supreme rule.... We are always in fear of shame, and we fear it as much as a criminal fears the police. We are surrounded by the eyes of shame. As Yoshi of 'Kichigai buraku Shūyūkiko' says: 'Our conscience is the others inside us' (*Ryōshin to wa, jibun no naka no tanin na no de aru* 良心とは、自分の中の他人なのである.) ... As you have followed the prescribed pattern, people will not criticize your actions. And, consequently, as people do not speak up, the others in our heart, who are our conscience, will not make too much difficulty.... If one follows the customary pattern, there will be no question of his personal responsibility.... Sometimes it may be considered a sacrifice to comply with this *taimen*, to*

What do present-day Japanese youth think of this prevalent traditional concept of morality? It is evident that a great majority of them are ignorant of the explicit *giri* theories as we have explained them here. Neither have they thought seriously of the principles or foundations of some morality. Although moral education has again been instituted in the schools, the students are not given a basic theoretical grounding in human morality either in the courses on morality that they take or in the textbooks which they use. It is equally evident, however, that they feel and have a moral conscience, and that, without knowing how to formulate them, they follow certain moral principles which are what, to all intents and purposes, govern their human conduct.

The older generation often complain that the younger generation do not know *giri*. It is a fact that the young Japanese today frequently goes too far in what he calls the spirit of democracy. The postwar environment brought with it the loss of a sense of submissiveness, a noticeable lack of educational discipline, a tremendous egoism, and outstandingly marked hedonistic tendencies. All this, owing to a misconception of the philosophies of freedom and equality, has enormously weakened all concept of authority, especially parental authority. A Japanese author writes, "The young generation of Japan has gone to the limits of the opposite extreme of obsessive individualism and of unlimited freedom."[53]

*have to do as other people. However, in return for this sacrifice, even what is considered wrong may, without any twinge of conscience, be silently permitted or overlooked. . . . When one says that the culture of Japan is a shame culture, it should be made clear that in this case shame refers to the group to whom one belongs. . . . People who are opposed to shame culture may feel that if it is a heavy burden to uphold the honor of one group, it may become unbearable to have this relationship multiplied. However, those who consciously or unconsciously support this kind of culture, do not feel the burden of those complications. Moreover in some circumstances this relationship to various groups may become the only salvation for the individual. For instance, an individual who, on account of his wild conduct has become a black sheep in his village, may be able to quiet the pangs of his conscience by becoming a member of the right kind of gang and by observing its laws and conventions," Tada Michitarō 多田道太郎 "Haji to taimen" 恥と体面 (Shame and Honor) in *Gendai rinri*, VI, Chikuma Shobō, 1958, pp. 234-240) (The English translation has been taken from F. Uyttendaele's article "Shame and Honor," *Missionary Bulletin*, 1963, XVII,

665-668. Hardly anywhere else could we find such a remarkable description of moral conscience as something purely extrinsic, something essentially connected with the views and reactions of those who live with us in the same group and society. Nevertheless as J. J. Spae writes in his article about the Japanese concept of sin, "The concept of sin implying guilt—and consequently responsibility to a higher order, if not a higher being—is found in literature and in daily parlance under many guises." (*Missionary Bulletin*, 1965, XIX, 456-464). Even granted that the "feeling of shame" acts as the driving force of Japanese behavior, it would be too much to affirm that any consciuosness of personal, internal guilt, independent from the shame-anxiety complex, is totally inexistent in the Japanese. The same author writes: "I have a feeling that this nobler and truer aspect of the Japanese sense of sin is rapidly gaining ground while the Confucianist notion of good and evil which is based upon one's attitudes towards one's elders and superiors as well as upon the moral judgement of the community, is declining" (Ibid. p. 464).

[53] Editorial of *The Japan Times,* February 1, 1964.

We are of the belief, however, that, considering the tragic crisis which Japan underwent in her defeat in World War II, which meant not only material capitulation but also surrender of many of her traditional spiritual values, this is one of the phenomena which is wont to go hand in hand with national crises of such magnitude as Japan's defeat, surrender and occupation. We are confident, though, that this period of moral crisis will pass.

We must not forget our remarks on question number 25 in our survey, in which we mentioned Japanese writers who believe that a new morality is emerging which, although it may appear superficial and without ideological consistency, embodies in itself a universal human element very much in harmony with the intuitive-emotional character of the Oriental. As the well-known writer Hasegawa Nyozekan tells us, it is not a morality based upon idealistic principles which take moral laws as the objective norms of morality; rather, it is an intuitive and practical morality which, based on experience and intuitive moral judgement, shows what is good and what is evil.[54]

The questions which we framed for the questionnaire on morality were aimed at discovering if, in this new emerging morality, the moral accent is placed more upon the internal and personal conscience of the individual than upon the *giri* code in relation to others.

The students who were our subjects in this study were the same group of 109 university young men who were asked to answer the questions regarding an afterlife.

We found that 89% of the students clearly admit that one should never do anything against the dictates of his own conscience, even when such an act is sanctioned or allowed by the laws or customs of the society in which he lives. This problem was propounded in one postulate as follows:

TABLE 59

	Agree	Disagree	Don't Know
1 If you think something is wrong but society approves of it, don't mind doing it.			
	%	%	%
	5.5	88.9	5.5

With two other statements we openly proposed the idea that the feelings of shame and guilt, which one has upon doing something which he deems morally bad, are born exclusively of the fear and shame of criticisms by others, because of the fact that one besmirches his reputation in society and among other men. A great majority completely disagree with this opinion.

[54] See note 33.

TABLE 60

Agree	Disagree	Don't Know
%	%	%

2 The anxiety and fear you feel when you do something wrong is nothing more than anxiety and fear of criticism and punishment from others.

23.8	71.6	4.6

3 The feeling of shame, ugliness, and impurity felt with sin is born only from the fact that one loses face before society and other people.

25.7	67.9	6.4

It is most interesting, however, that yet about 25% clearly declare their approval of the stated opinion, which represents the exclusiveness of a morality of shame in the crudest terms.

As a complement to these two questions, we added another on the idea of sin as something merely devised by men and society.

4 The idea of sin is nothing but that which has been created by men and society.

TABLE 61

Agree	Disagree	Don't Know
%	%	%
23.8	68.8	7.3

As was to be expected, the results were identical with the outcomes on the two preceding questions. The 25%, who agree with the idea that feelings of shame and guilt which one has after doing something wrong are due to shame of losing one's reputation with respect to others, also accept, quite logically, the concept of sin as something which man has merely invented.

Finally, two other questions ought to discover the moral criterion of the young man about what we of the West call internal sins.

TABLE 62

Agree	Disagree	Don't Know
%	%	%

5 If you secretly cherish in your heart jealousy and hate toward someone, you don't need to think that such internal feelings are wrong unless others notice them.

34.8	55.0	10.2

6 Whatever simply remains in your heart, and does not become an act, cannot become a sin.

33.9	54.2	11.9

Taking all of these results as a whole, we believe we can say that 55% of the young men, who admit the morality of man's internal acts, show most clearly a very personal and internal consciousness of sin, a consciousness that what is morally good or evil is fully independent of mere external criteria set up by society and irrespective of the external consequences which an evil act may bring with it. Even if there were no external consequences, even if one were not to lose his reputation with others, the internal workings of a heart that envies and hates are by themselves morally evil.

But even among those who admit that only external acts can be morally bad, there is a sufficient number of students who vigorously deny the idea that guilt-consciousness is due only to the external consequences which wrong doings can bring. The knowledge of having done evil is something personal and internal, independent of what men and society might say, without any relation to losing prestige or not, unrelated to the shame one might feel in front of others. Of the subjects, 75% feel that consciousness of sin is something deeper and more internal, something intrinsic in the human heart.

Furthermore, among the 25% who consider consciousness of sin as nothing more than feelings of shame before others for having lost reputation before them, there are not a few who contradict themselves by affirming that one should not do that which he thinks is not right, even if society, the law and custom were to accept and recognize it as proper. At least, with such an implicit statement, it can be discerned that there is recognition of the difference between consciousness of sin and consciousness of shame in front of others. We have seen that the students who think this way reach 88.9% of our sample.

We are of the belief that these results offer a sufficient guaranty that the concepts of individual and personal responsibility, true guilt morality, internal consciousness of sin, profound sincerity toward the dictates of one's own heart—all are essential elements of the moral conscience of a great majority of Japanese young men. This leaves to a very low secondary level the notion of shame and loss of reputation before others which, after all, is not only a natural fear but something which everyone must have.

Appendix I

BIBLIOGRAPHY OF SURVEYS ON THE RELIGIOUS
ATTITUDE OF JAPANESE STUDENTS

IN THIS appendix we offer the list of the main surveys on religion conducted among Japanese high school and university students during the period 1955–65. We only mention the surveys we have perused.

For a more general view of literature on religious surveys in Japan, see the bibliography given in the article of Imada Megumi 今田恵, "Shūkyō ishiki no hattatsu" 宗教意識の発達 (Development of Religious Consciousness), *Seinen shinrigaku kōza* 青年心理学講座 (Lectures on Psychology of Youth), Kaneko shobō 金子書房, Tokyo, 1955, I, 145–146. See also Suzuki Norihisa 鈴木範久, "'Nihonjin no shūkyō ishiki' kenkyū ni tsuite"「日本人の宗教意識」研究について (Studies on the Religious Consciousness of the Japanese), *Shūkyō kenkyū* 宗教研究 (Religious Research), 1965, No. 182, pp. 119–130.

The English translations given in this bibliography are almost always taken from the original Japanese sources.

1 Oka Dōko 岡道固, "Sengo gakusei no shūkyō ishiki 戦後学生の宗教意識 (Religious Consciousness of Postwar Students), *Jimbungaku kenkyū* 人文学研究 (Studies in the Humanities), Ōsaka shiritsu daigaku bungakukai 大阪市立大学文学会 (The Literary Association of Osaka City University), 1955, VI, 89–103.

2 Imada Megumi, "Shūkyō ishiki no hattatsu," pp.99–146.

3 Koike Naoatsu 小池直淳, "Shūkyōteki shinkō o motsu seinen no ningenzō" 宗教的信仰を持つ青年の人間像 (Human Image of the Believing Youth), *Nihon daigaku bungakubu kenkyū nempō* 日本大学文学部研究年報, 1955, VI, 191–200.

4 Okabe Yatarō 岡部弥太郎, "Jijoden ni arawareta kokuritsu daigaku gakusei no shūkyō to shakai shisō" 自叙伝にあらわれた国立大学学生の宗教と社会思想 (Religious Beliefs and Social Toughts of Students of a Representative State University), *Kyōiku kenkyū* 教育研究 (Bulletin of Educational Research), Kokusai kirisutokyō daigaku 国際基督教大学 (International Christian University, 1956, No. 3, pp. 80–101.

5 Horiuchi Haruyo 堀内治世, "Raisekan o chūshin to shita shūkyō ishiki no kenkyū" 来世観を中心とした宗教意識の研究 (Religious Consciousness about the Afterlife), *Bunkagaku nempō* 文化学年報 (Annual Report of the Faculty of Letters), Dōshisha daigaku 同志社大学, 1956, No. 5, pp. 68–99.

6 Kawai Iroku 河合伊六, "Shūkyō ni taisuru taido no kenkyū" 宗教に対する態度の研究 (A Survey About Attitudes Towards Religion), *Ronshū* 論集 (Bulletin), Hiroshima jogakuin daigaku 広島女学院大学, 1956, No. 6, pp, 11–21, 23–30; 1957, No. 7, pp. 45–52; 1958, No. 8, pp. 81–92.

7 Sakurai Masanobu 桜井正信, Wada Kenju 和田謙寿, Iwami Yoshie 岩見美栄 and Misawa Sanzō 三沢三蔵, "Shūkyō gyōji chōsa ni arawareta toshi seishōnen gakuto no mondai" 宗教行事調査にあらわれた都市青少年学徒の問題 (Problems of Younger Generation in Urban District Shown in the Religious Events Investigation), *Shūkyō shakai kenkyūjo nempō* 宗教社会研究所年報 (Bulletin of the Religious Research Institute), Komazawa daigaku 駒沢大学, 1957, III, 34–47.

8 Ide Masashi 井出正, "Shūkyō shinjō yori mita seishōnen shinri no ichidammen" 宗教心情より見た青少年心理の一断面 (A Psychological Profile of Children and Adolescents from the

View point of Religious Consciousness), *Matsuyama shōka daigaku ronshū* 松山商科大学論集, 1958, No. 29, pp. 111-162.

9 Picher René, O.P., "Quand les jeunes regardent le Christ," *Rythmes du Monde*, 1959, nouvélle série 7, pp, 320-332.

10 Ikeda Yoshisuke 池田義祐 and Naka Hisao 中久郎, "Shūmon daigakusei no jittai" 宗門大学生の実態, *Ōtani daigaku tetsugaku ronshū* 大谷大学哲学論集 (The Otani Philosophical Studies), 1959, v, 64-80.

11 Takahashi Yoshimi 高橋省己, "Shūkyō ni taisuru gendai seinen no taido" 宗教に対する現代青年の態度 (The Attitude of Today's Students Regarding Religion), *Kyōiku gakubu kenkyū shūroku* 教育学部研究集録 (Bulletin of Researches of the Faculty of Education), Kōbe daigaku 神戸大学, 1959, No. 19, pp. 87-96.

12 John C. Puivis, "Students on Religion," *Missionary Bulletin*, 1960, xv, 526-530.

13 Nakajima Sei 中島誠 and Tsushima Tadashi 津島忠, "Gendai gakusei to shūkyō" 現代学生と宗教 (Religion and Contemporary College Students), *Tetsugaku kenkyū* 哲学研究 (Philosophical Studies), 1960, xLI, 199-238.

14 Ushiyama Yoshitomo 牛島義友, *Seiō to Nihon no ningen keisei* 西欧と日本の人間形成 (The Building of Man in the West and in Japan), Kaneko shobō, Tokyo, 1961, pp. 326-332.

15 "Kansai gakuin ni okeru shūkyō katsudō no genjō to hyōka" 関西学院における宗教活動の現状と評価 (Present Condition and Evaluation of Religious Activities in Kansai gakuin University), *Kansai gakuin 'shūkyō to kyōiku' kenkyūkai shiryō* 関西学院「宗教と教育」研究会資料 (Publication of the Students' Religious and Educational Association of Kansai gakuin University), 1961.

16 Mizoguchi Yasuo 溝口靖夫, Sasabe Taketoshi 雀部猛利 and Namba Monkichi 難波紋吉, "Kirisutokyōshugi joshi daigaku gakusei no shūkyō ishiki ni tsuite no jisshōteki kenkyū" キリスト教主義女子大学生の宗教意識についての実証的研究 (Research on the Religious Consciousness of Students in Women's Christian Colleges in Japan), *Ronshū* 論集 (Studies), Kōbe jogakuin daigaku 神戸女学院大学, 1962, No. 25, pp. 23-44, No. 26, pp. 79-94.

17 Kuzutani Takamasa 葛谷隆正, "Seinen gakuto no shūkyōteki ishiki to sono kōdō" 青年学徒の宗教的意識とその行動 (Students' Religious Consciousness and Practice), *Kēsu kenkyū* ケース研究 (Case Studies), 1962, No. 73, pp.20-29.

18 Tōhoku daigaku katorikku kenkyūkai 東北大学カトリック研究会, "Gendai gakusei no shūkyōkan no dōkō" 現代学生の宗教観の動向 (Trends in the Religious Mentality of Contemporary Students), *Fukyō* 布教 (Missionary Bulletin), 1962, xVII, 400-406.

19 Kuzutani Takamasa, "Daigakusei no shūkyōteki taido to shūkyōteki ishiki" 大学生の宗教的態度と宗教的意識 (Students' Religious Attitudes and Consciousness), *Kyōiku shinri kenkyū* 教育心理研究 (Studies on Educational Pscychology), Kumamoto daigaku 熊本大学, 1963, III, 50-54.

20 Shiroiwa Yoshio 白岩義夫, "Shūkyō chōsa: tandai daigakusei taishō" 宗教調査：短大大学生対象 (A Religious Survey on Students of Junior Colleges), *Shūkyō shimbun* 宗教新聞 (Religious Journal), Kinjō gakuin daigaku 金城学院大学, December 1963.

21 Yokoyama Tetsu 横山哲, "Chōsa ni okeru chūgakkō, kōkōsei no dōtoku, shūkyō ishiki to kōdō" 調査に於ける中学校，高校生の道徳，宗教意識と行動 (A Survey on the Morality, Religious Consciousness and Behavior of Junior and High School Students), *Shūkyō kenkyū* 宗教研究 (Religious Researchs), 1963, No. 174, pp. 127-130.

22 Tanaka Hiroko 田中弘子, "Joshi daigakusei no seikatsu kūkan no shūkyōteki sokumen ni kansuru kenkyū" 女子大学生の生活空間の宗教的側面に関する研究 (Research on the Religious Aspect of the Life Environment of Female University Students), *Shinrigakka shiryō* 心理学科資料，Tōhoku daigaku 東北大学, 1963 (unpublished).

23 Tanaka Hiroko, "Joshi kōkōsei no shūkyōkan" 女子高校生の宗教観 (Religious Mentality of Hight School Girls), *Shinrigakka shiryō*, Tōhoku daigaku.

24 M.E. Troyer, "Nihonjin gakusei no shūkyōteki kachi shikō ni tsuite" 日本人学生の宗教的価 値指向について (On the Religious Values and Behavior of Japanese Students), *Kirisutokyō bunka gakkai nempō* キリスト教文化学会年報 (Annual Report of the Cultural Christian Association), 1964, XI, 67-82.

25 Kuzutani Takamasa. "Shūkyō to henken to no kankei ni tsuite" 宗教と偏見との関係につい て (On the Relationship Between Religion and Prejudice), *Kyōiku gakubu kiyō* 教育学部経 要 (Memoirs of the Facutly of Education), Kumamoto daigaku, 1964, No 12, pp. 70-77.

26 Kuzutani Takamasa, "Daigakusei no shūkyōteki taido to sono haikeiteki yōin ni tsuite" 大学生 の宗教的態度とその背景的要因について (A Study of the Effect of Personal and Sociocultural Backgrounds on the Religious Attitude of University Students), *Kyōikugakubu kiyō*, Kumamoto daigaku, 1965, No. 13, pp. 81-87.

27 "Jinsei ni kansuru setsumon: Hitsuyōsei kanjiru shūkyō 人生に関する設問: 必要性感じる 宗教 (Questioning Human Existence: Necessity of Religion), *Jōchi daigaku shimbun* 宗教上智 大学新聞, June 1965.

Appendix II

THE "t" VALUE FOR EACH QUESTION
OF THE SURVEY

The "t" value for each question of the survey.[1]

$$(1) \quad t=\frac{\overline{X}_H-\overline{X}_L}{\sqrt{\dfrac{S_H{}^2}{n_H}+\dfrac{S_L{}^2}{n_L}}}$$

$\overline{X}_H$ = The mean score on a given statement for the high group.

$\overline{X}_L$ = The mean score on the same statement for the low group.

$S_H{}^2$ = The variance of the distribution of responses of the high group to the statement.

$S_L{}^2$ = The variance of the distribution of responses of the low group to the statement.

n_H = The number of subjects in the high group.

n_L = The number of the subjects in the low group.

Because we selected the same percentage of the total number of subjects for the high and low groups, $n_H=n_L$; and then formula (1) can be written:

$$(2) \quad t=\frac{\overline{X}_H-\overline{X}_L}{\sqrt{\dfrac{\sum(X_H-\overline{X}_H)^2+\sum(X_L-\overline{X}_L)^2}{n(n-1)}}}$$

where $\quad \sum(X_H-\overline{X}_H)^2=\sum X_H{}^2-\dfrac{(\sum X_H)^2}{n}$

and $\quad \sum(X_L-\overline{X}_L)^2=\sum X_L{}^2-\dfrac{(\sum X_L)^2}{n}$

We present a full example of the calculation of "t" in terms of formula (2) for the 1st. question of our inquiry.

| Response | | Low Group | | | High Group | | | |
Categories	X		fX	fX²	X	f	fX	fX²
Strongly agree	0	8	0	0	0	1	0	0
Agree	1	12	12	12	1	5	5	5
Don't know	2	3	6	12	2	2	4	8
Disagree	3	1	3	9	3	7	21	63
Strongly disagree	4	1	4	16	4	10	40	160
Sums		25	25	49		25	70	236
		n_L	$\sum X_L$	$\sum X_L{}^2$		n_H	$\sum X_H$	$\sum X_H{}^2$

$$\overline{X}_L=\frac{25}{25}=1.00; \quad \overline{X}_H=\frac{70}{25}=2.80$$

$$\sum(X_L-\overline{X}_L)^2=49-\frac{25^2}{25}=24.00; \quad \sum(X_H-\overline{X}_H)^2=236-\frac{70^2}{25}=40.00$$

$$t=\frac{2.80-1.00}{\sqrt{\dfrac{40.00+24.00}{25(25-1)}}}=5.4$$

---

[1] Cfr. Allen L. Edwards, *Techniques of Attitude Scale Construction* (pp. 152-156) Apple-ton-Century-Crofts, Inc., New York, 1957.

TABLE OF "t" VALUES

Question	t value	Question	t value	Question	t value
2	5.5	14	6.1	26	7.1
3	4.3	15	7.7	27	7.1
4	2.9	16	6.8	28	5.7
5	7.0	17	8.8	29	4.9
6	7.1	18	6.2	30	6.3
7	8.8	19	3.7	31	5.9
8	5.8	20	4.2	32	6.5
9	9.0	21	7.2	33	6.8
10	7.7	22	7.9	34	7.5
11	6.4	23	3.0	35	9.1
12	8.1	24	3.9	36	7.9
13	6.2	25	6.4		

Appendix III
THE STANDARD ERROR
OF THE ESTIMATED PERCENTAGES

The Standard Error of the Estimated Percentages

Item		Total		Male		Female	
		Estimated Percentage	Standard Error	Estimated Percentage	Standard Error	Estimated Percentage	Standard Error
1	TA	61.4	1.29	63.8	0.99	48.7	2.12
	TD	26.7	1.19	24.2	0.84	39.8	2.70
	DK	11.9	0.50	12.0	0.63	11.5	1.26
2	TA	53.9	1.13	55.6	1.09	44.9	1.85
	TD	32.7	0.90	31.4	0.96	39.4	1.70
	DK	13.4	0.95	13.0	1.09	15.6	2.08
3	TA	46.7	1.20	47.7	1.06	41.4	2.48
	TD	31.7	1.13	30.8	0.85	36.2	2.86
	DK	21.6	0.79	21.4	0.79	22.4	2.44
4	TA	72.7	0.72	72.7	0.74	72.8	2.34
	TD	11.7	0.72	11.5	0.74	12.6	1.65
	DK	15.6	0.56	15.8	0.53	14.6	1.80
5	TA	45.6	0.95	46.3	1.08	41.6	2.32
	TD	41.9	1.02	40.4	0.77	49.7	2.90
	DK	12.5	0.76	13.2	0.68	8.7	1.82
6	TA	40.1	1.13	41.2	1.18	34.1	2.61
	TD	48.3	1.21	46.7	1.09	56.7	3.16
	DK	11.6	0.66	12.1	0.69	9.1	1.50
7	TA	39.7	1.65	41.0	1.56	33.4	2.98
	TD	50.6	1.51	49.1	1.32	58.7	2.53
	DK	9.6	0.39	10.0	0.48	7.9	1.16
8	TA	31.9	1.24	32.2	1.02	30.2	2.91
	TD	48.3	1.68	47.4	1.55	53.3	3.63
	DK	19.8	1.01	20.4	0.94	16.5	2.09
9	TA	14.6	0.81	15.4	0.91	10.5	1.59
	TD	67.6	1.29	66.2	1.41	75.0	2.70
	DK	17.8	1.16	18.4	1.18	14.5	2.10
10	TA	24.9	1.00	25.9	1.25	19.7	1.62
	TD	56.9	1.25	55.3	1.18	65.3	2.49
	DK	18.2	1.07	18.8	1.06	15.1	1.99
11	TA	23.2	1.25	24.9	1.29	14.4	2.24
	TD	65.7	1.41	63.7	1.13	76.6	3.24
	DK	11.0	0.65	11.4	0.64	9.0	2.07
12	TA	23.5	1.43	25.0	1.54	16.1	2.11
	TD	56.3	1.56	54.1	1.31	67.5	3.13
	DK	20.2	0.87	20.9	0.87	16.4	2.15
13	TA	17.7	0.67	18.3	0.78	14.9	1.59
	TD	68.3	1.23	67.7	0.94	71.6	3.38
	DK	14.0	0.75	14.1	0.71	13.4	2.50
14	TA	12.5	0.98	13.8	0.96	5.7	1.43
	TD	75.8	1.20	73.6	0.96	86.9	2.48
	DK	11.7	0.76	12.6	0.70	7.3	1.70
15	TA	13.3	0.99	14.4	1.07	7.0	1.66
	TD	74.4	1.56	72.4	1.54	84.4	2.55
	DK	12.4	0.84	13.1	0.80	8.6	1.16

The Standard Error of the Estimated Percentages

Item		Total		Male		Female	
		Estimated Percentage	Standard Error	Estimated Percentage	Standard Error	Estimated Percentage	Standard Error
16	TA	22.1	0.73	23.0	1.01	17.8	2.39
	TD	53.7	1.41	52.4	1.74	60.4	3.07
	DK	24.1	1.19	24.6	1.26	21.8	2.79
17	TA	21.6	1.44	22.5	1.45	17.1	2.31
	TD	61.3	1.78	59.6	1.58	70.6	2.53
	DK	17.0	1.00	17.9	0.99	12.3	1.08
18	TA	16.7	1.09	17.6	1.27	11.8	1.55
	TD	67.5	1.60	65.5	1.65	77.6	2.24
	DK	15.8	1.06	16.9	1.07	10.6	1.40
19	TA	66.7	0.91	65.2	1.19	74.1	1.74
	TD	13.2	0.64	13.8	0.97	10.1	1.37
	DK	20.2	0.66	21.0	0.64	15.8	1.59
20	TA	59.3	0.82	57.6	0.44	68.0	2.01
	TD	18.2	0.99	19.0	1.05	14.6	1.76
	DK	22.5	0.56	23.4	0.80	17.4	1.37
21	TA	57.2	1.05	55.9	1.17	63.8	2.57
	TD	30.1	1.16	30.9	1.37	25.6	1.39
	DK	12.8	0.50	13.2	0.53	10.6	1.69
22	TA	42.4	1.58	41.2	1.56	48.8	3.04
	TD	34.1	1.07	34.6	1.25	31.1	2.08
	DK	23.5	1.09	24.1	1.08	20.2	1.80
23	TA	32.1	0.62	30.1	0.91	42.4	2.39
	TD	32.4	1.43	33.2	1.55	28.7	1.61
	DK	35.4	1.56	36.7	1.97	28.8	2.71
24	TA	37.4	0.83	36.7	0.70	41.1	2.50
	TD	42.8	1.03	42.8	0.92	42.8	2.67
	DK	19.8	0.81	20.5	1.01	16.1	1.79
25	TA	56.5	1.38	55.4	1.40	62.2	2.84
	TD	25.6	1.43	26.4	1.34	21.3	2.01
	DK	17.9	0.77	18.2	0.88	16.5	2.21
26	TA	56.1	0.83	55.0	0.82	62.0	1.47
	TD	23.7	0.95	24.2	0.98	20.8	1.40
	DK	20.2	0.52	20.8	0.63	17.2	1.31
27	TA	36.6	1.20	34.5	1.17	47.8	2.78
	TD	30.9	1.28	31.7	1.55	26.7	2.99
	DK	32.5	1.15	33.9	1.06	25.5	2.18
28	TA	51.7	1.08	50.8	1.20	56.6	3.15
	TD	30.8	1.17	31.6	1.44	27.0	2.97
	DK	17.4	1.11	17.6	1.11	16.4	1.79
29	TA	38.5	1.21	37.4	1.32	44.5	2.04
	TD	39.1	1.41	39.5	1.54	37.0	1.86
	DK	22.4	1.32	23.1	1.43	18.6	1.65
30	TA	55.7	1.48	54.7	1.23	61.2	3.08
	TD	28.8	1.13	29.2	1.31	27.1	2.18
	DK	15.4	1.27	16.2	1.33	11.7	1.91
31	TA	31.7	1.26	30.8	1.19	36.6	2.95
	TD	48.1	0.88	48.8	0.98	44.5	2.56
	DK	20.2	0.90	20.4	1.04	18.9	2.80
32	TA	53.1	0.80	52.8	0.86	54.8	2.14
	TD	19.7	0.73	19.8	0.99	19.4	1.58
	DK	27.2	0.64	27.4	0.55	25.8	1.84
33	TA	20.4	0.95	19.1	1.10	27.3	2.87
	TD	61.1	1.30	62.4	1.55	54.4	2.89
	DK	18.5	0.82	18.6	1.01	18.3	1.45

The Standard Error of the Estimated Percentages

Item		Total		Male		Female	
		Estimated Percentage	Standard Error	Estimated Percentage	Standard Error	Estimated Percentage	Standard Error
34	TA	18.8	1.01	18.1	1.17	22.9	1.94
	TD	62.5	1.02	63.5	1.02	57.4	1.94
	DK	18.7	0.70	18.5	0.85	19.7	1.14
35	TA	12.8	0.51	11.9	0.45	17.4	1.52
	TD	75.2	0.94	75.8	1.02	71.9	1.84
	DK	12.0	0.99	12.3	1.05	10.8	1.47
36	TA	73.5	1.39	72.3	1.40	79.4	2.30
	TD	12.8	0.80	13.1	1.00	11.3	1.44
	DK	13.7	1.07	14.6	1.07	9.3	1.50 (1)

The use of this table:

If, for example, the results of the investigation show that 25% of the students are in agreement with a given question and the table indicates that the corresponding standard error is 1.08%, then at the 2% level of significance the true value of the percentage of the students in agreement with this questions will be

$$(A)\ 25\% \pm (3)(1.08\%)$$

That is to say that the true percentage will lie between 21.76% and 28.24%. In other words, the probability that statement (A) is correct is 98%.

1 It seems that the rather high standard error that can be observed in the female column of this table is due to the fact that the female population in the subsamples differs substantially in number and quality; consequently we should be very cautious in the interpretation of this column.

Note

In the method of "replicated sampling" the "k" subsamples are drawn completely independent of each other. Therefore the theory to be used for the variance of an estimate is the simple theory of the single stage. In this case the ratio estimate for proportion is found through the formula:

$$p = \frac{\text{The y — population in the sample with a given answer.}}{\text{The x — total population in the sample.}} = \frac{y}{x}$$

Let x_i, y_i be the x, y population in the ith subsample.

The estimate of the standard error of p is given by the formula:

$$\hat{\sigma}_p = \sqrt{\frac{1}{k(k-1)}\left(\frac{\sum\limits_{i=1}^{K} x_i}{k}\right)^2 \sum\limits_{i=1}^{K}(y_i - px_i)^2}$$

$$= \sqrt{\frac{k}{(k-1)x^2}\sum\limits_{i=1}^{K} x_i^2(p_i-p)^2}$$

(Cf.: W. G Cochran, *Sampling Techniques,* New York, John Wiley & Sons, Inc., 1953 (pg. 125))

When the estimated p is normally distributed about the population values, confidence limits for the population are as follows:

$$\hat{p} = p \pm t\hat{\sigma}_p \qquad \text{(Cf. Cochran, op. cit., pg. 20)}$$

Where "t" is the value of the normal deviate corresponding to the desired confidence probability. If the sample size is less than 30, the percentage points of confidence probability may be taken from Student's t-table with (k-1) degrees of freedom in the estimated variance. In our case the number of subsamples is 10; therefore, for the percentage points of confidence probability we must take the following Student's t-values.

Confidence probability %	50	75	90	95	98	99
t (Student's t values with 9 degrees of freedom)	0.70	1.23	1.83	2.26	3.00	3.25

Appendix IV

1 Religion is unnecessary for those who have self-confidence.

2 For a person who is satisfied with his life, religion is not really necessary.

3 The decision to acknowledge religion or not depends only on man's feelings and moods.

4 There are many kinds of religion, and their viewpoints differ. Therefore, it is all right if people choose that religion which suits their own taste.

5 Religion is a means to escape from the troubles of the real world.

6 Religion is nothing more than a kind of sedative.

7 Religion is nothing more than calling upon the gods in time of trouble.

8 Religion is in contradiction to science and reason.

9 The case of scientists with religious beliefs reflects an improper attitude from the scientific point of view.

10 Religion weakens one's individuality and blocks the development of one's personality.

11 Religion in our present state of advanced civilization is close to superstition.

12 Religious belief is born from man's ignorance.

13 Religion is nothing more than a heritage from primitive ancestors.

14 Religion is now out of date.

15 It may be that religion is something fitting for old people, but for young people it is something you may take or leave.

16 Religion is founded on man's hallucinations.

17 Religion is nothing more than a drug which makes man submissive and resigned.

18 Religion is a means of exploitation for the ruling class; it is of no use for ordinary people.

19 Religion instills peace in the depths of a man's heart.

20 Religion saves man from his emptiness and loneliness.

21 Religion is extremely worthwhile as a support for man's heart.

22 Religion gives meaning to a man's life and clarifies the purpose of his existence.

23 Religion dispels the uneasiness about drifting into nothingness with man's death.

24 Religion offers a solution to man's anxieties.

25 The teaching of religion is morally excellent, and, because it fosters kindred human love, it is quite important for mankind.

26 Religion gives discipline and moral training to the whole man.

27 Religion unceasingly stirs up in man aspirations for his self-improvement.

28 Religion can make a great contribution to the realization of peace among mankind.

29 Religion has the power to solve the disorders of society and to overcome personal egoism.

30 Man must have an attitude of understanding and respect for religion.

31 It can be said that a life based on religion deserves respect.

32 If religion should ever disappear from this world, it would be a loss to mankind.

33 Religion which makes a man grasp the highest truth, beauty and goodness is most important for man.

34 Religion is necessary to obtain true happiness.

35 Religion is to man as a way of incomparable richness, and therefore man must enter upon this way.

36 It is necessary that at least once in his life man investigate religion.

Original version of the 36 basic questions concerning religion
submitted to the students.

1 自分に強い自信があれば，宗教はその人にとって必要ではない。

2 人生に満足していれば別に宗教の必要はない。

3 宗教を認めるか認めないかの決心は，人間の気持と感情だけによるものである。

4 宗教にはいろいろあり，それぞれ立場もちがうが人は自分の肌に合ったものを選べ
　ばよい。

5 宗教は現実のわずらわしさからの逃避である。

6 宗教は一種の鎮静剤にすぎない。

7 宗教は苦しい時の神だのみにすぎない。

8 宗教は科学と理性に矛盾するものである。

9 科学者が宗教を持つ場合，それは科学の立場からはふさわしくない態度である。

10 宗教は人間の個性をよわめ，人格の発達をさまたげる。

11 宗教は今日のように文明の発達した時代においては迷信に近い。

12 宗教的な信仰は人間の無知からうまれるものである。

13 宗教は原始的民族の遺産にすぎない。

14 宗教はもはや時代おくれのものである。

15 宗教は老人にふさわしいかもしれないが，若い人々にはどうでもよいことである。

16 宗教は人間の錯覚にもとづいている。

17 宗教は人のあきらめと忍従を強いるアヘンにすぎない。

18 宗教は支配者の搾取の手段であって一般の人々のためにはならない。

19 宗教は深い心の落着きを人々に与える。

20 宗教は人生のはかなさと孤独からの救いを与える。

21 宗教は人間の心のよりどころとして大変望ましいものである。

22 宗教は人間の生活に意味を与え，人間の目的を明らかにする。

23 宗教は人間の死によって無に帰すことへの不安を解消してくれる。

24 宗教は人間の悩みを解決してくれる。

25 宗教の教えは道徳的に立派であり，人間同志の愛を養うから人間には大切である。

26 宗教は心身の鍛練になり，よい修養になる。

27 宗教は絶えず人間に向上しようとする心を起させる。

28 人類の平和の実現のために宗教は大いに貢献することができる。

29 宗教は社会の乱れと個人の利己主義をなくす力を持っている。

30 人は宗教に対して理解と尊重の念をもつべきである。

31 宗教にもとづいた生活態度は尊敬に値する。

32 この世の中に宗教がなくなるならば，それは人類にとってマイナスとなる。

33 宗教は最高の真理，最高の善，最高の美を把握させるから，人間にとって一番大切
　なものである。

34 真の幸福を得るためには宗教が必要である。

35 宗教は最も豊かな人間の道であるから，人間はその道を歩かなければならない。

36 人は宗教について，せめて一度はまじめに研究する必要がある。

Appendix V

ORIGINAL VERSION OF THE STUDENTS' COMMENTS
ON RELIGION WHICH HAVE BEEN USED
IN THE ENGLISH TEXT

Question 1 自分に強い自信があれば宗教はその人にとって必要ではない

1 宗教に頼る人間は弱い人間だ。強い人間には宗教は必要ではない。いやむしろ人間を弱めさせるのは宗教だ。

2 宗教は強く生きている人間には不必要であり，弱者の強力な救いの神となるものだと思っている。

3 強い意志さえもっていれば宗教なんぞは無用の長物であるということになる。

4 宗教は意志を持っている人間には必要ない。

5 宗教に頼る人は自分自身に自信がないからではないか。私は少くとも強い人物となりたい。

6 宗教を信仰している人は何か人間的に弱いところのある人間ではないか。

7 もし自分に自己を本当に生かせる考え方があるとすれば，必らずしも宗教を信仰しなくてもそれで充分と思う。

8 本当に自分をつきつめて反省し，明日を目指して進む人にとっては無宗教であってさしつかえない。

9 無宗教でも個人の意志をしっかりもって進めば幸福も得られると思う。

10 自分に自信がある時は無神論，気が弱い時に有神論。

Question 2 人生に満足していれば別に宗教の必要はない

1 幸福なときなどは我々は宗教なんか"ウエット"の代表だとか我々には全然無関係なものなんだと考え，ある程度軽蔑の念を持つものである。

2 希望にもえ，ある目的に向ってつっ走っている青年にとっては何の不安もなく不満もないので宗教を必要としない。

3 宗教とは現在の僕にはなにか遠いものに思えてしようがない。それは僕が不幸でなく，むしろ幸福な環境に生活しているためである。

4 健康で自分の生活に満足している人間，意志を持っている人間には宗教は必要ない。

5 もし，私が経済的に生活に困り，その為精神的にも不安定になり，本当に，せっぱつまったりした場合には，心の支えとして信仰することはありうるでしょう。

6 心に悩みも何もなければ神にすがる筈はない。

7 僕も悩みごとができたり，自分が信じられなくなったら，宗教に入るかも知れないが，いまのところ僕には関係のない存在だ。

L

8 宗教などを信じている人は病人や貧乏人ばかりと思っている。

9 現代のこの安定した世界においては宗教など必要ないように思われる。 なぜならば日常生活において不安なこともなければ，とくに心配することもないからである。

10 社会の物質的，精神的水準を高めて，宗教の必要をなくすことが望ましい。

Question 3 宗教を認めるか認めないかの決心は人間の気持と感情だけによるものである

1 宗教というものはその人々の気持次第で必要なものになり， 不必要なものにもなると思うのであります。

2 神に従う多くの人々がいることを知っている。 その人達にとって神は常に自分を見つめてくれ励ましてくれるものかも知れないけど， それはその人の気持の持ちようだと思う。

3 日本人は宗教を直感的， 感覚的に受け入れ，それを理論的に信仰するという点に欠けている。

4 宗教は感情の世界であり安堵の世界である。

5 信仰ということはどういうことであろうかということは，実際に宗教を信仰していないので客観的な立場からの考えをのべる。教会は大変壮厳で心が安らかになるような所であると思う。なぜそう思ったかは，二，三度教会に行ったが始めて入った時の第一印象がそうであった。その様な場所で静かに祈っているといつのまにか神と自分ひとりがそこにいて，自分の心のわだかまりを打ち明けるような状態になるのではないかと思う。即ち信仰とは催眠術にかけられたような状態になっているのではないだろうか。

6 信者が神を信じることは， これが神を認めたとか， 神の存在を知ったとかのためでなく自分にとって神というものの存在性を認めた方が有益であり， 神がいた方が自分は幸福であろうと考えたためであろう。

7 宗教はあくまでも感情的なものである。

8 宗教は自分が困った時，お寺， 教会， 神社等に行って自分の悩みを話す， たゞそれだけのことで自分が助かった， あるいは気持が楽になったように思うのである。

9 人が本当にある宗教を信仰している場合， それを良いとか悪いとか判断すべきでなく，人個人が満足していればそれでよいのである。

10 宗教は知的であるよりも感情的な現象であり， 知的な理解により撰択されるのではないと思う。

Question 4 宗教にはいろいろありそれぞれ立場もちがうが人は自分の肌にあったものを選べばよい。

1 僕自身は宗教は思想であると思っています。 だから僕にとっては神の実在，非実在の問題は意味がありません。「思想」なのですからその考え方に僕が共鳴出来れば信じるし，共鳴出来なければ信じないのです。

2 宗教のうちどれを選ぶという最後的なことは人の好みによる。

3 宗教とは人生の目的ではなくその手段，方法である。それ故いく通りかの方法があって当然ではないかと思う。

4 僕は人々が信仰を持つことはいいことだとは思いますが人々にはそれぞれの好みがあるわけですからどの信仰を選ぶかは常に自由であっていいと思います。

5 宗教は人間の精神のよりどころであると思う。だから神を特別に限定する必要はないと思う。要するに個人個人が精神のよりどころであると思って信じるものが神であろうと何であろうと信じること自体が宗教であると思う。

6 どんな宗教を選んでもよいと思います。

7 宗教は必要な人々には必要だし，不必要な人にはいらないと思います。

8 宗教は個人の問題であり必要とするものにとって無くてはならないものであろうし，無関心なものには結局何ものでもないものだろう。

9 宗教とは人の精神を安定させるための一種の哲学で私にとってはあってもなくてもよいものだ。

10 現在世界の人が信じている宗教がキリスト教であろうと，仏教であろうと，回教であろうと，また他のいかなる宗教であろうとかまわないと思います。

Question　5　宗教は現実のわずらわしさからの逃避である。

1 信者というものは現実からのがれるというかどうも卑怯者のように思える。

2 宗教は人間の現実逃避と良心の問題にすぎないと思います。

3 宗教というものはひどく他力本願的であり，現実逃避的である。

4 宗教は一般の社会の問題，現実問題より遠ざかり，現実より遊離し，観念的に自己の内にひとつの個人的な安心境を作って，その中に安住しようと欲することである。

5 宗教のあるべき意味としては現実からの逃避ではなかろうか。

6 僕は困難に直面しても決して逃げ道的な信仰へは行かないと確信しています。

7 要するに弱い人間，悩みごとのある人が自分で解決できず，現実逃避になり，修道院へ入ったりするようになるんだと思う。

8 日本人が宗教に近づいて行くのは精神的な不安から逃避しようとするときだけである。

9 現代のようにあまりにも機械化された時代に於ては，宗教は単なる現実からの逃避の手段にすぎなくなっている。

10 宗教＝逃避の手段ということである。"神に救いを求める"それは自分で努力すること，現実を見つめることからの逃避であり，"人間の力でどうにもできない，それを可能にするのが神である"というもので逃避と思える。

Question　6　宗教は一種の鎮静剤にすぎない。

1 キリスト教は，一種の精神安定剤のような働きをするのではないだろうか。

2 宗教は利己的要求の対象であり催眠術である。

3 宗教とは何の意味もないおまじないと同じであり，結局はつらい現実からの逃避の手段にしか思われない。

4 宗教は自分自身の支えにすぎない。 この悪い世の中にあっては自分自身が段々とそれに適応して行ってしまう。それに我慢できない人が宗教なるものによって自分自身を忘れる「無我の境」になり，その休息の場とし，気持を新たにする。

5 熱烈なる信仰者は一種の大酒のみにたとえられる。

6 宗教などというものは一種の気休めにすぎない。

7 宗教によって精神安定を少しでも保つことが出来ることは意義がある。

8 我々は一時的に宗教という木陰で休んでもよいけれども年中そこにいることができないことを知るべきだ。その中にいるために我々は何もせず弛緩してしまう恐れがあるのではないか。我々は休み終ったら，木陰に未練を残さず，つまり宗教をのりこえる準備を怠ってはならない。

9 宗教は精神安定剤の役割を果しているにすぎない。

10 普通，一般の人達には，何か精神的欠陥があるんでしょうか。その欠陥をおぎなうものとして，又助ける意味に於いて，何らかの宗教が必要となってくるのではないかと思います。

Question　7　宗教は苦しい時の神頼みにすぎない。

1 「溺れるものわらをもつかむ」とか「困った時の神だのみ」とかいった諺のように人間がいざ困った時に，困難を切りぬけるひとつの手段として行うものである。

2 "苦しい時の神だのみ" 私の宗教観はこの一語につきます。

3 "苦しい時の神だのみ" まさに私はそれである。一心不乱に身も心もつくして神を信じる気にはなれない。

4 自分の力ではどうしょうもない時，例えば病気の時，死の危機に直面した時，神の存在を願い，神の助けを乞う。

5 悩みに直面した時，心のよりどころとして何か自分よりもっと能力のあるものにたよりたいという願望から神が生れたのだろう。

6 不治の病とか貧しい階層の人とか悩みごとのある人とか，要するに心に不安のある人が困った時の神だのみで，すがりついているように見える。

7 困った時の神だのみというようにせっぱつまった時などは考えの片隅に神の存在を認めている。

8 諸宗教に共通する点は何か人間が困難や災難に出あった時に，何かに頼りたいという気持から，その宗教に入って困難に立ち向うということである。

9 自分ではどうにもならなくなった事件や手におえないことが起った時，神によって助けてもらうように思う。結局は自分が弱いためではないか。

10 健康で悩みもない時は宗教は存在しないが，一度肉体的，精神的に悩みを生じた時，我にもなく神の名を口に出すようなことがある。私は健康な時，そうでない時では，まるで矛盾するようなことを平気でやっている。

Question　8　宗教は科学と理性に矛盾するものである。

1 宗教と科学は両立することはできない。科学は自然や人間の現象を追求するのに反し，宗教は人間が作り出した人為的なものである。

2 神がいるとかいないとか，非科学的なことは興味がない。現代のように科学の発達した世の中で神の存在を論じても仕方のないことである。

3 合理的な社会科学の勉強をしている僕にとって非合理的な宗教など信じる気にはなれない。

4 今日では宗教は非科学的，非時代的と見なされ，一般の人々には受け入れられていない。

5 日本の場合，小学校の時，宗教と科学は反対語として，我々は習っている。

6 この科学の発達した現代に於て人間を超越した崇高偉大な神が存在するのだろうか。疑問に思うよりも先に馬鹿々々しくて考えようもない。それを信仰する者は馬鹿と思う。いやましてその人物をあわれむといった方がよい。

7 宗教が科学の発展をさまたげることは歴史に於て事実である。

8 私は宗教に対立するものとして科学を考える。自然を支配する整然たる法則性，その神秘性，秩序を科学は少しづつ解明して来た。その根源（とくに生命の起源など）はいまだ誰にもわからない。だから，私はそれらについては今はただ「わからない」と頭を下げるだけ。宗教がその間の関係を何とか説明しようとして神なる創造主にその根源を求めることは賛成し得ない。そうした神が今度は逆に教義の形でもって人間をしばりつけるのは困るし，それを恐れる。

9 現代のように科学の進歩した世界でも神を信じ敬う人がいるのを疑問に思う。

10 理工学部，電子電気工学科で学んでいる僕には，たゞ現実に起る絶対的な現象のみが対象であって神の様な抽象的なものは絶対に認められない。

Question 9 科学者が宗教を持つ場合，それは科学の立場からはふさわしくない態度である。

1 神の力にたより自分の力を信じて生活して行きたいのです。もし，教養もあり人格もある人ならもう少し自分の力を信じてよいものだと思う。

2 宗教を信じる人の中には教養の低い人が多いと思います。しかしこの事はおかしいどころか当然だと思います。

3 先生はノーベル賞を授与されたような偉大な科学者が最後には無神論をすてて信仰の道に入ったという例をあげたことを記憶しますが，その時，私の感じた卒直な感想を述べますと「俺だって死期が近づけば……」という気持です。

4 現代の知識人が何故神を信ずるかというと，一般民衆の上に立っている人物であるけれども平生の生活の孤独な面に対処するために，また彼らは生活に対する彼等自身の責任を転換するために，また逃避するためではないだろうか。また気をまぎらすためではないだろうか。

5 教養もあり人格がすぐれている人が，「信ずる」と聞いた時，私が一番つよく感ずることは，その人々の生れた時からの環境というものを考えずにはおれない。

6 宗教を信じている人のうちには立派な学者がいることを耳にした。これにはどうも嫌な気持がしてたまらない。人間の精神的弱味をついた宣伝にほかならない。

Question 10 宗教は人間の個性を弱め人格の発達をさまたげる。

1 信者となるのは人間がある一面からすると人間としてかたわになっているみたい。

2 我々は自己に確固たる信念を持つべきであって宗教は自身を他力本願なよわい人間にするような気がしてならない。

3 人間の本当の美しい姿は人間自身が作り出すものであって，他のもの一神一に依存することにより作り出されるものではないと思う。そこには人間自身の主体性がないからである。

4 私は思うに宗教を信仰することによって，あらゆる面であるきまった思想に陥し入れられてしまって，自己の個性などなくしたも同然となるといった如き信仰は決してしたくありません。

5 宗教は，卑怯な自己逃避である。ある点に於いては，自己成長の最大の敵だと考えている。なぜなら，苦しみや，悩みを真向うから受け入れ，正々堂々とそれと戦おうとせず，ただ祈ったり，おがんだりすることで，苦しみや，悩みから逃れようとし，本当に考えるという事をも努力しないからだ。

6 私は宗教の必要を認めない。私は主体性というものを大切にしたい。

7 何か神を信ずることによって自分がよわくなってしまったような気がしてしまう。

8 宗教について考えるということは，日常生活からかけはなれたことのように思われる。更にもし自分が宗教を深く研究してその信者になったとすれば，自分の日常生活ばかりか思想までが極度に制限されて，しかもまわりの人からは何か特別な人間ででもあるかのように思われる。

9 宗教は人から努力をとり去り，依頼心を強くさせるもの，とくにこれは若いものにとって最大の害であると思う。

10 信者は個性的でないと思います。すべての信者は固苦しくて，同じ型にはまっている者のように見えます。

Question 11 宗教は今日のように文明の発達した時代に於ては迷信に近い。

1 宗教という言葉をきいて最初に感じたことは，坊主が出て来て暗い陰気な場所で仏像に向ってお経を読んでいたり，きびしくて迷信をそのまゝ受け入れる非近代的な人々の集まりとか一度信じてしまったら気が狂ってしまうような感じを受けました。

2 僕の父親は毎日，神様と仏様にお祈りします。それを僕は毎日見聞するのですが，何か魔力に魅せられ，子供のような卒直な心を失った人のように父が思われるのです。

3 宗教はおまじないと同じであると思っている。

4 日本社会に於ては，宗教が学校に於て教育されてこなかったので，まだ宗教をマジックとする見方が否定されていない。

5 信仰というものは，概して迷信的要素を含んでいるものであり，教養のない学問的程度の低い人がそれを持つものと一般的に考えられている。

6 宗教はとかく迷信的なことが多いと思う。

7 宗教はきわめて迷信的で科学的でない。そして生活に不必要であるとさえ思っている。

8 どんな宗教にも非科学的，迷信的な教義が残るのではないでしょうか。

Question 12 宗教的な信仰は人間の無知から生れるものである。

Question 13 宗教は原始的民族の遺産にすぎない。

1 宗教は原始人の自然への無知から発生したものである。現代の人間は古代の人間より精神面で，あるいは思想の面で発達していると自認したいため，古代人が信じている宗教（太陽・月・光）にふりかえらずしてキリスト教などに目を向けているが，キリスト教と古代宗教とは根本的に全然，差異がないのである。

2 宗教を信仰するということについて，それは無知な人間が神に対する絶対的な考えを持ち始めその中にオールマイテイな力を見出し，あるいはそのようなものを発見したと自分で思った時それが信仰である。

3 宗教は無知な，普段の生活に安心出来ずにいる人のよりどころとなるものである。

4 昔の人間は今から考えれば色々な点で無知でありました。それ故その様な空想的なものを信ずることもできたでしょう。現在は科学の世の中，何の根拠もないそのようなものに頼らなくても，人間の生活には何のさしつかえもないのです。

5 宗教は生活に根ざしている原始的，歴史的，伝統的なものである。

6 宗教と科学は両立しえない。なぜなら宗教は原始的なものであるのに対して，科学は文明的・進歩的なものであるからである。

7 神という言葉が出て来てこれには本当に抵抗を感じた。今までは神という言葉をきいてもただ莫然としており，キリスト教信者についても“めくらの現代人”であるものぐらいにしか思っていなかった。

Question 14 宗教はもはや時代おくれのものである。

1 宗教は現実の悲惨から人々の目をそらさせ科学的，合理的に現実をみる能力を奪ってしまう。だから上智大で宗教学が必須であることについては時代に逆行することだと思う。

2 宗教的信仰は新しい変化に対処できないのではないか。非現代的な形式化が現代の生活の中で無駄を作っているのではないか。

3 日本人の大部分の人は宗教を信じていなく非常に現代的でよいと思う。

4 現代において宗教はあまり盛んになれない。我々は科学に依存する生活をしているからです。

5 現代には時代思潮として神がない。現代は神の無信への方向を極限にいきつめてきた時代だ。

6 神（人間が空想した偶像）に対する考え方が人類が発達するために常にかわらねばならないし，また変って来たと思う。神への信仰は非近代的なものである。

7 宗教は古くして変らない不変の真理を尊ぶものと思われます。先へ先へと進んで行こうとする人達の目にはこのことが時代に逆行するかのように強く映ずるようです。

8 宗教というと，何か今の科学の時代に相反するものだという気がする。

Question 15 宗教は老人にふさわしいかもしれないが,
若い人にはどうでもよいことである。

1 宗教ときくと僕の場合古くさい何か年よりの人々が近づくもののように感じ，我々のような若い連中がついて行くのはばからしい。

2 宗教は現在の若い人には何の関係もない。宗教など腹の足しにもならない言葉を吐いているより他の方に時間をさいた方がよさそうだ。

3 私は日本に於ては宗教は50歳以上の人達の間にのみ存在するようなものに思える。つまり宗教は近代的でない，そして今日全くそれを必要としないで生活していて一向不自由を感じないのである。

4 僕も今よりももっと年をとり人生の荒波にもまれる時，心の安らぎとして宗教の重要性に関して深く感じることがあると思う。年をとるにしたがって神を信じたくなるらしい。しかし私はまだ若いのだ。

5 うちの父も前は信仰などしなかったが，最近神棚の前で両手を揃えて拝んでいるのを見るが，父もあの世行きが近くなったのではないかと兄と笑ったこともある。

6 僕はまだ若いからイエス様も仏様も信じないのである。

7 宗教というのはこれから行くあの世に不安をいだく老人とか，治る見込みのない重病人が救いを求めるためのものだと思います。ですから私達健康な若い者にとっては，宗数は関係がないと思われるのです。

8 日本に於ては，宗教というものは若い人達にとってはお年寄の杖のように思われて来たのではないでしょうか。

Question 16 宗教は人間の錯覚にもとづいている。

1 宗教について心配なことは，よりどころを求めて錯覚のようなものを信ずるようになるということである。人間は瞬間的に，また一時的に錯覚を感じることがある。しかし無数の人が朝から晩まで一生涯錯覚を信じ，そのために生きるということは話しにもならない。

2 熱心に祈っている人達を見て不思議な気持がする。この人達は意志が弱く，心の支えとなるように幻想的なものを信ずる哀れな人達であろうかと思ったぐらいで，私は信じるということが何か恐しい気持さえします。

3 あこがれの偶像である神に対し信仰を希望している中に実際に神が存在し，神の教えを信仰しているという錯覚に陥入ってしまう。

4 宗教というと寺院，教会の霊前でひざまずき，神に祈り続けて，あるいは死者の魂をまつりあげている姿を思い出し，それらに対して非現実的，非科学的，空想的また神秘的なものであると感じる。

5 一般に宗教心理は異常心理，またはそれに近いものとされている。

6 信仰心というものも人間の平常的な生活心理からみれば，やはり異常な心理現象であり，どちらかといえば原始衝動に近いものだと解釈している。

7 結局自分自身をだますことのできる人が宗教を信じることのできる人という気がします。

8 私は人が宗教を信じようという気になる心理がわからない。私の場合，それはただ
の虚構としか思えない。

Question 17 宗教は人のあきらめと忍従を強いるアヘンにすぎない。

1 宗教とは麻薬であるという言葉を耳にするし，また私自身もある程度本当だと自分
自身に云い聞かせている。

2 真の人間の解放にとって宗教はアヘンであり害である。

3 神にすがるのみですませるのは「あきらめ」であり，あきらめてしまうならば問題
は確かにそれで終るが，もしすべての問題をそのようにばかり処理してしまうとした
ら生きている必要までがなくなってしまうと思います。その意味でいわゆる「信者」
という人達に対して「弱虫」とか「逃避的」であるとかいう言葉があてはまるのでは
ないでしょうか。

4 宗教はアヘンであるとも云う。これもまた一面の真理をもっている。

5 宗教とは奴隷的状態に耐えるための精神的支柱であると思うこともあります。

Question 18 宗教は支配者の搾取の手段であって
一般の人々のためにならない。

1 宗教は人間による人間の搾取に支配が始った時（人間疎外）から不可避的に発生した。

2 開祖は別として宗教団体となると権力者と結ぶのが常であったし，いつも保守的で
ある。宗教団体が権力を握った場合，非人道的なことを行っていることが多い。

3 現在社会における宗教団体の権力というものは大したものである。政治にまでせん
風を巻き起さんばかりであるが，これからもこの宗教団体は大きく成長するでしょう
か。

4 古来，日本の宗教は現実的性格をおびていて常に権力者はその権力を維持するのに
役立ったようだ。

5 日本に於ては宗教は独裁者が人民をひきつけるための一手段にすぎなかった。

6 宗教そのものは純なるものであっても現実の社会では，いろいろ不純な手によって
利用されている。金集めの手段として，政権獲得の支配者が被支配者を懐柔する手段
などに利用する。

Question 19 宗教は深い心の落着きを人々に与える。

1 宗教というものはそれを信ずることによって心の落着きが得られる。

2 信仰することによって人間が冷静になり，安心して落着くことは確かに有益であ
り，必要なことである。

3 宗教は我々の日常生活にゆとり，心のやすらぎを与えてくれる。

4 心のやすらぎを得ることが人生に於て最も幸福なもののひとつだとしたらそれを目
標とすることが宗教だと思います。

5 宗教は人間の心のやすらぎをもたらすのに必要であると思う。

6 本来，宗教とは人間の心にやすらぎを与えるものである。

7 宗教とは人間のあらゆる面に於て，また信ずることによってその信者の欠点や不安感をいやし，やすらぎを与えるものである。

8 信仰をもっている人の厳しさを感じると共に，信仰を持った人の心の平静さ，やすらぎを感じる。

9 人間は常にその生活に於て，内面的価値と外面的価値の両者に対してバランスのある追求をするわけであるが，このバランスがくずれる時，人は不安の状態に陥入るのであり，これを解決する手段として宗教が存在する。

10 宗教は心を落着けるためのひとつの道具としてしか考えていない。

Question 20 宗教は人生のはかなさと孤独からの救いを与える。

1 自分自身を孤独なものと認めた時，神の存在を知るのではないかと思う。

2 人間は自分の力のなさを感じた時，または孤独感の強い時，神仏を求めるから宗教を否定しない。

3 宗教は自己の孤独をのがれる手段にすぎない。

4 宗教を孤独からの解決の場としてみる。

5 宗教の起源を考える時，人間の孤独感あるいは死の恐怖を救ってくれて頼りになる絶対的なものを人間は求める。そこに人間は神というものを考え出した。だから宗教は人間の弱い一面であると考える。

6 ひとり孤独でいる時，自分ひとりの世界に入りこむ時，我々は非常な孤独感におそわれる。無の状態が出現するのである。その様な全く，無気味な世界から自分の味方を見出そうとする。つまりこの味方こそ神なのである。

7 宗教とは結局，人間の孤独の心のよりどころとして存在するのではないかと思う。

8 人間は時々恐しい孤独感に恐われることがある。そうした時人間は何か絶対的な力を持ったものにすがりつき，そのもとで自己の安全を守りたくなる。そこに宗教が生れ，信仰が生れる。

9 人間があることにぶつかった時，例えば母が死んだり，また愛すべき妻の死や肉親の死によったり，自分自身が孤独になったりする時に宗教は私達の支えとなり慰めとなってくれる。

10 人生は孤独で空しいものである。だから人は少しでもしあわせに暮したいと思う。そこにひとつの宗教を考える。

Question 21 宗教は人間の心のよりどころとして大変望ましいものである。

1 科学が発達して人間のメカニック化，人間疎外などによって人間相互の信頼はうすれ慈愛の念もうかんでこない社会になると人間の心のよりどころとして宗教が必要となってくるのではないだろうか。

2 人々が神によって心の安らぎを得，心のよりどころとすることは良いと思う。

3 宗教は精神面で支えになる点で肯定する。従って全面的に否定するわけではない。

4 宗教は心の動揺などが起った時の心のよりどころとして，また，人間形成の過程において大切だと思う。

5 人間より神を作って，それに頼る方がいろいろと都合のよいこともあるから宗教を否定したくはない。

6 神の存在を信じてそれによって自分が幸福になることが出来るような人がいたならばそれは大変よいことである。

7 人間には一種の弱さがあり，よりどころのようなものを求めて信じるようになったということはある意味で正しいと思う。

8 何かに頼ろうとして神を信ずる気になるのだと思う。 それによってその人の心が柔らぎ顔にほほえみがわくようになったのならそれは一番よいのではないか。

9 今では一般に願望，心のよりどころとして神の存在を認めている。

10 人生に於いて人は宗教に自分のよりどころを見つけ，いこいの場所となす。

Question 22 宗教は人間の生活に意味を与え，
人間の目的を明らかにする。

1 宗教を信ずることにより自分の不安をなくして目的に向って進むことも出来るであろう。

2 人は何のために生きているのか， 如何に生きたらよいのかを考える時に始めて宗教に顔を合わせる。

3 人生の目的と意義について考えた時にこそ本当の意味での宗教が生れる。

4 人間が宗教を真に信ずるならばその人の人生は何かまとまったものになると思う。

5 宗教はすべての人間の行動をひとつの目的に導く。だからもしその宗教が真理であるなら，その宗教にたよった人の人生は非常に筋の通ったものとなる。しかしその宗教は真でなくてもかまわない。人生の目的をつかみ得ないものは宗教によってそれを得，宗教を信じることによりその人生を有意義な目的に向けるのである。

6 私自身について云えば「人生は何か」という問題に答えてくれるものとしての“宗教”を考える。

7 人間が一体人生とは何であろうか， また何のために人間は生きているのかということを考えた時，そこに宗教が生れてくる。

8 宗教は人間生活を解決してゆくものである。

9 宗教というものには暗黙に人生の目的というものが示されているのである。

10 私は人間の発展の目的を知りたいのである。 そこには何か目的が存在するであろうことを確信する。この答はもしかすると宗教の中に存在するのかもしれない。

Question 23 宗教は人間の死によって無に帰することへの
不安を解消してくれる。

1 生物である限り死をまぬがれることは出来ようもない。 そこに絶対的なもの―神や仏―を求めるものが存在する理由である。

2 宗教は偉大な力である。人間の死に対する解決だと思う。 人間にとって永遠のナゾである「死」に対して答を出し，それを信ずる者は常に一種のやすらぎを持ち，常に落着いて人生を送ることが出来ると思う。

3 人の生命とははかなく短いものだ。そして限られた人間は永遠で不滅のものをあこがれ求めている。そしてそれが宗教ではないだろうか。

4 「生あるものは死す」の諺の通り人が宗教を論ずるには一応「死」ということを考えているからだと思う。その精神的不安のよりどころを宗教に求めるのではないか。

5 人間はこの世に生を受けたからには死を経験しなくてはならない，しかし人間は死を恐れている。どの宗教も人間の死について考え始めたころから出発している。

6 宗教の信者は死後の生活を恐れるが故に信ずる。

7 もし人間に死というものがなかったら宗教は生れてこなかったであろう。人間のこのはかない運命を少しでも自分自身で慰めるために宗教が起ったように思われる。

8 この死を考えるとある種の不安が起り，その不安を何らかの方法でまぎらすため，何かにすがりたい一心で宗教を信仰したといってもいいすぎではないと思う。

9 「死」に直面した時又はそれを感じた時には必ず恐怖心が起ると思う。その恐怖心を少しでも柔らげようとして宗教というものに心をひかれるのではないかと思う。

10 我々は生命がこの世限りのはかないものだと理論ではわり切って考えることもできるがしかしそれではものたらないし，そんな風にも考えたくない。そういった心から宗教を作り，それを信じ込んで満足を得ようとするのではなかろうか。

Question 24 宗教は人間の悩みを解決してくれる。

1 人間は大変よわいものであり，人生に於けるあらゆる問題や困難に直面した場合，宗教の存在によって切りぬけられるのである。

2 宗教とは人間の生活のありとあらゆる悩みを解決するものである。

3 現代人には悩みが多すぎる反面，本当に信頼できる人が殆んどいない。このようなことを解決し，信頼できるものが宗教であると思う。

4 宗教を信仰することによってその不安，悩みを緩和することができる。

5 人間はその悩み，弱点，まよいから自分を救おうとして宗教にたよります。

6 宗教は心の分裂を統一するところにある。

7 現代のように明日のわからぬ毎日に不安をもつ人々がふえ，種々の人間的悩みが増してくると，宗教が要求されてくる。

8 人間に精神活動がある以上，そこには精神的悩みがある。それをあるひとつの方向に，つまり解決へと導くのが宗教である。

9 宗教は社会的不安，人間の精神的分裂をいやすものである。

10 自分の悩みや罪への責任などを神や仏を信ずることによって自分の内部にひそませておかず，いくらかでも他へ語ることにより，悩みや罪の責任をかるくしょうとする。この点で宗教は日常生活にずい分役立っている。

Question 25 宗教の考えは道徳的に立派であり，
人間同志の愛を養うから人間には必要である。

1 宗教は生活の根本的道徳原理である。

2 全ての人に人間性のモラルを浸透させるために宗教が必要である。

3 キリストの教えは人生を道徳的に導く，正しい宗教のように思われる。

4 宗教的愛の教え，宗教的道徳性の確立が存在しなければ，人間とはいえないかもしれない。

5 宗教の核心は愛であるとする。宗教は人間に対して精神的ささえとなり，人間相互の精神的結びつけをする役割であろう。

6 宗教は“人間がいかに生きるべきか”を学ぶものである。

7 宗教の最大の役割りは愛と精神的喜びである。

8 宗教とは人間道徳の理想を説いたものである。

9 漠然とつかみどころのない人間の心を正しいよい方面に導いてくれるのは宗教と思います。

10 キリスト教では愛というものをとても強調するが，実際に世界中の人々が愛情に結ばれていけば，これほど幸福なことはないと思う。

Question 26 宗教は心身の鍛錬になり，よい修養になる。

1 僕は宗教を人間の道徳，行為のひとつの手段と考えている。

2 宗教の基礎なしに道徳教育はありうるのでしょうか。

3 僕は人間を育成するのが宗教ではないかという気がする。

4 宗教とは精神的なもの。それによって修養をたかめる。

5 宗教は人間に道徳的基準を与える。

6 宗教とは人間のためのものであり，人間のよりよき精神生活を支えるものである。

7 現代のような刺激のつよい世の中だとやっぱり宗教をもった学校に育った方がよいと思います。

8 禅宗の座禅などのような修練により，心身を清め，本性を悟り，心の落着いた人間を作るということはよいことであると思う。

9 私は信仰をもたないけれども宗教に対して関心をもつことには賛成である。道徳的にプラスとなる面が多いから。

10 宗教が与える思想は道徳的に善なるものが多いから，我々は人生を歩むのにこの宗教をよく理解し，そのあとに行動しなければならない。信仰心のある人は，無信仰の人よりも，人生を正しく歩むことができる。

Question 27 宗教は絶えず人間に向上しようとする心を起させる。

1 宗教は人格の向上を目的とする。

2 宗教は人格を向上させるために働かなければならぬ。

3 宗教の真の教は「現世利益」「身上相談」「先祖崇拝」などではなく，自己を向上し他人と共に幸福を喜びあうところにある。即ち宗教は“生活”なのである。

4 人間の生長力の向上のために生きようとする上に宗教は必要なのである。

5 神を信じることによって自身以上に高められ自信と勇気をもって自ら進んで困難に対処しうるのだ。

6　真の宗教とは人間の弱さを補い，全ての人間を真の人間として高めて行けるもので
なければならない。

Question　28　人類の平和の実現のために宗教は大いに貢献することが出来る。

1　現代社会に於て全ての人類がよりよく平等に，また平和に生きるために自己を見つ
め，信じあい願いあい共に立ちゆく社会を作りあげる必要がある。このために仏教，
キリスト教などの宗教が必要となる。

2　宗教の目的とするところは人類の平和，幸福ということであると思う。

3　現代では社会共同体を無視して宗教をのべることはできない。即ち宗教と社会は相
互に関連しあって，人類の幸福のために貢献すべきものであると信じている。

4　現代のような世界には，世界平和のため宗教が大いに貢献しなければならないので
はないかと思う。

5　現代は文明がかなり発達して来たので宗教（正しい宗教）に従って行けば現代の危
険もかなり防止できると思う。

6　人類がもしひとつの発想法のもとに物を考えることができたたなら，（たとえばひとつ
の世界的宗教を信ずるとか）いかにこの世に平和が訪れることであろうか。

Question　29　宗教は社会の乱れと個人の利己主義をなくする力を持っている。

1　宗教は人間の道徳的な面に影響を与え社会秩序を保つ上に重要である。

2　宗教は社会の結合，一致に多大な影響を与える。

3　宗教は人間の気持を柔らげ，社会の中でお互いにいやな思いをなくす。

4　宗教は人間の心の乱れを鎮めると思う。

5　宗教の本質は己れに対して厳しく，個人の集合体である社会に対しては奉仕するこ
とにある。

6　神をもつことは社会生活を円滑にする働きを推進することになる。

Question　30　人は宗教に対して理解と尊重の念をもつべきである。
Question　31　宗教にもとづいた生活態度は尊敬に値するといえる。

1　信仰し，神に祈り，邪欲をさけ，慎しい生活をしている人々は大変偉いと思いま
す。

2　自分自身は将来何を信ずるかわからないし，たぶん信じないであろうが宗教を信じ
ている人は何か強いものを感じる。

3　僕はクリスチャンではなく，平凡なる俗人である。つまらないことに腹をたて喧嘩
もよくする。しかし哲学の時間になると，いつも先生（神父さん）が羨ましくなり，
自分が恥ずかしくなる。自分もあのような落着いた心をもって全てのものを純粋に愛
しえたらどんなに幸福だろうと思う。先日僕は "The Sound of music" という映画を
みたが，その中で修道女の美しい姿には強く心をうたれた。神に自分の愛をささげた
人はあんなにも美しくなるのかと心の中で快い嬉しさがこみあげてくる。なんだかこ
の世には神が存在するような気もする。

4 僕は多くの信者が熱心に奉仕活動をするのを見て偉いと思います。

5 ひとつのある宗教を本当に心から信じ得る人をうらやましく思い，自分もそのような状態に達したいと思っている。

6 私は種々の宗教を信ずる人と話す機会に恵まれた。 みなそれぞれやすらかな雰囲気をもったひとでした。信仰によって作り出されたものだろうか。その様な人々を見ていると，自分も信仰してみようかと思う時もある。

7 信者の明るい生活をみて羨しく思います。

8 宗教の信者をみると非常にうらやましく思う。 何故なら彼らは私達が自分というものきり信頼出来ないこの世界で，他にもうひとつ自分が信頼をおけるものをもっているのだから。

9 僕は現在この複雑な社会では， もっと冷静に考えるという必要性からもっと宗教を重視した方がいいと思う。

10 熱心な信者に多大の敬意と羨望を感じ自らを哀れと思っている。

Question 32 この世の中に宗教がなくなるならば，それは人類にとってマイナスとなる。

1 社会に於て宗教がなかったならもっと混乱すると思う。

2 宗教的愛の教えがなければ弱肉強食の思想がはびこり，人間は動物化してしまう。

3 もし本当に科学的思想によってのみ行動するなら，この世界はいっぺんで吹きとんでしまうであろうし，また亡んでしまうことは絶対間違いない事実であるから宗教に基づいた人間崇拝，地球崇拝主義を定着させねばならない。

4 宗教は根本的には自分で自分をはっきりつかむことだと思います。 人間は外へ外へと拡大を求めるならば，それに伴って内へ内へと集結するものを求めることを忘れてはならない。外へ外へと拡大するものが科学であれば内へ内へと集結するものは宗教である。宗教は決して滅びないと思う。

5 この世の中に宗教というものが必要であることは事実である。 宗教は全般的にいって世の中のきまりというものの役目を果す役割が大である。

6 青少年の犯罪を含め社会は混乱してしまうかもしれません。 こういう世界にこそ宗教は必要となってくるのです。

7 人生観とは云うまでもなく価値評価の問題に関係します。 科学は決して価値の問題を解決することはできない。従って科学のみで人間は生きることはできないと思います。科学は決して"如何に生きるべきか"を教えるものではないのです。そして，この問題こそ人間が生きて行くにあたって何者にもまして重要な，切実な問題なのであり，人間はどうしてもこの問題の解決を求めなければならない。この問題の解決を求め救いとなるものが宗教であるとするならば，宗教というものは決して消滅しないといっていいと思います。

Question 33 宗教は最高の真理，最高の善，最高の美を把握させるから人間にとって一番大切なものである。

1 私は「心の支え」としてより「真理を愛す」という点で神を求めている。

2　真理を求め，真理の前にひざまずく心は何か宗教の本質にふれるものではなかろうか。

3　真の宗教とは真理の道しるべとならなければいけない。

4　宗教というものは，人間が自然の美，宇宙における多くの神秘的現象などを目の前に見たとき必然的に生まれてくる。

5　人間は無限な美を追求するそれが宗教である。

Question　34　真の幸福を得るためには宗教が必要である。

1　全ての人は宗教に幸福と心のやすらぎを求める。

2　宗教は人間の精神的な幸福をいかにして実現せしめるかを追求してゆくものと思う。

3　幸福生活確立が信仰の目的である。

4　人間の内分裂を統一し，生命の拡充をもたらし幸福にするのが宗教である。

5　宗教とは神仏など超人間的・絶対的なものを思慕崇拝・信仰して，それによって慰め，安心，幸福を得ようとする働きだと思う。

6　人生と幸福に対する無限の欲望を絶対的なものの力をかりて，現世，もしくは来世に於て充たそうとするところに宗教の本来の意義がある。

7　幸福を求めるために人間以上の能力をもつと思われるものを人間は尊敬し，崇拝する。ここで宗教というものができたのではないだろうか。

Question　35　宗教は最も豊かな人間の道であるから，
人間はその道を歩かなければならない。

1　宗教は何かしら精神生活を豊かにしているように思える。

2　宗教は生活を豊かにすると思う。

3　よい信仰は人を豊かにするものと思います。

4　宗教は人間の心を豊かにし，心のひろい寛大な人間を作りあげるのに役立つ。

5　宗教にたよって楽をしようと云うのではなく，それによって少しでも自分が豊かになるような信仰をしたいと思っている。

6　この世のむなしさをなんとか救って人生をよりよく豊かに内面性のあるものにしようとする努力が宗教なのである。

7　宗教というものは人々の心を慰め，人生を豊かにする。

Question　36　人は宗教についてせめて一度はまじめに研究する必要がある。

1　宗教はそれを認める認めないにかかわらず，宗教自体は人間として一度は学ばなければならない必須のものである。

2　この人生をまじめに生きている人間であるならば，我々人間の存在の根本と通ずる宗教は一度は研究する義務があると思っている。

3　ひとつの宗教ではなく多くの宗教を学ぶ必要があると思う。

Appendix VI

STATISTIC TABLES SHOWING THE RESULTS OBTAINED FROM BELIEVING STUDENTS

	Catholics	Protestants	Buddhists and other Religions
Boys:	76	162	312
Girls:	78	86	76
Total:	154	248	388

Q 1	% Cath.	% Prot.	% B.Oth.	Q 2	% Cath.	% Prot.	% B. Oth.	Q 3	% Cath.	% Prot.	% B.Oth.
SA	1.29	9.67	13.11	SA	1.29	7.25	14.28	SA	3.24	6.85	13.11
A	11.03	11.69	25.07	A	10.38	8.46	20.40	A	11.03	14.11	22.15
TA	12.32	21.36	38.18	TA	11.67	15.71	34.68	TA	14.27	20.96	35.26
D	25.97	29.83	30.32	D	18.83	35.48	28.57	D	22.72	25.40	25.36
SD	53.89	41.53	24.78	SD	58.44	40.72	26.23	SD	50.64	35.48	13.99
TD	79.86	71.36	55.10	TD	77.27	76.20	54.80	TD	73.36	60.88	39.35
DK	7.79	7.25	6.70	DK	11.03	8.06	10.49	DK	12.33	18.14	25.36

Q 4				Q 5				Q 6			
SA	14.28	24.19	34.48	SA	0.64	4.83	2.33	SA	0.00	0.80	5.24
A	29.22	26.20	27.69	A	9.09	12.90	18.36	A	5.84	8.06	14.28
TA	43.50	50.39	62.17	TA	9.73	17.73	20.69	TA	5.84	8.86	19.52
D	26.62	14.91	6.70	D	19.48	29.43	27.40	D	18.83	25.40	23.90
SD	14.28	24.99	17.20	SD	62.98	49.99	45.18	SD	70.77	62.49	49.56
TD	40.90	39.90	23.90	TD	82.46	79.42	72.58	TD	89.60	87.89	73.46
DK	15.58	9.67	9.91	DK	7.79	2.82	6.70	DK	4.54	3.22	6.99

Q 7				Q 8				Q 9			
SA	0.00	2.41	5.53	SA	0.64	2.41	3.49	SA	0.00	0.40	1.74
A	4.54	5.64	10.78	A	5.19	16.53	14.57	A	0.64	5.64	8.45
TA	4.54	8.05	16.31	TA	5.83	18.94	18.06	TA	0.64	6.04	10.19
D	14.28	24.19	37.31	D	18.18	27.01	27.69	D	8.44	13.30	21.86
SD	76.62	64.51	43.14	SD	70.12	43.95	35.27	SD	85.71	72.98	55.68
TD	90.90	88.70	80.45	TD	88.30	70.96	62.96	TD	94.15	86.28	77.54
DK	4.58	3.22	3.20	DK	5.84	10.08	18.95	DK	5.19	7.66	12.24

Q 10				Q 11				Q 12			
SA	1.29	5.24	4.66	SA	0.64	0.40	1.45	SA	0.00	0.40	3.20
A	3.89	7.66	9.62	A	0.64	4.03	7.58	A	2.59	4.87	8.74
TA	5.18	12.90	14.28	TA	1.28	4.43	9.03	TA	2.59	5.27	11.94
D	20.77	16.93	27.98	D	12.98	16.93	31.19	D	11.53	19.36	25.07
SD	65.58	66.12	48.68	SD	85.06	75.40	53.64	SD	75.97	58.46	46.93
TD	86.35	83.05	76.66	TD	98.04	92.33	84.83	TD	87.50	77.82	72.00
DK	8.44	4.03	9.03	DK	0.64	3.22	6.12	DK	3.89	8.89	16.03

M

Q 13	% Cath.	% Prot.	% B. Oth.	Q 14	% Cath.	% Prot.	% B. Oth.	Q 15	% Cath.	% Prot.	% B.Oth.
SA	0.00	2.01	3.79	SA	0.00	0.00	0.58	SA	0.00	0.80	1.45
A	2.59	4.03	6.70	A	2.59	0.80	4.08	A	0.00	0.80	3.79
TA	2.59	6.04	10.49	TA	2.59	0.80	4.66	TA	0.00	1.60	5.24
D	11.68	15.72	24.19	D	3.89	9.27	24.78	D	6.49	20.56	25.65
SD	79.22	72.58	57.72	SD	91.55	88.30	66.47	SD	92.85	77.82	63.84
TD	90.90	88.30	81.91	TD	95.44	97.57	91.25	TD	99.34	98.38	89.49
DK	6.49	5.64	7.58	DK	1.94	1.61	4.08	DK	0.64	0.40	5.24

Q 16				Q 17				Q 18			
SA	0.00	2.01	1.74	SA	0.00	0.40	2.04	SA	0.00	0.40	2.33
A	5.19	4.43	6.12	A	0.64	1.20	6.99	A	0.64	4.03	5.53
TA	5.19	6.44	7.86	TA	0.64	1.60	9.03	TA	0.64	4.43	7.86
D	14.28	18.14	25.07	D	14.93	22.98	18.07	D	12.33	14.11	24.48
SD	75.97	64.11	48.68	SD	80.51	70.16	62.39	SD	83.76	74.59	61.22
TD	90.25	82.25	73.75	TD	95.44	93.14	80.46	TD	96.09	88.70	85.70
DK	4.54	11.69	18.36	DK	3.89	5.24	10.49	DK	3.24	6.85	6.41

Q 19				Q 20				Q 21			
SA	52.59	56.04	36.73	SA	29.22	39.11	22.44	SA	42.85	45.96	31.77
A	40.90	35.88	51.60	A	48.70	48.79	52.18	A	43.50	43.54	48.39
TA	93.49	91.92	88.33	TA	77.92	87.90	74.62	TA	86.35	89.50	80.16
D	2.59	3.22	3.49	D	11.03	5.64	8.16	D	11.68	6.45	9.32
SD	0.00	0.80	0.58	SD	3.89	0.00	3.49	SD	1.29	0.80	4.66
TD	2.59	4.02	4.07	TD	14.92	5.64	11.65	TD	12.97	7.25	13.98
DK	3.89	4.03	7.58	DK	7.14	6.45	13.70	DK	0.64	3.22	5.83

Q 22				Q 23				Q 24			
SA	66.23	47.98	25.94	SA	32.45	18.14	14.86	SA	14.93	20.96	17.49
A	27.92	41.12	38.19	A	40.25	39.51	27.11	A	52.59	49.59	40.81
TA	94.15	89.10	64.13	TA	72.70	57.65	41.97	TA	67.52	70.55	58.30
D	3.24	5.24	13.41	D	14.93	9.67	12.53	D	24.67	14.51	13.41
SD	0.00	0.80	4.95	SD	4.54	10.48	12.24	SD	2.59	5.24	11.07
TD	3.24	6.04	18.36	TD	19.47	20.15	24.77	TD	27.26	19.75	24.48
DK	2.64	4.83	17.49	DK	7.79	22.17	33.23	DK	5.19	9.67	17.20

Q 25				Q 26				Q 27			
SA	44.15	45.56	36.15	SA	30.51	34.27	29.73	SA	53.89	38.30	24.19
A	42.85	41.12	43.73	A	53.24	41.53	44.60	A	29.87	40.72	34.11
TA	87.00	86.68	79.88	TA	83.75	75.80	74.33	TA	83.76	79.02	58.30
D	7.79	10.48	10.20	D	4.54	8.06	8.45	D	5.19	8.06	13.70
SD	0.64	0.80	2.04	SD	0.64	3.62	7.28	SD	1.94	0.40	4.95
TD	8.43	11.28	12.24	TD	5.18	11.68	15.73	TD	7.13	8.46	18.65
DK	4.54	2.01	7.87	DK	11.03	12.49	9.91	DK	9.09	12.49	23.03

Q 28				Q 29				Q 30			
SA	56.49	49.99	33.81	SA	22.07	23.38	21.57	SA	66.88	50.40	41.10
A	33.76	38.70	38.19	A	48.05	49.99	38.77	A	25.97	34.67	39.94
TA	90.25	88.69	72.00	TA	70.12	73.37	60.34	TA	92.85	85.07	81.04
D	5.84	2.82	7.87	D	14.28	12.49	15.74	D	1.94	6.85	8.16
SD	0.00	2.01	7.28	SD	2.59	2.82	11.95	SD	0.64	2.32	3.49
TD	5.84	4.83	15.15	TD	16.87	15.31	27.69	TD	2.58	9.17	11.65
DK	3.89	6.45	12.82	DK	12.98	11.29	11.95	DK	4.54	5.24	7.28

Q 31	% Cath.	% Prot.	% B. Oth.	Q 32	% Cath.	% Prot.	% B. Oth.	Q 33	% Cath.	% Prot.	% B. Oth.
SA	41.58	35.88	19.53	SA	68.18	53.22	50.72	SA	40.25	30.50	20.11
A	39.61	41.93	38.88	A	20.12	18.95	21.57	A	38.96	33.89	29.44
TA	81.19	77.81	58.41	TA	88.30	72.17	72.29	TA	79.21	64.39	49.55
D	12.33	13.30	15.74	D	1.29	6.04	4.66	D	7.14	20.33	26.53
SD	1.29	2.01	9.91	SD	1.29	4.83	5.53	SD	3.89	5.08	11.95
TD	13.62	15.31	25.65	TD	2.58	10.87	10.19	TD	11.03	25.41	38.48
DK	5.19	6.85	16.03	DK	9.09	16.93	17.49	DK	8.44	10.16	11.95

Q 34	Cath.	Prot.	B. Oth.	Q 35	Cath.	Prot.	B. Oth.	Q 36	Cath.	Prot.	B. Oth.
SA	53.24	37.49	19.82	SA	27.27	15.72	12.82	SA	88.31	66.93	58.60
A	22.72	27.82	25.07	A	44.15	36.29	29.44	A	7.14	19.25	30.02
TA	75.96	65.31	44.89	TA	71.42	52.01	42.26	TA	95.45	86.18	88.62
D	11.03	13.30	21.28	D	14.28	30.24	25.94	D	1.29	3.22	3.49
SD	1.29	6.85	15.16	SD	6.49	8.46	19.82	SD	0.00	2.41	2.62
TD	12.32	20.15	36.44	TD	20.77	38.70	45.76	TD	1.29	5.63	6.11
DK	11.68	14.51	18.65	DK	7.79	9.27	11.95	DK	3.24	8.06	5.24

NB: Q: Question; SA=Strongly agree; A: Agree; TA=Total agree
SD: Strongly disagree; D=Disagree; TD=Total disagree; DK=Don't know.

Appendix VII
ORIGINAL VERSION OF THE QUESTIONS
CONCERNING GOD, THE AFTERLIFE AND MORALITY
SUBMITTED TO THE STUDENTS

1　神が人間を作ったのではなく，人間が神を作ったのである。

2　神は人間の考えの中に単なる概念ではなく，実際に存在する。

3　神というものはそれは結局，それぞれの民族の祖先である。

4　神は死んだ偉人の霊である。

5　神というものは神々のことである。

6　神というのは人間や自然を超えた絶対者である。

7　神はひとつだけしかない，最高で偉大な存在者である。

8　神は真・善・美の極致で聖なるものである。

9　神は大自然と同じものである。

10　神はなにか強大なエネルギーのかたまりのようなものである。

11　神といえば，結局それは理想化された自分の心のことである。

12　神は人間の祈りに耳を傾けて，理解と心をそなえたものである。

13　神は人間にたたりを与える恐ろしいものである。

Original version of the questions about the afterlife
submitted to the students

1　来世があるなどということは空想から出た作り話である。

2　来世は実際にはないものであるが，人は死後にかける願いによって来世があると信ずるのである。

3　死んでしまえばそれまでといわれているが，死は人にとってすべての終りである。

4　死後の世界を見て来た人は誰もいないのであるから，来世があるなどということは全くあてにはならない。

5　世の中には来世を信ずる人と信じない人があるが，それはその人の性格や性質の問題である。

6　人生の春にある若い人々は人生を如何に充実して生きるかということを考えるだけでよいのであって，来世のことなどは全く必要はない。

7　この世で悪いことをした人と，よいことをした人が全くふさわしく罰せられたり報いられたりする世界は死後にある。

8　人は生れつき，かぎりのない幸福への欲求をいだいているが，それが完全に満たされるのが死後の世界である。

9　来世があるかないかは，はっきりしないが，来世があるような気がする。

10　人がいかに死後の世界を否定しても，来世は厳然として存在する。

Original version of the questions about morality submitted to the students

1 自分が悪いと思うことでも，社会が是認するならばそのような行為をしてもかまわない。

2 人が悪いことをした時に感ずる不安や恐れは，人の非難や罰に対する不安や恐れにすぎない。

3 罪に伴う恥ずかしさ，みにくさ，汚れなどの感じは社会や他人の目を意識することによってのみ生ずるものである。

4 社会や他人に気付かれないかぎり，他人に対するねたみや憎みのような心をひそかにいだいても悪いと思う必要はない。

5 実際行為にでないで心の中だけにとどまっているかぎりどんなことでも罪にはならない。

6 罪の概念は人間や社会が作りあげたものにすぎない。

Appendix VIII

ORIGINAL VERSION OF THE STUDENTS' COMMENTS
ON GOD AND PRAYER WHICH HAVE BEEN USED
IN THE ENGLISH TEXT

1 神が存在するかどうかという問題は大変おかしいと思います。苦しみからの解放を神に求めることは不当に馬鹿らしいことでもあり，つまらないことだと思います。

2 宗教とはあくまでも人為的なものである。神の存在を否定したい。神の話はすべてフィクションである。神は人間を創造したといわれるが，神が人間を創造したのではなく，人間が神を創造したのである。

3 神というのはただ幻想的な観念である。

4 人間ははじめに神を作りあげ，後に神に服従し，神をあがめるようになったのだ。

5 頼りになる絶対的なものを人間は求める。その人間は神というものを考えだした。

6 神は心の中の精神的なものであるから，存在すると思えばするし，しないと思えばしない。

7 人間は不安でしようがないのである。何かにすがりたい，そこで神という絶対的，万能なものを作り，それを信じすがるのである。

8 神と言われるものは自分の心の中の良心であると思います。

9 人間はなぐさめ，安心，幸福を得ようとして，神というものを自分の心の中に存在させる。

10 あくまでも，宗教とか神とかは認識だけであって，人間の心の問題である。しかし人間は一般的には心の事だけに依存出来ない。だから，神というものを偶像化している。

Original version of the students' comments on prayer
which have been used in the English text

1 盲腸を手術したことがありましたが，あまりの痛さに神さまどうぞもっと痛まないようにして下さいと心で願いましたし，また手術をする段になって手術がうまく行くようにとも願いました。

2 一度，風邪をひいて40度近い熱を出した時，死ぬのではないかと思い神に祈った。

3 自分が苦しい立場，入学試験とか病気になったりした場合，神に頼りたくなることもあったのは事実です。

4 何か自分の力ではどうにもできなくなったり，急に何かが起ったりしたような場合によく神様を思うことです。これは私にとって矛盾したことです。

5 僕は何も心配ごとのない時は宗教のことは少しも考えないが，いざという時はやはり神ということを考える。

6　私は今だかつて神さまと出会ったことはないが，自分でもわからぬままに「かなわ
　ぬ時の神だのみ」という言葉にかなりの信頼性をおいている。

7　苦しいことに出会うと誰でも神に助けを求めるだろう。

8　全然無信仰の人でも何か困った時 "あゝ神さま" などと呼んでみたくなる。